Kenkyusha's Bilingual Dictionary of Japanese Cultural Terms

和英 日本文化 表現辞典

研究社辞書編集部 [編]

研究社

© 2007　KENKYUSHA Co., Ltd.

PRINTED IN JAPAN

まえがき

　本辞典は日本最大の和英辞典として定評のある『新和英大辞典　第5版』から主に日本特有の文化，風物，習慣，季節の行事，食べ物などに関する語を精選して加筆し，さらに流行語や新語を加えて編集しました．

本辞典の特色は以下のようになります．
（1）　収録語は見出し語と複合語を含めて約 3500 語．『新和英大辞典』に比べて文字も大きく，携帯に便利．
（2）　日本固有の文化，風物，行事などを表わすことば，「歌舞伎」，「枯山水」，「福助」，「盆踊り」，「縁日」，「千歳飴」，「炬燵」，「大入り袋」，「しゃぶしゃぶ」などをわかりやすい英語で説明しています．日頃外国人に接する機会の多いビジネスマンやホームステイのホストファミリーだけでなく，これから海外旅行や留学を予定している人には最適です．
（3）　日本人特有のメンタル面を表わすことば，「お蔭様」，「腹芸」，「根回し」，「内弁慶」，「判官贔屓」，「もったいない」などを収録しています．文化の違いで外国人にはなかなか理解できない日本人固有の物の見方を用例で補足しながらより具体的な文脈で理解できるように配慮しました．
（4）『新和英大辞典』に未収録の新語・流行語である「振り込め詐欺」，「スローライフ」，「大人買い」，「音楽配信」，「萎え」，「駅ナカ」，「さくっと」などの語を研究社オンライン辞書検索サービス，KOD から収録しました．簡潔な英語で外国人に説明する際に役立ちます．

　校閲は南九州短期大学教授 David P. Dutcher 氏にお願いしました．ダッチャー氏はアメリカのニューヨーク州のご出身で，在日期間は 30 年以上にもなり，平安時代後期の『狭衣物語』でハーバード大学の文学博士号を授与されたほど日本の古典文学や日本文化に精通しておられる．同氏はすべての項目と用例に目を通され，それにより内容が細かな点まで行き届いた辞典になりました．同氏に心から感謝申し上げます．

　終わりに，本書の刊行に際して関係者は遺漏のないよう努めたつもりでありますが，なお不備の点がございましたならば，利用者の皆様の忌憚のないご意見・ご批判を賜れば幸いです．

2007 年 3 月

　　　　　　　　　　　　　　　　　　　　　　　　研究社辞書編集部

凡　例

1 見出し語
 （1）　配列は五十音順．同一のかなは清音・濁音・半濁音の順とした．
 （2）　カタカナ見出しの長音符(ー)は，その直前の文字を長く伸ばした音を「あ」行の音に置き換えた場合の位置に配列した．
　　　例：「インターホン」→「インタアホン」，「カレー」→「カレイ」，「キューマーク」→「キュウマアク」

2 準見出し：用例の下に，ゴシック体・漢字交じりで五十音順に配列した．準見出しで扱うのは次の語句である．
 （1）　「～な」や「～する」があるとき．
　　　いき【粋】 smartness; stylishness; chic; high spirit; verve.　**～な**〔あか抜けしている〕refined; elegant; stylish; …
　　　がいしょく【外食】…**～する** eat [dine] out.
 （2）　慣用句の類
　　　かた　【肩】〔人や動物などの肩〕a shoulder.
　　　肩が凝る[張る]〔肩の筋肉が固くなる〕feel stiff in *one*'s shoulders; …

3 注意すべき記号の使い方
 （1）　**【　】**　見出し語の代表的な漢字表記を示す．
　　　あい【藍】
 （2）　**■**　複合語が始まることを示す．
　　　あさがお【朝顔】…■**朝顔市** a morning glory market; …
 （3）　〚　〛　専門語の分野を示す．
　　　あおぶさ【青房】〚相撲〛
 （4）　〔　〕　見出し語について解説したり，用例の文脈を補足説明するときに示す．
　　　あくび【欠伸】〔あくびをすること〕yawning;〔1 回の〕a yawn.
 （5）　**◐**　用例がここから始まることを示す．
 （6）　〈　〉　訳の英語について文法上の注記を行う必要があるとき．
　　　うま²【馬】 a horse《*pl.* ～s, ～》;〈集合的に〉horseflesh; …
 （7）　《　》　訳語句の連語を示す．

     あぐら【胡坐】◐ あぐらをかく sit cross-legged 《on a cushion》

(8) / 用例と用例の区切りを示す.

(9) [ ] 直前の語句と言い換え可能な語句を示す.

   あまがえる【雨蛙】a tree「frog [toad]; a hyla.

(10) 「 [ ] の箇所と入れ替え可能な語句の始まりを示す. (9) の「あまがえる」の用例は a tree frog または a tree toad を表わす.

(11) ( ) 省略可能な語句, 簡単な補足を示す.

   あいいろ【藍色】indigo (blue).

(12) 〚 〛 語源を示す.

   あうん【阿吽】〚<Skt *a-hūm*〛

(13) < (12) の記号の中で用いて日本語の語源を示す.

(14) ⇨ 参照を示す.

   あきのななくさ【秋の七草】the seven flowers of autumn [⇨ ななくさ].

(15) ▶ 日本語についての付加的情報, また訳の英語についての注記を示すのに用いた.

   おかげさま【お蔭様】◐ おかげさまでみんな元気です. We are all fit and well. ▶ 特に "thank you" を付け加える必要はない/

(16) ▷ 派生的な情報を示すのに用いた.

   おおばん【大判】1 〔紙・本などの普通より大きい型〕a large「size [sheet]; (a) folio size. ▷ large-sized; folio(-sized) (形容詞)

(17) * と ": この記号が左肩に付された英語がそれぞれ * は Americanism (米国用法), " は Briticism (英国用法) を表わす.

4 主な用法指示

 《口》口語 《文》文語 《俗》俗語 《古》古語 《卑》卑語

5 専門語の分野名

〚医〛医学	〚史〛歴史(学)	〚動〛動物(学)
〚化〛化学	〚植〛植物(学)	〚法〛法律, 法学
〚建〛建築	〚数〛数学	〚物〛物理(学)
〚鉱物〛鉱物(学), 鉱山	〚聖〛聖書	
〚昆〛昆虫	〚天〛天文(学)	

6 外国語

Du	オランダ語	Port	ポルトガル語
F	フランス語	Russ	ロシア語
It	イタリア語	Skt	サンスクリット語
L	ラテン語		

7 ローマン体で表記した日本語：複数の米国の辞典に収録されて，ほぼ英語化した日本語

aikido	合気道	Bunraku	文楽	Bushido	武士道
daikon	大根	daimyo	大名	fusuma	襖
futon	布団	geta	下駄	go	碁
haiku	俳句	judo	柔道	Kabuki	歌舞伎
kana	仮名	kanji	漢字	karate	空手
kimono	着物	koto	琴	miso	味噌
ninja	忍者	Noh	能(楽)	obi	帯
origami	折り紙	sake	酒	samisen	三味線
samurai	侍	sashimi	刺身	shiatsu	指圧
shiitake	シイタケ	Shinto	神道	shogun	将軍
sukiyaki	すき焼き	sumo	相撲	sushi	寿司
tanka	短歌	tanuki	タヌキ	tatami	畳
tempura	天ぷら	teriyaki	照り焼き	tofu	豆腐
tokonoma	床の間	torii	鳥居	wasabi	わさび
yakitori	焼き鳥	Zen	禅	zori	草履

8 イタリック体で表記した日本語：7 で示した以外の日本語はイタリック体[斜体]で示した．

Bon mochi oden soba tabi など．

9 その他

pl. は plural（複数形）の略：**おび**【帯】〔和装の〕an obi 《*pl.* ~s》

あ

あい【藍】 1 〘植〙〔タデ科の 1 年草, 東南アジア原産の染料植物〕true indigo.　2〔染料〕indigo; indigo dye.　3〔色名〕indigo; indigo blue.　◐ 藍に染める dye 《jeans》deep blue.

あいあいがさ【相合い傘】◐ 相合い傘で行く walk [go] under the same umbrella; share *one*'s umbrella 《with *somebody*》.

あいいろ【藍色】 indigo (blue).

あいかぎ【合い鍵】〔同じ鍵〕a「spare [duplicate] key;〔どの錠にも合う鍵〕a master key; a passkey.　◐ 合い鍵作ります.〔掲示〕Keys Cut (Here). 合い鍵屋 a key cutter; a key maker; a keysmith.

あいかた【相方】 1〔一緒に物事をする人〕a [*one*'s] partner.　◐ 漫才で相方をつとめる partner *somebody* [be *somebody*'s partner] in a two-person comic team.　2〔相手の遊女・敵娼〕formerly, the courtesan or boy who waited on the pleasure of a customer in a licensed bordello.

あいがも【間鴨】 a cross-breed of wild and domestic ducks.　■ 間鴨農法 a method of organic rice cultivation; *aigamo* ducklings introduced to paddies eat insects and weeds while providing manure and stimulating rice roots by their paddling.

あいきどう【合気道】 aikido; a purely defensive martial art by means of which an attacker's strength and momentum are used to throw or immobilize him.

あいきょうげん【間狂言】 a simple description of the thematic elements of a Noh play spoken by a player (*kyōgen-kata*) who comes on stage when the leading actor (*shite*) goes off.

あいくち【匕首】 a「dagger [dirk, stiletto] without a guard.

あいこ【相子】 1〔無勝負・引きわけ〕a tie; a draw; a drawn [an inconclusive] game [match].　◐ あいこになる be drawn; be tied; end in a「draw [tie]; end inconclusively / じゃんけんぽんよ, あいこでしょ.

Let's「play [do] the fingers game, paper, stone, or scissors. Nobody won, so we'll「play [do] it again. ▶日本の風物について言っているので，このように説明しないと英語圏の人々にはわかりにくい．［⇨じゃんけん］ **2**〔五分五分〕◐あいこになる get [be] even 《with *somebody*》; be quits 《with *somebody*》/ さあこれであいこだ．Now we are「quits [all even].

あいせき【相席】相席する share a table 《with *somebody* at a restaurant》. ◐相席でもよろしゅうございますか．〔込んだレストランに入ってきた人に向かって〕Would you mind sharing a table?

あいなめ【鮎魚女・鮎並】〖魚〗a rock trout; a greenling.

あうん【阿吽】〖<Skt *a-hūm*〗〔初めと終わり〕alpha and omega;〔呼吸〕inhalation and exhalation;〔狛(こま)犬の〕an open mouth and a closed mouth. ◐あうんの呼吸〔相撲などの〕the harmonious timing required of two or more people engaged in a mutual endeavor.

あえもの【和え物】vegetables, fish, or shellfish dressed with miso, sesame, or vinegar. たとえば「野菜の酢和え」なら vegetables dressed with vinegar と言える．

あおいまつり【葵祭り】the Aoi Festival, held at the Upper and Lower Kamo Shrines in Kyoto on May 15.

あおこ【青粉】〔アオノリの粉末〕powderized green laver; green laver in powder form.

あおざかな【青魚】fish with blue backs, such as sardines and herrings.

あおじそ【青紫蘇】〖植〗〔シソ科の１年草；シソの一品種で茎・葉ともに緑色〕green perilla; a green beefsteak plant.

あおじる【青汁】〔緑色野菜をすりつぶした汁〕puréed green-leaf vegetables.

あおにさい【青二才】〔若僧〕a green [raw, callow] youth;《口》a young squirt;〔未熟者〕a greenhorn. ◐青二才のくせに生意気な奴だ．You're pretty cocky for「someone who's still a kid [a greenhorn].

あおのり【青海苔】green laver.

あおひげ【青髭】〔歌舞伎で〕blue makeup, often worn by a villain in a Kabuki play; it indicates that the character has shaved his face from his sideburns to his chin.

あおぶさ【青房】〖相撲〗the blue tassel hanging from the northeast corner of the roof over a sumo ring.

あおほん【青本】an illustrated storybook (published in the mid Edo period).

あおやぎ【青柳】1 〔柳〕a leafy green willow.　2 〖貝〗〔バカガイのむき身〕the meat of a「trough shell [surf clam].

あかいはね【赤い羽根】〔共同募金の〕a (Community Chest) red feather.　▷赤い羽根をつけている wear a red feather 《on *one*'s coat lapel》.　■ 赤い羽根共同募金運動 the Red Feather campaign; the Community Chest drive.

あかおに【赤鬼】a red「ogre [troll].

あかがい【赤貝】〖貝〗an ark shell.

あかぎれ【皸】chaps [cracks] 《in the skin》.　▷冬になると毎年あかぎれが切れる. Every winter my「skin [hands, fingers] get chapped.

あかすり【垢擦り】〔垢をこすり落とすこと〕scrubbing [rubbing] grime off the skin; 〔その道具〕(布) a rough-textured cloth to remove grime from the skin; (軽石) a pumice stone; (へちま) a loofa(h).　■ 韓国式垢擦り Korean-style *akasuri*. 垢擦り布[タオル] an *akasuri*「cloth [towel].

あかだし【赤出し】a *misoshiru* made from reddish-brown miso.

あかたん【赤丹】the three red hanafuda for January, February, and March; the bonus points for this combination.

あかちょうちん【赤提灯】〔提灯〕a red lantern; 〔飲み屋〕a place (advertised by a red lantern) where one can eat and drink inexpensively.

あかチン【赤チン】〖商標〗Mercurochrome; a red antiseptic formerly used to disinfect minor cuts and grazes.　▷赤チンを塗る put on [apply] Mercurochrome.

あかとんぼ【赤蜻蛉】a red dragonfly; 〔薄羽黄トンボ〕a wandering glider; 〔ショウジョウトンボ〕a scarlet skimmer.

あかねいろ【茜色】madder (red).　▷入日が山頂を茜色に染めた. The setting sun dyed the mountaintops「crimson [(a) dark red].

あかぶさ【赤房】〖相撲〗the red tassel hanging from the southeast corner of the roof over a sumo ring.

ア・カペラ〖音楽〗〔無伴奏で・無伴奏の〕*a capella*; *a cappella*.　▷ア・カペラで歌う sing *a cappella*.　■ アカペラ・グループ an *a cappella* group.

あかぼう【赤帽】a *redcap; a (station) porter.　▷赤帽に荷物を運ばせ

る get a「*redcap ["porter] to carry *one*'s「bags [luggage] / 赤帽を頼む get [hire] a「*red cap ["porter].

あかほん【赤本】**1**〔江戸時代の草双紙〕a red-covered storybook.　**2**〔安本〕cheap [pulp] fiction; *a dime novel; a "penny dreadful.

あかみそ【赤味噌】*akamiso*; reddish-brown miso.

あがりかまち【上がり框】a thick plank that one steps on when ascending from the vestibule to the entrance hall of a Japanese dwelling.

あきたけん【秋田犬】an Akita (dog).

あきのななくさ【秋の七草】the seven flowers of autumn [⇨ ななくさ].

あく　1〔灰〕wood ash.　**2**〔灰汁〕lye.　◐あくに漬ける soak《sliced burdock》in lye.　**3**〔野菜の渋味やえぐみ〕a (disagreeable) bitter [acrid, sharp] taste.　◐ホウレンソウのあく the harshness in spinach / ゴボウのあく the bitterness in burdock / あくを抜く remove the harsh taste《from fiddlehead ferns》.　**4**〔煮汁に浮く濁った泡〕scum.　◐材料が煮立ってあくが浮いてきたらすくい取ります. When the ingredients come to a boil and scum gathers on the surface, skim it off (with a「spoon [ladle]). / あくをおたまですくう skim off (the) scum with a ladle.　**5**〔人間や文章などの強い個性・癖〕a strong personality.　◐あくの強い親分肌の政治家 a godfather-like politician with a「strong personality [distinctive character].

あくび【欠伸】〔あくびをすること〕yawning;〔1回の〕a yawn.
　～する　yawn; give a《big》yawn.　◐口を手で覆いながらあくびする cover *one*'s mouth and yawn / あくびをかみ殺す stifle [suppress, strangle, smother] a yawn.

あぐら【胡坐】◐あぐらをかく sit cross-legged《on a cushion》; sit down with *one*'s legs crossed.

あげえん【揚げ縁】a hinged shutter that is lowered to serve as a porch during the day and raised to shut up shop.

あげぜんすえぜん【上げ膳据え膳】◐早く隠居して上げ膳据え膳で暮らしてみたいものだ. I can't wait to go into retirement and be waited on hand and foot.

あげだしどうふ【揚げ出し豆腐】lightly fried tofu.

あげだま【揚げ玉】bits of batter that fall into the oil when frying tempura and that also get fried.

あけのみょうじょう【暁の明星】the morning star; the daystar; Lucifer; Venus.

あげはちょう【揚羽蝶】〖昆〗a swallowtail (butterfly).

あげパン【揚げパン】a deep-fried ball of dough or filled bun.

あげまき【総角】**1**〔昔の子供の髪型の一種〕an ancient style of boys' hairdo, parted in the middle and bound in loops at the sides. **2**〔明治時代の女性の髪型の一種〕a Meiji-era (1868–1912) women's hairdo, piled in a pompadour and held in place with a pin. **3**〔総角結び〕=あげまきむすび.

あげまきむすび【総角結び】a style of decorative cord knot tied in trefoil shape.

あげまく【揚げ幕】〔歌舞伎・能舞台の〕a curtain at the entrance to the Kabuki or Noh stage.

あけむつ【明け六つ】the sixth hour of the morning (=approximately six o'clock in the present-day counting of hours).

あげもち【揚げ餅】a deep-fried rice cake.

あごあしつき【顎足付き】〔食事代・交通費付き〕◐あご足付きの招待旅行 a complimentary ⌈trip [tour] with all expenses paid; an ⌈all-expenses-paid [ǁall-in, *all-inclusive] (complimentary) trip; a (complimentary) trip for which ⌈everything is [travel and all meals are] paid (by the company).

あこうろうし【赤穂浪士】the forty-seven rōnin of the Akō domain who broke into the Edo residence of Kira Kōzukenosuke on January 30, 1703 (Dec. 14, 1702 by lunar reckonig), to avenge the death of their Lord, Asano Naganori.

あさいち¹【朝一】(the) first thing in the morning. ◐明日朝一で彼女に電話をします. I'll give her a call (the) first thing in the morning.

あさいち²【朝市】a market held during the morning; a morning market. ◐週末になるとここに朝市が立つ. A market is held here on weekend mornings.

あさがお【朝顔】〖植〗〔ヒルガオ科のつる性1年草〕(近縁の数種を含む) a morning glory; a Japanese morning glory. ■**朝顔市** a morning glory market;〔東京入谷の〕the morning glory market held early in July at Iriya in Tokyo.

あさぎ(いろ)¹【浅黄(色)】〔うすい黄〕light yellow; pale yellow.

あさぎ(いろ)²【浅葱(色)】〔緑がかったうすい藍色〕(a) ⌈pale [light] greenish blue; a pale blue-green. ◐ 浅葱色の着物 a pale「greenish-blue [blue-green]」kimono.

あさぎまく【浅葱幕】 a pale「greenish-blue [blue-green]」curtain suspended behind the main curtain in the Kabuki theater.

あさぎもめん【浅葱木綿】 a pale「greenish-blue [blue-green]」cotton cloth.

あさくさがみ【浅草紙】 coarse「toilet [lavatory]」paper (originally made at Asakusa in Tokyo).

あさくさのり【浅草海苔】〔アマノリ属の総称〕purple laver (cultivated at Asakusa during the Edo period);〔乾海苔〕nori; *amanori*; laver.

あさシャン【朝シャン】 a morning「hair-wash [shampoo]」; washing *one*'s hair in the morning.

あさつき【浅葱】〘植〙chives.

あさづけ【浅漬】 a vegetable pickled for a short time (in salted rice-bran paste [with salt]). ◐ キャベツの浅漬 cabbage pickled for a short time / 浅漬のたくあん white radish pickled for a short time.

あさのはもよう【麻の葉模様】 a geometric hemp-leaf pattern.

あさむし【浅蒸し】 (cooking by) light steaming.

あさり【浅蜊】〘貝〙a「Japanese littleneck [baby-neck]」clam; a Manila clam.

あじ【鯵】〘魚〙a jack mackerel; a saurel; a jack;〔マアジ〕Japanese jack mackerel. ◐ アジの南蛮漬け deep-fried「jack mackerel [saurel]」marinated in a marinade of chopped shallots, cayenne pepper, etc / アジの開き a「jack mackerel [saurel]」cut open lengthwise and dried / アジの干物 (sun-)dried「jack mackerel [saurel]」. ■ 豆鯵 a small「jack mackerel [saurel]」.

あしがる【足軽】〔最下級の武士〕a samurai of the lowest rank.

あしくち【足口】〔靴下の上端〕the open end of a sock;〔ショーツなどの下端〕the leg holes of a pair of underwear. ■ 足口ゴム ◐ 足口ゴム入りの靴下 socks with elastic tops.

あじさい【紫陽花】〘植〙〔ユキノシタ科の半常緑低木〕a Japanese hydrangea;〔セイヨウアジサイ・ハイドランジア〕a (common) hydrangea; a French hydrangea; a garden hydrangea.

あしずもう【足相撲】 leg wrestling.

あしだ【足駄】 (a pair of) high clogs; rain clogs.

あしづかい【足遣い】〔文楽の〕in Bunraku, the puppeteer who manipulates the feet of a puppet.

あじつけのり【味付け海苔】seasoned dried laver.

あしゆ【足湯】a footbath. ◐足湯を使う have a footbath; soak *one*'s feet in warm water.

あじろ【網代】wickerwork (of split bamboo or wood);〔捕魚のしかけ〕a fish weir. ■網代垣 an *ajiro* [a wicker(work)] fence. 網代笠 a wicker hat. 網代車 a wickerwork bullock carriage.

あじろあみ【網代編み】weaving thin strips of bamboo or other material into wickerwork; a wickerwork「weave [pattern]. ◐網代編みの天井 a wickerwork ceiling.

あすかじだい【飛鳥時代】the Asuka period (600–710).

あずき【小豆】an adzuki bean. ◐母は小豆を煮てあんこを作った. Mother boiled adzuki beans and made sweet bean paste. ■小豆アイス adzuki-bean sherbet. 小豆粥 adzuki-bean gruel. 小豆飯 rice boiled with adzuki beans.

あずきいろ【小豆色】reddish-brown; russet.

あずまおとこ【東男】a man from Eastern Japan. ◐東男に京女. A gallant Edo youth and a gracious Kyoto beauty.

あずまや【東屋】a summerhouse;《文》a gazebo;《文》a bower.

あぜくらづくり【校倉造り】a type of storehouse construction, exemplified by the eighth-century Shōsōin, made of interlocked timbers triangular in section.

あぜみち【畦道】a「raised footpath [ridge] between rice paddies.

あせも【汗疹】prickly heat; (a) heat rash. ◐あせもがかゆい. Heat rash is itchy. / 赤ちゃんの首にあせもができた. The baby has developed a heat rash on its neck.

あそん【朝臣】a prestigious title initially conferred, in the Nara period, on princes who had been reduced to the commonalty.

あだうちもの【仇討ち物】Bunraku or Kabuki plays whose theme is revenge.

あたまきん【頭金】a deposit; a down payment;〔保証金〕(a) security; money paid as (a) security;〔借家人が払う保証金〕key money. ◐1割の頭金 a 10%「deposit [down payment]; a「deposit [down payment] of 10% / 頭金を払う pay [put down, make] a deposit; make a down payment.

あたまだし【頭出し】 ■ 頭出し機能 a cue [search] function. 音響機器メーカーによって Automatic Music Sensor, Automatic Music Search, Music Search など様々の呼び名がある. ◐頭出し機能を使ってテープの必要な箇所を呼び出した. I used the「cue [search] (function) to find the place I needed on the tape.

あちゃらづけ【あちゃら漬け】 white radish [lotus root, turnips] pickled in sweetened vinegar seasoned with cayenne pepper.

あつあげ【厚揚げ】 *atsuage*; thick deep-fried「tofu [bean curd].

あつかん【熱燗】 hot sake.

あっちむいてほい〔日本の遊びの1つ〕*acchi muite hoi*; The winner of a rock, paper, scissors game calls out *acchi muite hoi* ("Look this way!) while simultaneously pointing up, down, left, or right. The opponent must, without breaking tempo, look in a different direction and compounds the loss by hesitating or pointing in the same direction.

あづちももやまじだい【安土桃山時代】 the Azuchi-Momoyama period (1573-1603).

あっぱっぱ a plain, loose one-piece dress (for summer wear).

あつもの【羹】 broth; hot soup. ◐あつものに懲りてなますを吹く. A burnt child「dreads [fears] fire.〘諺〙| Once bitten, twice shy.〘諺〙

あつやき【厚焼き】 ■ 厚焼き卵 a thick「omelette [omelet].

あてうま【当て馬】 1〔馬〕a stallion brought near a mare to see whether the latter is in heat. 2〔人〕a person sent to test another's intentions;〔選挙の〕=あてうまこうほ.

あてうまこうほ【当て馬候補】 a dummy candidate put up against the favorite; a stalking horse.

アド〔能狂言の〕an actor supporting the protagonist in a Kyōgen play. ■ 主(おも)アド the「principal [main] supporting player to a Kyōgen protagonist.

あとざ【後座】〔能舞台の〕the rear stage.

アトピー〘医〙atopy. ■ アトピー患者 an atopy sufferer; a patient suffering from atopy; an atopy case. アトピー性喘息 atopic asthma. アトピー性皮膚炎 atopic dermatitis.

あとやく【後厄】 the year following *one*'s climacteric (chief among which are the ages 42 for a man and 33 for a woman, calculated by considering a person one year old at birth).

あなご【穴子】〔アナゴ科の魚の総称〕a conger (eel).

あねさま(にんぎょう)【姉様(人形)】a doll in bridal costume, made from paper and bits of cloth.

あひる【家鴨】〔マガモを家畜化したもの；総称および雌〕a (domestic) duck;〔雄〕a drake.　◐ アヒルが鳴いている. A duck is [Ducks are, The ducks are] quacking. / アヒルの子 a duckling.

あぶなえ【危な絵】a genre of ukiyo-e woodblock prints depicting women in mildly erotic poses.　[⇨ しゅんが]

あぶらあげ【油揚げ】deep-fried「tofu [soybean curd].　◐ 油揚げ1枚 a piece of deep-fried「tofu [soybean curd].

あぶらぜみ【油蟬】〘昆〙a large brown cicada.

あぶらとりがみ【脂取り紙】〔顔などの〕absorbent paper.

あぶらな【油菜】〘植〙〔アブラナ科の2年草；栽培植物〕rape; colza (セイヨウアブラナ); Chinese colza (在来のアブラナ).

あぶらむし【油虫】**1**〘昆〙〔ゴキブリ〕a cockroach.　**2**〘昆〙〔アリマキ〕a plant louse 《*pl.* plant lice》; a greenfly; an ant cow.

あべかわもち【安倍川餅】a rice cake dusted with bean flour.

あま【海女】(ama) a woman diver; an *ama* 《*pl.* ~(s)》.　◐ 真珠採りの海女 a「female [woman] pearl diver.

あまあし【雨脚】〔筋のように見える雨〕the intensity of the rain;〔雨が通りすぎていくさま・その速さ〕(the speed of) a passing shower.　◐ 激しい雨脚 a「heavy [driving] rain. / 雨脚が速い. The rain is passing rapidly.

あまおち【雨落ち】the eavesdrop.　■雨落ち石 stone slabs lining the eavesdrop (to prevent drip erosion).

あまがえる【雨蛙】a tree「frog [toad]; a hyla.

あまくだり【天下り】"parachuting"; the practice of well connected government officials finding employment in the private sector after retiring.

あまぐり【甘栗】sweet roasted chestnuts.

あまざけ【甘酒】a sweet drink made from fermented rice or sake lees.

あまてらすおおみかみ【天照大神】the Sun Goddess.

あまなつ(かん)【甘夏(柑)】a Watson Pomelo.

あまなっとう【甘納豆】candied beans.

あまのいわと【天の岩戸】the Gate of the Celestial Rock Cave.

あまのはごろも【天の羽衣】the Celestial Feather Cloak.

あまみそ【甘味噌】sweet「miso [bean paste].

あみ【糠蝦】〚動〛〔小エビ〕a mysid; an opossum shrimp. ◐アミの佃(だく)煮 mysids boiled down in soy (sauce).

あみがさ【編み笠】a broad-brimmed hat woven of rushes or rice straw and worn for protection from the sun or to disguise *one's* identity.

あめおとこ【雨男】a "rain man" who brings rain with him wherever he goes; a man who seems to cause it to rain when he is present. 英語には日本語のような決まった言い方はない．[⇨ あめおんな]

あめおんな【雨女】a "rain woman" who brings rain with her wherever she goes; a woman who seems to cause it to rain when she is present.

あめざいく【飴細工】〔飴の細工菓子〕figures made of soft *ame*; wheat-gluten figures.

あめに【飴煮】〔料理〕a culinary method or dish in which a fish or other food is simmered in a mixture of its natural juices together with a spiced sweet syrup.

あめゆ【飴湯】a drink made of thick malt syrup dissolved with grated cinnamon in hot water, said to be effective against the summer heat.

アメリカン・コーヒー〔日本で好まれる濃いコーヒーと区別して〕mild [weak] coffee. ▶英語圏では普通 coffee といえばアメリカン・コーヒーのことである．

あめんぼ【水黽】〚昆〛a water strider; a pond [water] skater; a water「skipper [spider].

あゆ【鮎】an *ayu* (fish); a sweetfish.

あら【粗】1〔魚の〕bony parts 《of a fish》． 2〔欠点〕a fault; a defect; a flaw.

あらい【洗い】〔刺身の一種〕slices of raw fish rinsed in cold water. ◐鯉(こい)の洗い sliced [slices of] (raw) carp washed in cold water.

あらいはり【洗い張り】unstitching of the parts of a kimono, the washing and drying of each, and removal of creases prior to restitching.

あらがみ【荒神】a vigorous, powerful(, sometimes impetuous) deity.

あらかん【阿羅漢】an arhat; an arahat; an arahant; a Hinayana Buddhist monk who has attained nirvana.

あらぎょう【荒行】rigorous ascetic exercises; asceticism.

あらこ【粗粉】〔干菓子の材料〕rough-ground rice flour.

あらごとし【荒事師】〔歌舞伎の俳優〕an actor who plays robust and roistering characters.

あらし【嵐】〔激しい風〕a gale; a wind storm;〔暴風雨〕a deluge; a tempest;《文》the fury of the elements.

あらじお【粗塩】unrefined [solar] salt.

あらに【粗煮】bony portions of fish stewed in shoyu, sweet sake, and sugar.

あらひとがみ【現人神】an emperor; a living god; a god incarnate.

あらまき【荒巻, 新巻】〔鮭〕a slightly salted salmon;〔わらなどで巻いた魚〕a fish wrapped in「straw [rush leaves].

あられもち【霰餅】rice cake cut into roughly cubically chunks then dried, roasted, and flavored (with「shoyu [salt, sugar, etc.]).

あり【蟻】an ant. ◐蟻のように働く work like「an ant [ants]. ■働き蟻 a worker ant; a worker. 兵(隊)蟻 a soldier ant; a soldier.

ありたやき【有田焼】Arita「ware [porcelain].

アレルギー〖医〗an allergy;〔過敏な反応〕an allergy. ◐うちの子供たちはみんな卵に対してアレルギーがある. Our children are all allergic to eggs. / アレルギーになる develop an allergy / アレルギーを治す cure an allergy. ■花粉アレルギー an allergy to pollen. 食物アレルギー ◐大豆が原因の食物アレルギー a food allergy caused by soybeans. 薬物アレルギー an allergy to a medication. アレルギー性の allergic. ◐アレルギー性の炎症 an allergic inflammation. アレルギー性疾患 an allergic disease; an allergy. アレルギー性鼻炎[皮膚炎, 喘息] allergic「rhinitis [dermatitis, asthma].

あわおどり【阿波踊り】〔徳島を本場とする盆踊り〕(the) Awa Odori, a group folk dance of Tokushima Prefecture; (the) Awa Dance.

あわせ【袷】a lined kimono. ■袷羽織 a lined「haori [Japanese half-coat]. 袷仕立〔仕立て方〕lining《a garment》;〔衣類〕a lined garment.

あわび【鮑】〖貝〗an abalone; an ear shell; an *awabi*.

あわもち【粟餅】millet「dough [cake].

あわもり【泡盛】a clear liquor (60〜80 proof) produced in Okinawa Prefecture; it is distilled from rice fermented with black yeast.

あん【餡】bean jam;〔くずあん〕a thick clear sauce for foods that is prepared from broth mixed with a paste of arrowroot starch. ■うぐ

いす餡 a sweet paste made from green peas.　栗餡 a sweet white paste made from finely ground chestnut meal or steamed and strained chestnuts.　こし餡 smooth sweet red-bean paste.　さらし餡 red-bean paste in dry powder form.　白餡 a sweet white paste made from white beans.　つぶし[つぶ]餡 lumpy [coarse] sweet red-bean paste.　みそ餡 a sweet paste made from lima beans and soybean paste.　餡ドーナツ a doughnut with bean-jam filling.

あんか【行火】a foot warmer; a bed warmer.　■電気行火 an electric ˈfoot [bed] warmer.

あんかけ【餡掛け】food with a sauce of broth thickened with (powdered) ˈkudzu [arrowroot starch].　■餡掛けうどん wheat-flour noodles in soup thickened with a paste of arrowroot starch.　餡掛け豆腐 tofu [bean curd] with topped with a savory broth thickened with arrowroot starch.

あんこう【鮟鱇】〖魚〗an anglerfish; an angler; a frogfish; a sea toad.　◐ あんこうの吊るし切り boning and slicing of anglerfish while the fish is hung on a hook under its chin.　■鮟鱇鍋 anglerfish hotpot; a (winter) dish of anglerfish, tofu and other ingredients boiled in a pot at the table.

あんころ(もち)【餡ころ(餅)】soft *mochi* wrapped in sweet bean-jam.

あんず【杏】〔植〕〔バラ科の落葉小高木；中国北部原産の果樹〕an apricot; 〔果実〕an apricot.　◐ あんずのジャム apricot jam.

あんどん【行灯】a paper-covered lamp stand.

あんパン【餡パン】a ˈbean-jam [beanpaste] bun; a bun with bean jam inside.

あんまん【餡饅】a small ˈsteamed bun filled with sweet beanpaste flavored with sesame oil.

あんみつ【餡蜜】a dessert of boiled beans, cubes of agar gelatin, and bits of fruits topped with a sweet syrup.

い

い【亥】〔十二支の〕the Boar; the last of the twelve animals of the oriental zodiac. ◐亥の日 the day of the Boar / 亥の刻(ｺｸ) the hour of the Boar (9-11 p.m.) / 亥の方(ｶﾀ)〔北北西〕the direction of the Boar(; north-northwest). ■**亥年** the year of the Boar. ◐亥年生まれの born in the year of the Boar.

いあい【居合い】drawing a sword quickly from a sitting position to cut *one*'s adversary down. ■**居合い腰** the crouch assumed when the sword is drawn from a sitting position.

いえもと【家元】〔宗家〕the head family;〔人〕the head of a school 《of Noh players》. ◐茶道の家元 the head of a school of the tea ceremony / 家元を継ぐ take over [succeed to] the headship of a school. ■**家元制度** the *iemoto* system; the monopolized licensing of teaching a Japanese art by the head of that school of art.

イオマンテ〔アイヌの熊祭り〕*i-omante*; the Bear Festival, an Ainu ritual to thank the bear deity for providing bearskins and meat.

いか【烏賊】〘動〙a cuttlefish; a squid; a calamari. ◐イカの甲 a cuttlebone; a pen / イカの墨 squid ink; cuttlefish ink. ■**イカ釣り船** a squid fishing [boat].

いかいちょう【居開帳】temporary [seasonal] opening of a section of a (Buddhist) temple to allow public viewing of the「principal [chief]「image(s) [statue(s)].

いかいよう【胃潰瘍】an ulcered stomach; a「gastric [stomach] ulcer.

いかそうめん【烏賊素麺】thin strips of (raw) cuttlefish eaten dipped in wasabi and soy sauce.

いかだ【筏】a raft. ◐いかだで運ぶ raft; send [transport] by raft. / いかだで川を下る go「down a river [downstream] on a raft; raft downstream.

いかどっくり【烏賊徳利】 a sake bottle made from a dried「squid [cuttlefish].

いかなご【玉筋魚】『魚』a sand「eel [launce, lance]; a launce; a lance.

いかめし【烏賊飯】 stuffed squid; (boiled) squid stuffed with steamed glutinous rice.

いカメラ【胃カメラ】 a gastroscope; a gastrocamera; an endoscope. ◐ 病院で胃カメラを飲まされた. I「had [was given] a gastroscopy at the hospital. | They photographed the inside of my stomach.

いがもの【伊賀者】〔伊賀忍者〕ninjas from Iga domain in service to the Tokugawa Shogunate; they were famed for their skill as spies and assassins.

いがやき【伊賀焼き】 Iga ware; pottery [earthenware] from「Iga [the Iga area in Mie Prefecture].

いがん【胃癌】 gastric [stomach] cancer; cancer of the stomach.

いかんそくたい【衣冠束帯】 traditional formal court dress.

いき【粋】 smartness; stylishness; chic; high spirits; verve. 〜な〔あか抜けしている〕refined; elegant; stylish; fashionable;〔さばけている〕with good sense; worldly-wise; sophisticated; aware of the latest trends; *au fait*. ◐ 粋な男 a sophisticated man; a man of urbane tastes / 粋な女 a「stylish [fashionable] woman.

いきりょう【生き霊】 the baleful apparition of a living person who has a grudge against one.

いぐし【斎串】 a decorated branch of bamboo or *sakaki*, waved by a priest during a Shinto rite.

いくび【猪首】 a bull neck; a short and thick neck. ◐ 猪首の男 a「bullnecked [thick-necked] man / 彼は猪首だ. He has a short thick neck.

イクラ〖＜Russ. *ikra*〗salmon roe. ■ イクラ丼 a bowl of rice topped with salmon roe.

イケイケ〔慎重さを欠いた積極性・抑制のきかない奔放性〕■ イケイケムード a go-go mood. イケイケギャル a girl with a go-for-it attitude. イケイケドンドンの拡大路線 go-go expansionism.

いげたかすり【井桁絣】 ikat-dyed cloth with a pattern in the form of doubled crosses.

いけづくり【活け作り】〔調理法〕filleting a fish while it is still alive, slicing the meat into sashimi, and replacing it on the fish before serving;〔料理名〕a fish served whole with its meat sliced and replaced in position while it is still alive.

いけばな【生け花・活け花】〔術〕ikebana; (the art of) Japanese flower 「arrangement [arranging];〔生けた花〕flowers arranged in a 「vase [bowl]; a floral arrangement.

いご【囲碁】(the game of) go.　■囲碁棋士 a professional go player.　囲碁将棋教室 classes in go and *shōgi*.　囲碁名人戦 the battle to determine the grand champion in go.

いざ〔さあ〕come (now); now (then); well (now).　◐いざという時(に) in the「day [hour] of peril; in the moment of danger; when an emergency arises; in case of emergency; in an emergency; at zero hour; at the 「crucial [critical] moment.　■いざ鎌倉〔一大事が起こった場合; いよいよ行動を起こす時〕It's time to come running. | The time has come (to rush to the aid of the Kamakura Bakufu). / いざ鎌倉という時彼はきっと役に立つ人間です。He's someone you're sure to find「useful [helpful] when you're in serious trouble.

いざかや【居酒屋】a tavern; a bar; a bistro; *a saloon; ‖a pub;《口》an alehouse;《文》a public house.　◐居酒屋の主人 *a barkeeper; a saloon keeper; ‖a 「public-house [pub] keeper; a publican.

いさき【伊佐木】〖魚〗a grunt.

いざなぎのみこと【伊奘諾尊・伊邪那岐命】Izanagi-no-mikoto; In Japanese myth, the male divinity who with his divine female consort created the lands of Japan.

いざなみのみこと【伊奘冉尊・伊邪那美命】Izanami-no-mikoto; In Japanese myth, the female deity who with her divine male consort created the lands of Japan.

いしかりなべ【石狩鍋】〖料理〗a meal cooked in a pot at the table in which pieces of fresh salmon, vegetables, tofu, and other ingredients are boiled in a kelp and miso broth.

いしじぞう【石地蔵】a stone image of *Jizō*.

いしどうろう【石灯籠】a stone lantern.

いじめ〔特に子供同士の〕bullying《in school》; teasing; (集団的) group victimization [harassment]; (新入生などへの) hazing.　◐ひどいいじめ brutal teasing / 情容赦ないいじめ merciless teasing / 陰湿ないじめ

sly [furtive] bullying / クラスでのいじめ bullying in the classroom.

いしやき【石焼き】 roasting「on a heated slab of stone [in hot pebbles].　■**石焼きいも** a sweet potato roasted in hot pebbles.　**石焼き豆腐** tofu roasted on a metal pan (originally on heated stones).

いじん【異人】〔外国人〕a foreigner; an alien;〔西洋人〕a Westerner.　■**異人館**〔外国人, 特に西洋人の居住する洋館〕a Western-style「residence [merchant's office] built for Westerners in Japan in the Meiji period.

いずものかみ【出雲の神】 the Izumo Shrine deity who presides over matchmaking; the god of marriage.

いせえび【伊勢海老】 a spiny lobster; a large edible marine crustacean of the genus *Panulirus*; *Panulirus japonicus*.　◐伊勢海老の活け作り *Ise ebi* served live, with the flesh sliced and displayed in the shell.

いせまいり【伊勢参り】 a「pilgrimage [visit] to Ise Shrine.　◐伊勢参りの人 a pilgrim to Ise Shrine.

いそべやき【磯辺焼き】 a grilled 《rice cake》 wrapped in laver paper.

いたこ a necromancer, almost always female and usually blind, in northeastern Honshū.

いたち【鼬】 a (yellow) weasel.　◐いたちの最後っぺ the final desperate tactic of a cornered weasel; a last desperate resort.

いたちごっこ【鼬ごっこ】《口》a rat race.　◐物価と賃金のいたちごっこ a spiral of prices and wages; a vicious circle of wage rise and price hike; a《runaway》wage-price spiral.

いだてん【韋駄天】『仏教』〔四天王の一人である増長天の八大将軍の一人〕Idaten;《Skt》Skanda; one of the eight great generals of Zōjōten [《Skt》Virūḍhaka], he protects Buddhism and is popularly known for the ability to travel at great speed;〔足の速い人〕a swift runner; a strong endurance runner.　◐韋駄天のごとく走る run like「the wind [greased lightning]; run like a bat out of hell.　■**韋駄天走り** running at「lightning [headlong] speed.

いたどこ【板床】〔板張りの床の間〕a decorative alcove with a plank floor.

いたばさみ【板挟み】 a dilemma; a double bind.　◐義理と人情の板挟み the predicament of being duty-bound to take an action contrary to *one*'s sympathetic inclinations / 板挟みになる[なっている] be (placed

[put]) in a dilemma 《between…》; be in a fix; be [get] caught in a double bind; be on the horns of a dilemma / 上司と部下の板挟みになって困っている. I was troubled by my ⌈contrary [mutually contradictory] obligations to my superiors and subordinates.

いたみわけ【痛み分け】〚相撲〛 a draw in a sumo wrestling match declared because of an injury suffered by one of the contestants; 〔争いごとで双方が犠牲を払いながら勝敗なしとすること〕 a draw reached after sacrifices on both sides.

いために【炒め煮】〔調理法〕 sautéing; (a method of) cooking in which ingredients are first (stir-)fried and then ⌈cooked [boiled] in a liquid sauce; 〔料理〕 (a) sauté; food that has been first (stir-)fried and then simmered in broth. ◐ ひじきの炒め煮 (a dish of) *hijiki* seaweed that has been first pan-fried then cooked in soy sauce and other condiments / ナスの炒め煮 sautéed ⌈*eggplant [‖aubergine]; (a) sauté of ⌈*eggplant [‖aubergine].

いためもの【炒め物】 a stir-fry; stir-fried food. ◐ 肉と野菜の炒め物 (stir-)fried meat with (mixed) vegetables.

いたやき【板焼き】〔杉板焼き〕 domestic or wild fowl sliced thin, seasoned with soy and sweet sake, and grilled on a cedar board; 〔板焼き豆腐〕 tofu sliced thin and cooked between two cedar boards spread with miso.

いたわさ【板山葵】 slices of *kamaboko* served with grated wasabi.

いちげん【一見】〔旅館・料亭などで〕 appearing 《at an inn or a Japanese-style restaurant》 without an introduction from a regular customer; 〔その客〕 a first-time customer who arrives 《at an inn or a restaurant》 without an introduction. ◐ 一見の客 a chance customer. ■ **一見さん** a chance customer; a first-timer. ◐ 京都の高級料亭はほとんどが一見さんお断りだ. Almost every ⌈expensive [first-rate] restaurant in Kyoto turns away customers who have no introduction.

いちご【苺】〚植〛〔バラ科の多年草; 栽培イチゴ〕 a strawberry; 〔果物〕 a strawberry. ◐ 摘みたてのイチゴ freshly picked strawberries / イチゴ一粒 a (single) strawberry / イチゴを採る harvest strawberries / イチゴを摘む pick strawberries / 氷いちご shaved ice covered with strawberry syrup. ■ **いちご狩り** an outing to a strawberry farm (to pick strawberries). **いちご栽培** the cultivation of strawberries; strawberry farming. **いちごジャム** strawberry jam. **いちご酒** strawberry liqueur. **いちごシロップ** strawberry syrup. **いちご畑** a strawberry「bed [field, patch]. **いちごミルク** 〔イチゴに牛乳などをかけたもの〕 strawberries with milk; 〔イチゴ味の牛乳〕 strawberry-flavored milk.

いちごいちえ【一期一会】〔一生に一度きりの出会い・経験〕a uniquely precious「encounter [experience]; 〔茶道の教え〕Each occasion on which hospitality is offered and accepted is to be cherished as a unique experience in *one*'s life.

いちじく【無花果】〔クワ科の落葉小高木; 小アジア原産の果樹〕a (common) fig; 〔果実〕a fig. ◑ イチジクの葉 a fig leaf / イチジクのコンポート a fig compote; a compote of figs.

いちじゅういっさい【一汁一菜】a meal consisting of one soup and one main dish (besides rice); rice with soup and one other dish; a simple meal; plain [simple] fare.

いちのぜん【一の膳】the「principal [main] course of a traditional Japanese-style dinner.

いちのとり【一の酉】〔11月の最初の酉の日〕the first day of the cock in the eleventh month; 〔一の酉に行われる酉の市〕the market held on the first day of the cock in the eleventh month.

いちばん【一番】〔第一番〕the first; No. 1; the first place.

いちひめにたろう【一姫二太郎】first a daughter, then a son(, traditionally an auspicious order for the birth of children); 〔俗解: 娘一人に息子二人〕one daughter, two sons.

いちぶ【一分】〔10分の1〕one-tenth; 〔100分の1〕one-hundredth; one percent; 〔10分の1寸〕one-tenth of a *sun*; 〔4分の1両〕a quarter of a *ryō*.

いちふじにたかさんなすび【一富士 二鷹 三茄子】first Mt. Fuji, second a hawk, third an「*eggplant ["aubergine] (, the order of the three objects that are traditionally believed to「be auspicious [bring good luck] if they appear in *one*'s first dream of the New Year). [⇨ はつゆめ]

いちまつにんぎょう【市松人形】an Ichimatsu doll (with movable legs and arms attached to a torso of compacted sawdust on which a head sits, with all parts coated with white chalk).

いちまつ(もよう)【市松(模様)】checks; a checked [checkered, chequered] pattern; 〔細工〕checkerwork.

いちやづけ【一夜漬け】pickles made overnight. ◐白菜の一夜漬けを作った. I made some lightly salted pickles of Chinese cabbage. / 一夜漬けで歴史の試験勉強をする spend the whole night before the history examination cramming / 一夜漬けの青物 greens「pickled [salted] overnight / 一夜漬けの知識 knowledge obtained by last-minute cramming / 一夜漬けの勉強 overnight cramming.

いちょう【銀杏】〔イチョウ科の落葉高木; 中国原産〕a ginkgo; a maidenhair-tree.

いちょうぎり【銀杏切り】◐いちょう切りにする cut 《carrots》 in four lengthwise before slicing, so that each slice produces a quarter-circle (that resembles the leaf of the ginkgo tree).

いっかんばり【一閑張り】a kind of lacquered papier-mâché.

いっきのみ【一気飲み】drinking down [downing] a jug of beer in one go; drinking a large glass 《of beer》 without pausing for breath; *《口》 chugalugging. ～する drink down [down] a large glass of beer in one go; drink a large glass 《of beer》 without pausing for breath; *《口》 chugalug 《beer》.

いっけん【一間】a [one] *ken*; (about) six feet. ◐一間の床の間 an alcove one *ken*「wide [in width].

いっこん【一献】a cup (of sake); 〔小酒宴〕a small drinking party. ◐一献すすめる offer somebody a「drink [cup of sake] / 近々一献差し上げたく存じます.〔人を招待する言葉〕One of these days I would like to「take you out for a few drinks.

いっし【一矢】an arrow. ◐一矢を報いる get a blow in; get back at *somebody* [retaliate, strike back at *somebody*] / 試合終了直前に得点して相手チームにようやく一矢報いた. Just before the final whistle they scored a goal, finally managing to get back at the other team.

いっしゅうき【一周忌】the first anniversary of *somebody's* death. ◐その日は亡父の一周忌に当たる. That day is the first anniversary of my father's death.

いっしょうます【一升枡】a one-*shō* (=1.8 liters)「measuring box.

いっすん【一寸】〔尺貫法における長さの単位〕a *sun* (=約 3.03 cm). ◐一寸先も見えない闇である be pitch-dark; be too dark to see *one's* hand in front of *one's* face / 一寸先も見えない吹雪 a blinding「blizzard [snowstorm] / 霧のために一寸先も見えなかった. We could not see an inch ahead (of us) on account of the dense fog. / 一寸の虫にも五分の魂. Even a worm will turn. | Tread on a worm and it will turn.〖諺〗| The fly has her spleen, and the ant her gall.〖諺〗/ 一寸の光陰軽んずべからず. Carpe diem. | Life must be lived every moment. | Every moment (that we have) is precious.

いっすんぼうし【一寸法師】〔童話の〕(an) Inch Boy; (a) Tom Thumb;〔小男〕a dwarf; a pygmy; a pigmy; an elf 《*pl.* elves》; a manikin; a midget; a Lilliputian; a hop-o'-my-thumb.

いっせきにちょう【一石二鳥】killing two birds with one stone. ●一石二鳥の名案 a bright idea that will「make it possible [enable *one*] to kill two birds with one stone.

いっちょうら【一張羅】〔持っているなかで最上の衣服〕*one*'s best clothes; *one*'s Sunday best;〔持っている唯一の晴れ着〕*one*'s only smart clothes;〔持っている唯一の衣服〕the only suit of clothes that *one* has. ●一張羅を着て出かける go out in *one*'s Sunday best; go out dressed (up) to the nines.

いっとうぼり【一刀彫】〔技法〕a style of wood carving using a single (small) knife;〔作品〕a simple wood carving.

いっぴきおおかみ【一匹狼】a lone wolf; a loner; an independent (kind of) person. ●政界の一匹狼 a political「loner [lone wolf, maverick].

いっぷくかけ【一幅掛け】decorating the tokonoma, or alcove, in a traditional Japanese dwelling by juxtaposing a hanging scroll with a tea bowl or other aesthetic object placed at its foot.

いっぽんじめ【一本締め】a clapping of the hands by all present at a gathering, following a pattern of 3 claps, 3 claps, 3 claps, and 1 clap.

いっぽんば【一本歯】clogs with a single vertical support.

いっぽんばし【一本箸】one of a pair of chopsticks, especially one stood in a bowl of rice offered up to a deceased person.

いっぽんばな【一本花】the single blossom 《of the Japanese anise tree》 placed by the pillow of a deceased person.

いてざ【射手座】〖天・占星〗the Archer; Sagittarius (略: Sgr). ●射手座生まれの人 a Sagittarius; a Sagittarian.

いとあやつり【糸操り】〔南京操り〕the manipulation of「marionettes [string puppets].

いとごんにゃく【糸蒟蒻】*konnyaku* noodles.

いどぢゃわん【井戸茶碗】 a type of tea bowl with a pale yellowish-orange glaze produced in Korea from the late 16th to the early 17th century and highly esteemed by Japanese tea masters.

いとづくり【糸作り】 raw squid or other seafood sliced into thin strips.

いとなます【糸膾】 a dish of long, thinly sliced vegetables with fish, marinated in vinegar.

いとみち【糸道】〔糸爪〕a groove that develops on the left index fingernail of a samisen or koto player from being rubbed by the strings;〔三味線[琴]の演奏技能〕《a player's》samisen [koto] playing ability.

いともの【糸物】〔織物〕thread textiles; (textile) fabrics; 弦楽器 stringed instruments(: samisen, koto);〔三味線を伴う演芸〕a samisen performance; performance arts accompanied by a samisen.

いなおりごうとう【居直り強盗】 a sneak-thief who「turns aggressive [becomes violent high-handed attitude] when「discovered [caught] in the act.

いなかに【田舎煮】 a country-style dish of vegetables boiled in a broth strongly flavored heavily laced with soy sauce.

いなご【蝗】 a locust.

いなずま【稲妻】 (a flash [bolt] of) lightning. ◐ 空に稲妻が走った. A bolt of lightning raced across the sky. / 稲妻のように〔速く〕like lightning; as「quick [swift] as lightning; with lightning speed / 名案が稲妻のようにひらめいた. A wonderful idea came (to her) like a flash of lightning.

いなだ〔ブリの幼魚; 全長 40cm 前後のもの〕a yellowtail.

いなばのしろうさぎ【因幡の白兎】 the White Hare of Inaba an ancient tale of a hare that tricks crocodiles into forming a bridge for it to cross, but crowing over his deceit has his pelt skinned by the last crocodile.

いなり【稲荷】 the god of harvests; a local guardian deity;〔俗説〕the fox deity. ■ 稲荷神社 an Inari shrine.

いなりずし【稲荷ずし】 flavored boiled rice wrapped in fried bean curd.

いぬ【戌】〔十二支の〕the Dog, one of the twelve animals of the Oriental zodiac. ◐ 戌の日 the day of the Dog / 戌の刻(こく) the hour of the Dog (7-9 p.m.) / 戌の方(かた)〔西北西〕the direction of the Dog(: west-northwest) / 戌年 the year of the Dog / 戌年生まれの born in the year of the Dog.

いぬがみ【犬神】a dog spirit; a dog god. ◐犬神憑き〔状態〕possession by a dog spirit;〔人〕a person possessed by a dog spirit.

いぬくい, いぬぐい【犬食い】～する eat like a dog; eat greedily with *one*'s head down; (when eating with chopsticks) eat from a bowl without picking it up.

いぬくぼう【犬公方】〔徳川綱吉のあだ名〕the Dog Shogun (the nickname of the fifth Tokugawa shogun Tsunayoshi who decreed that animals should be protected).

いぬはりこ【犬張子】a papier-mâché dog (toy).

いねむりうんてん【居眠り運転】falling asleep「at the wheel [while driving]; dozing (off) at the wheel. ◐居眠り運転をする doze (off) at the wheel; fall asleep while driving 《a car》.

いのしし【猪】1 a wild boar;〔日本産の〕a white-whiskered boar. ◐イノシシの肉 wild boar meat. 2〔十二支の〕＝い.

いはい【位牌】a (Buddhist) memorial tablet; a tablet on which the posthumous Buddhist name of the deceased is inscribed, and which is kept in the Buddhist altar cabinet in the home. ◐先祖の位牌 an ancestral [a family] memorial tablet.

いばやし【居囃子】〔能の〕a short Noh piece performed by 3 performers who remain seated.

いぶしぎん【燻し銀】oxidized silver;〔色〕somber silver. ◐いぶし銀のような refined; sober; quiet / 彼の演技にはいぶし銀のような味がある. His performance is exquisitely understated.

いぼ【疣】〔小突起〕a wart;〚医〛(皮膚の) a wart; a verruca 《*pl.* -cae, ～s》;（ガマの）a pustule. ◐手にいぼができた. I got a wart on my hand. | A wart developed on my hand.

いまがわやき【今川焼】a Japanese muffin containing bean jam, served hot.

いまよう【今様】〔今様歌〕an ancient verse form consisting of 4 lines each divided into two couplets of 7 and 5 syllables.

いまりやき【伊万里焼】Imari ware. [＝ありたやき]

いも【芋】1〔ジャガイモ〕a potato 《*pl.* ～es》; *a white potato; 《口》a spud;〔サツマイモ〕a sweet potato;〔サトイモ〕a taro 《*pl.* ～s》;〔ヤマノイモ〕a yam. 2〔根瘤〕a root nodule. 3〔やぼったい人〕an unrefined person; a person with no「refinement [sophistication];（男）a clod; a bumpkin.

いもあめ【芋飴】sweet-potato paste.

いもがゆ【芋粥】rice porridge with sweet potato.

いもがら【芋がら】dried runners of the taro (plant).

いもじょうちゅう【芋焼酎】a liquor distilled from sweet potatoes.

いもでんがく【芋田楽】taros flavored with miso and「broiled ["grilled] on a skewer.

いもにかい【芋煮会】a party outdoors at which people eat a stew of taros, green onions, beef, etc.; a taro cookout.

いもばたけ【芋畑】〔ジャガイモの〕a potato「field [patch];〔サツマイモの〕a sweet-potato「field [patch];〔サトイモの〕a taro「field [patch];〔ヤマノイモの〕a yam field; a field of yams.

いもばん【芋版】a print made from the incised surface of a cross-section of a sweet potato; a "potato print." ◐いも版の年賀状 a new year's card with a potato print on it.

いもようかん【芋羊羹】(a bar of) jellied sweet-potato paste.

いもり【井守】〔イモリ科の両生類〕a newt; an eft. ◐イモリの黒焼〔惚れ薬〕a love potion powder made from charred newt.

いよかん【伊予柑】an Iyokan; an Iyo tangor.

いりこ^1【炒り子】dried small sardines.

いりこ^2【炒り粉】parched rice flour.

いりこ^3【海参】dried sea slug; dried sea cucumber; (dried) trepang.

いりざけ【煎り酒】〔酒に醤油・かつお節・梅干しなどを入れ半量に煮つめて作った調味料〕a liquid seasoning prepared by boiling down to half the quantity, a mixture of sake and soy sauce, fish stock, pickled plums, and other ingredients.

いりどうふ【煎り豆腐】boiled bean curd drained, seasoned, and heated.

いりどり【炒り鶏】finely chopped chicken meat and vegetables braised and then stewed.

いりに【煎り煮】◐煎り煮にする simmer in (soy-flavored) stock after roasting / 煎り煮にした里芋 taro (roasted and) simmered in soy-flavored stock.

いるか【海豚】a dolphin; a porpoise. ◐イルカ・ショー a dolphin show.

いろは 1〔仮名〕*iroha*; the traditional Japanese syllabary;〔歌〕⇨いろは

歌. **2**〔初歩・基本〕the ABC 《of...》; the「rudiments [basics, elements]《of...》; lesson [step] one; the first「step [rule]. ■ **いろは歌** a Heian-era verse, recited during calligraphy practice in which each of the 47 symbols of the syllabary is used just once.　**いろは歌留多** (a pack of) traditional playing cards, featuring proverbs each of which begins with a different letter of the *iroha* alphabet.　**いろは順** *iroha* order; traditional Japanese alphabetical order.　**いろは47文字** the 47 characters of the *iroha* syllabary.

いろむじ【色無地】a semiformal kimono of a solid color, unpatterned except for a crest; an unpatterned kimono.

いろり【囲炉裏】a sunken hearth; a sunken fireplace.

いわし【鰯】a sardine;〔小鰯〕a sprat.　◐ イワシのオイル漬け sardines in oil / イワシの缶詰 canned [tinned] sardines.

いわたおび【岩田帯】a maternity belt (worn from the sixth month of pregnancy).

いわな【岩魚】〔サケ科の淡水魚〕a Japanese char(r).

いん【院】**1**〔上皇〕an ex-emperor.　◐ 後鳥羽院 the ex-Emperor Gotoba.　**2**〔戒名に添える語〕the suffix -*in* used in posthumous Buddhist names.

いんかん【印鑑】〔印章〕a seal;〔押した形〕(the「mark [impression] made by) a seal; a seal mark.　■ **印鑑証明** registration of a seal (impression) by local authorities; seal certification.　◐ 印鑑証明書 a certificate proving that one has registered (the impression of) *one*'s seal with the local government; a seal-registration certificate.　**印鑑登録**〔市区町村の役所への〕registration of [registering] a seal (with the local government); seal registration.　◐ 印鑑登録証 a personal seal registration-card; a card used as evidence that one has registered a personal seal (with a local government).

いんげんまめ【隠元豆】〔マメ科の1年生つる植物; 食用作物〕a common bean; a kidney bean; a haricot bean; a French bean.

いんせい【院政】government by a retired emperor; the rule of a cloistered emperor; a cloister government.　◐ 前社長は表には出ないが, 実質的には院政をしいている. The retired company president is actually pulling the strings from behind the scenes.

いんぞう, いんそう【印相】〔仏像の〕the gesture of a Buddha's hands;

〔印章の〕 *one*'s fortune as told in *one*'s personal seal.

インターネット・カフェ an Internet café; a cybercafé.

インターネット・プロバイダー 〔接続業者〕an Internet service provider (略: ISP).

インターホン 〔内部電話〕an intercom; an interphone. ◐ インターホンが鳴った. The intercom buzzed. / インターホンに応(こた)える answer the intercom.

いんでん【印伝】〔革細工〕*inden*; a「handbag [wallet, purse] made of dyed tanned leather and decorated with dots of Japanese lacquer in a distinctive conventional pattern.

いんにく【印肉】 a seal pad; a pad saturated with a vermilion (or sometimes other-colored) mixture for "inking" a「seal [*hanko*] before impression.

いんろう【印籠】 a container made up of (usually) from 3 to 5 tiers of flat rectangular cases and a lid, initially used to carry seals and stamp pads and then (in the Edo period) for medicines;〔薬入れ〕an inro; a medicine case [box];〔印入れ〕a seal case. ◐ この印籠が目に入らぬか! Can't [Don't] you see (the crest on) this seal case!

う

う¹【卯】〔十二支の〕the Rabbit [Hare], one of the twelve animals of the oriental zodiac. 〔⇨ うさぎ〕 ◐ 卯の日 the day of the Rabbit / 卯の刻(こく) the hour of the Rabbit (5-7 a.m.) / 卯の方(かた)〔東〕the direction of the Rabbit (east). ■ 卯年 the year of the Rabbit.

う²【鵜】〔ウ科の鳥の総称〕a cormorant; a shag. 〔⇨ うかい〕 ◐ 鵜を使って魚を取る fish with cormorants; use cormorants for fishing. 鵜の目鷹の目 keen「eyes [eyesight]; vigilant attention.

ういろう(もち)【外郎(餅)】sweet rice jelly.

ウーロンちゃ【烏龍茶】oolong [oulong] (tea).

うおがし【魚河岸】a waterside area where a fish market is located; a fish market;〔東京・築地の中央卸売市場〕the Tsukiji wholesale fish market in Tokyo.

うおざ【魚座】『天・占星』the Fishes; Pisces (略: Psc.). ◐ 魚座生まれの人 a Pisces; a Piscean.

うおすき【魚鋤】〔魚介を用いた「すき焼き」風の鍋料理〕fish sukiyaki; sukiyaki with seafood instead of beef.

うかい【鵜飼い】cormorant fishing; fishing with cormorants. ■ 鵜飼い船 a boat for fishing with cormorants.

うきくさ【浮草】〔ウキクサ科の1年生水草〕greater duckweed;〔水面に浮かぶ水草の総称〕a floating aquatic plant. ◐ 浮草の生活を送る lead an「unstable [unsettled] life. ■ 浮き草稼業 a precarious trade; an unstable occupation; an itinerant trade.

うきよえ【浮世絵】an ukiyo-e 《pl. ~s》; a woodblock pictures of the Edo period. ■ 浮世絵師 an ukiyo-e artist; a woodblock print artist of the Edo period. 浮世絵風の ukiyo-e-style; as *one* might see in an ukiyo-e.

うきよぞうし【浮世草子】popular stories of everyday life in the Edo

period.

うぐいす【鶯】1〔ヒタキ科の鳥〕a (Japanese) bush warbler. ◐鶯の谷渡り the flight of a bush warbler from valley to valley;〔鳴き声〕the song of a bush warbler in flight. **2**〔色〕brownish green.

うぐいすばり【鶯張り】a nightingale floor; a squeaking floorboard. ◐鶯張りの廊下 a nightingale corridor; a corridor that announces approaching footsteps.

うぐいすまめ【鶯豆】an *uguisu* pea; a sweetened, boiled pea.

うぐいすもち【鶯餅】a cake of soft *mochi* filled with bean jam and powdered with green soybean flour.

うこん【鬱金】1〔ショウガ科の多年草;熱帯アジア原産の香辛料植物〕turmeric;〔香辛料〕(根茎) turmeric. **2**〔色〕=うこんいろ.

うこんいろ【鬱金色】saffron (yellow).

うさぎ【兎】〔飼いウサギ〕a rabbit;〔野ウサギ〕a hare;〔ウサギ目の動物〕a lagomorph;〔ウサギ科の動物〕a leporid. ◐月の中のうさぎ the rabbit in the moon / うさぎの肉 rabbit meat.

うさぎごや【兎小屋】〔箱型の〕a rabbit「hutch [cage, pen].

うさぎめ【兎目】〔フラッシュ撮影のとき人物の目が赤く写る現象〕the red-eye effect; red-eye.

うし¹【丑】〔十二支の〕the Ox, one of the twelve animals of the oriental zodiac. ◐丑の日 the day of the Ox / 日本には夏の土用の丑の日にウナギを食べる習慣がある. Japanese have a custom of eating eel on the midsummer day of the Ox. / 丑の刻(ﾞ) the hour of the Ox (1–3 a.m.); the wee hours of the morning / 丑の方(ﾞ)〔北北東〕the direction of the Ox (north-northeast). ■丑年 the year of the Ox.

うし²【牛】〔雌〕a cow;〔雄〕a bull;〔去勢牛〕an ox《*pl.* oxen》; a bullock; a steer;〈集合的に〉cattle; cows;〔子〕a calf《*pl.* calves》. ◐牛に引かれて善光寺参り just following a cow and ending up at Zenkō-ji Temple; going somewhere at another's request and having an unexpected happy experience as a result / 食べてすぐ寝ると牛になるよ. You'll turn into a cow if you lie down right after you eat!

うじ【蛆】a maggot;〔魚釣りの餌〕ᴵᴵa gentle. ◐うじだらけの maggoty / うじがわいている〈物・場所が主語〉be「infested with [full of] maggots; be maggot-ridden; be flyblown.

うしおじる【潮汁】a thin soup made from boiling fish or shellfish in seawater (or plain water seasoned only with salt).

うしおに【潮煮】fish or shellfish boiled in salted water.

うしがえる【牛蛙】〔食用ガエル〕a bullfrog.

うじがみ【氏神】a [the] local「tutelar [tutelary, guardian] deity; a [the] genius loci. ◐時の氏神 a person who appears at the right moment to lend a helping hand; a fairy godmother; a godsend.

うじこ【氏子】people [a person] under the protection of the local tutelar deity; a parishioner of a Shinto shrine. ■氏子総代 a representative of (shrine) parishioners.

うしのときまいり【丑の時参り】a visit to a shrine「around the hour of the Ox [in the wee hours of the morning] to lay a curse on *somebody*. (A straw doll, representing a person who is greatly disliked or hated, is nailed to a tree, and an incantation is said for the death of that person.)

うしみつ【丑三つ】■丑三つ時[頃] the third quarter of the hour of the Ox (approximately 3:00 to 3:30 a.m.); in the「small [wee] hours of the morning; at [in the] dead of night. ◐草木も眠る丑三つ時 in the「wee [small] hours of morning, when even the trees are asleep.

うしろがみ【後ろ髪】◐後ろ髪を引かれる思いだった. I found it hard to wrench myself away. | It was with great reluctance that I left *somebody* [*something*] behind.

うしろゆび【後ろ指】◐後ろ指をさされる be「talked about [spoken ill of] behind *one*'s back; be the object of「covert [surreptitious] finger-pointing / 人に後ろ指をさされないように気をつけなさい. Give no one cause to「talk about [point fingers at] you behind your back.

うすかわまんじゅう【薄皮饅頭】sweet bean paste in a thin envelope of dough.

うすちゃ【薄茶】〔茶道のお点前(てまえ)の１つ〕weak green tea prepared at a formal tea ceremony. ◐薄茶を立てる prepare a light tea.

うすべり【薄縁】rush matting bordered with cloth.

うすやき【薄焼き】pan-frying「thinly spread batter [beaten egg]. ■薄焼きせんべい a thin rice cracker. 薄焼き卵 a paper-thin omelette used to wrap, or lay on top of, other ingredients.

うずら【鶉】〖鳥〗a quail 《*pl.* ~(s)》. ◐ウズラの群れ a flock of quail(s); a bevy of quails / ウズラの卵 a quail('s) egg.

うずらまめ【鶉豆】a mottled kidney bean; a pinto bean.

うたあわせ【歌合せ】〔平安時代の〕a tanka poetry contest.

うたい【謡】〔謡曲〕〈総称〉*utai*; Noh chant. ◐謡を謡う recite [chant]「a Noh text [an *utai*]. ■謡本 an *utai* libretto; the libretto of a Noh drama.

うだいじん【右大臣】the Minister of the Right in pre-modern Japan; inferior in rank to a *sadaijin*, or minister of the left.

うたかい【歌会】a tanka「party [competition]. ■歌会始 the New Year's Poetry Party (held at the Imperial Court); the Imperial New Year's Poetry Reading.

うたがるた【歌がるた】cards on which are printed the opening three lines from famous tanka poems, used in a game whose object is to grab before other players the card on which is printed the closing couplet of the poem being read aloud by a nonplayer; poem [poetry] cards;〔遊び〕a poem- [poetry-] card game. [⇨かるた]

うたせゆ【打たせ湯】a steady stream of hot-spring water cascading onto a person's back; pelting water.

うだつ【梲】〔棟木を支える柱〕a short pillar set on a beam to support a ridgepole. うだつが上がらない cannot「get on [rise] in the world; do not「rise above mediocrity [get ahead, go places]; not be a success 《as …》. ◐この店にはうだつの上がらない連中ばかり寄ってくる. This bar attracts the going-nowhere set.

うたまくら【歌枕】〔和歌に詠まれる名所〕a place famed in classical Japanese poetry;〔枕詞や名所を記した書物〕a handbook of place-names and associated phrases used when composing tanka.

うたものがたり【歌物語】an early Heian-period genre of collected short tales centering around poems.

うちあげ【打ち上げ】**1**〔空へ上げること〕(花火などの) letting [setting] off 《fireworks》; a display 《of fireworks》; shooting (off [up]) 《fireworks》; (ロケットの) a launch(ing); (a) lift-off. **2**〔興行の終了〕the「close [end]《of a run of performances》;〔仕事じまい〕the「end [winding-up, completion]《of a project》. ◐いよいよこの仕事も打ち上げだ. At last we seem to have reached the end of this job. / きょうでこの公演は打ち上げだ. Today marks the last performance in this series. | The last performance is today.

うちいり【討ち入り】a raid《on…》; an attack《on…》. ◐四十七士の吉

良邸討ち入り the attack on Kira's mansion by the 47 *rōnin*.

うちいわい【内祝い】1〔内輪の祝い〕a family celebration.　**2**〔贈り物〕a small present (given on the occasion of a family celebration).

うちがし【打ち菓子】 molded confectionery; a molded sweet.

うちだし【打ち出し】〔演劇・相撲などの一日の興行の終わり〕the end; the close; the conclusion.

うちっぱなし【打ちっぱなし】1〔コンクリートの〕《buildings of》undressed [unfaced] concrete.　**2**〔ゴルフ練習場〕a driving range.

うちでのこづち【打出の小槌】 a mallet, figuring in fables, that produces *one*'s heart's desire at a wave; a magic wand; a cornucopia.

うちべんけい【内弁慶】 a person who「throws *his* weight around [behaves bossily] at home, but is「meek (and mild) [timid] outside. [⇨ べんけい]　◐彼は内弁慶だ. He is a lion at home, but a mouse「outside [abroad].

うちみず【打ち水】 watering; sprinkling.　◐庭に打ち水をする water [sprinkle water in] the「*yard [''garden] / 路地に打ち水をする sprinkle water on the「backstreet [alleyway]; sprinkle the lane with water.

うちわ【団扇】〔風を起こす道具〕a (round, rigid) fan.

うちわだいこ【団扇太鼓】 a hand drum shaped like a round fan.

うつびょう【鬱病】 depression; melancholia; melancholy; depressive psychosis.

うでずもう【腕相撲】 Indian [arm] wrestling.

うど【独活】〔植〕an udo (a plant of the ginseng family cultivated for its edible shoots).

うどん【饂飩】 thick white noodles made from wheat flour, salt, and water; *udon*.　■うどん屋〔食堂〕(店) an *udon*「restaurant [shop];〔製麺所〕a noodle-making factory.

うなぎ【鰻】 an eel; a Japanese eel.　◐うなぎの蒲焼 broiled eel; ''a spitchcock; an eel split down the spine or down the belly and grilled over a charcoal fire while being dipped several times in a thick, sweet soy sauce / うなぎの寝床のような家 a long and narrow house.

うなぎのぼり【鰻登り】　◐うなぎ登りに上がる advance [be promoted] rapidly; rise rapidly; shoot up; soar; (sky)rocket / 不景気の影響で失業率がうなぎ登りに上昇している. As a result of the recession the unemployment rate has「shot up [soared, skyrocketed].

うなじゅう【鰻重】broiled eel on rice, served in a lacquered meal box.

うなどん【鰻丼】a bowl of hot boiled rice topped with broiled eel.

うなりごま【唸り独楽】a humming top.

うに【海胆】1【海胆】a sea urchin; an echinoid; an echinus 《*pl.* echini》; a sea porcupine. 2【雲丹】〔食品〕(seasoned) sea urchin eggs.

うねめ【采女】a lady-in-waiting at court in ancient Japan.

うのみ【鵜呑み】鵜呑みにする〔かまずに飲み込む〕swallow *something*「whole [without chewing]; gobble (up); gulp (down); bolt 《food》;〔そのままを真(ま)に受ける〕swallow; accept *something* (as true) without question(ing); take [accept] *something* on faith; cram 《knowledge》;《口》buy. / 彼女はその話をうのみにした.《口》She swallowed the story hook, line, and sinker. | She bought the whole story.

うばい【烏梅】〔染料・薬料〕green「plums [Japanese apricots] that have been dried and smoked and are used in Chinese medicine and for dyeing.

うばがい【姥貝】〔ほっきがい〕a Sakhalin surf clam.

うばぐるま【乳母車】a (baby) buggy; *a baby carriage; ‖a perambulator; ‖《口》a (child) pram;〔折りたたみ式の〕*a stroller; ‖a pushchair;〔幌(ほろ)つきの〕a bassinet(te).

うぶすな(がみ)【産土(神)】the「tutelary deity [guardian god] of *one*'s hometown; the *genius loci*.

うま¹【午】〔十二支の〕the Horse, one of the twelve animals of the Oriental zodiac. ◐午の日 the day of the Horse / 午の刻(こく) the hour of the Horse (11 a.m.-1 p.m.) / 午の方(かた)〔南〕the direction of the Horse (south). ■午年 the year of the Horse.

うま²【馬】a horse《*pl.* 〜s, 〜》;〈集合的に〉horseflesh;《口》a nag;〔小型の〕a pony;〔家畜〕a horse;〔乗用馬〕a mount;〔軍馬〕a charger, a steed;〔子〕a colt. ◐野生の馬 a wild horse / 馬に乗る ride (a horse); mount [get on] a horse; get in the saddle.

馬が合う get「on [along] well 《with…》; hit it off 《with…》; have good rapport 《with…》;《口》click 《as friends, from their first meeting》. / 二人は馬が合うらしい. They seem to get along well with each other.

馬の耳に念仏(だ). It's「unprofitable [nonproductive, a complete waste of time]. ◐その講演会に彼が聞きに行っても馬の耳に念仏だろう. Even if he goes to the lecture it's likely「he won't get a thing out of it [it will be completely lost on him].

うまき【鰻巻】chopped eel rolled in an omelet(te).

うまじるし【馬印】a「banner [standard, flag] stood beside the horse of a「commander [general] leading warriors in battle (a practice initiated in the late 16th century); a commander's battle standard.

うまに【旨煮】fish [meat] and vegetables stewed in salt, soy sauce, sake, and sugar.

うまのほね【馬の骨】 ◐ どこの馬の骨だかわからない連中 people from who knows where; people of「doubtful [unknown] origin; suspicious strangers / どこの馬の骨だかわからない男だ. Nobody knows where he comes from. | His identity is a mystery.

うままわり【馬回り】〔大将の乗った馬の周囲〕the vicinity of a general on horseback;〔護衛の騎馬侍〕a general's mounted guard.

うみせんやません【海千山千】 ◐ 海千山千の実業家 a「shrewd [canny, sharp] businessman who knows every trick in the book / やつは女にかけては海千山千のプレイボーイだ. He's been around and has a way with women.

うみのひ【海の日】〔7月の第3月曜日（もと7月20日）〕Marine Day.

うみぼうず【海坊主】〔妖怪〕a roundheaded sea「goblin [monster]; a naked apparition with a bald head and bulging eyes whose appearance bodes ill for an ocean voyage.

うめ【梅】〔バラ科の落葉低木; 中国原産の観賞植物・果樹〕an *ume* (tree); a mume; a Japanese「apricot [plum];〔実〕a mume; a Japanese「apricot [plum]. ◐ 梅に鶯(うぐいす) a bush warbler in a blossoming *ume* tree; an auspicious「match [pair].

うめしゅ【梅酒】*ume*「brandy [liqueur].

うめぼし【梅干し】〔梅の塩漬け〕a pickled「*ume* [plum]. ■ 梅干し飴 a kind of candy that resembles an *umeboshi* in both shape and size. 梅干しばばあ a「wizened [wrinkled]「old woman [granny, hag].

うらしまたろう【浦島太郎】(a) Rip van Winkle. ◐ 20年ぶりに帰国したら, 東京はすっかり変わっていて, 浦島太郎になった気分だった. When I came back after twenty years overseas, Tokyo was so completely changed I felt like Rip van Winkle.

うらせんけ【裏千家】the Urasenke school of the tea ceremony (founded by Sen no Rikyū).

うらぼん【盂蘭盆】 the *Bon* Festival; the Feast of Lanterns (held from 13 to 15 July in honor of the spirits of ancestors).

うりもみ【瓜揉み】 thinly sliced cucumber rubbed with salt (and dressed in vinegar).

うるうどし【閏年】 a leap year; an intercalary [《文》a bissextile] year. ◐ 閏年は4年ごとにやってくる. A leap year comes along every four years. / 今年は閏年だ. This year is a leap year.

うるか salted entrails and roe of the *ayu*, or sweetfish.

うるし【漆】1 〔ウルシ科の落葉高木; 中国原産〕a varnish tree; a Japanese lacquer tree. **2** 〔漆の木から採った塗料〕lacquer; varnish; japan; Japanese [Chinese] lacquer. ■漆かぶれ[負け] lacquer poisoning; rhus dermatitis. 漆工芸 lacquerwork (art). 漆細工 lacquerware; japan. 漆職人 a lacquerer; a japanner; a lacquer worker. 漆塗り ◐ 漆塗りの箸(はし) lacquered chopsticks / 漆塗りの飾りだんす a 「japanned [lacquered] ornamental chest. 漆屋 a lacquer 「shop [dealer]. 漆蠟(ろう) *urushi* 「tallow [wax].

うろこ【鱗】 a scale;〔動〕a shard; a squama 《*pl.* -mae》. ◐ うろこでおおわれている be covered with scales; be scaly.

うわおび【上帯】 an outer 「sash [belt].

うわしき, うわじき【上敷】〔絨毯(じゅうたん)〕a rug; a carpet;〔敷布〕a sheet;〔薄べり〕a bordered (rush) mat; bordered matting.

うわばみ【蟒】〔大蛇〕a giant snake; an anaconda; a boa constrictor; a boa; a python. ◐ ウワバミのように酒を飲む drink like a fish.

うんざ【運座】 a meeting of haiku poets; a haiku contest.

うんしゅうみかん【温州蜜柑】 a satsuma; a satsuma 「mandarin [tangerine].

うんじょう【運上】 business taxes 《levied in the Edo period》.

うんすい【雲水】 an itinerant Zen 「priest [monk]; a 「wandering [mendicant] monk; a mendicant.

うんちく【蘊蓄】 a fund of knowledge; a great stock of knowledge; profound [extensive] knowledge; great erudition. ◐ 彼のワインについてのうんちく his extensive knowledge about wine / うんちくをひけらかす show off *one*'s knowledge.

え

えあわせ【絵合わせ】〔平安時代に流行した物合わせ遊技の1つ〕a game originated in the Heian period in which pairs of pictures are matched and judged for quality.

えいが【映画】 a moving [motion] picture; *a movie; ॥a film; 《口》a flick; 〈総称〉the screen; *the movies; ॥the pictures; the cinema ● 映画を見に行く go to「*a movie [॥a film, *the movies, ॥the pictures]; go see「*a movie [॥a film]; ॥go to the cinema. ■ 映画音楽 film music; screen music; the sound track.

えいがかん【映画館】 a motion-picture theater; *a movie「house [theater]; ॥a cinema; ॥a cinema「house [palace].

えいせいほうそう【衛星放送】 satellite broadcasting; broadcasting via satellite. ● 衛星放送で野球中継をやっている. They're showing baseball live by satellite. | Baseball games are being covered live on satellite TV. ■ デジタル衛星放送 digital satellite broadcasting. 衛星放送局 a (television) satellite broadcasting station; a TV station that broadcasts via satellite. 衛星放送受信アンテナ a satellite dish;《口》a dish.

えいたいくよう【永代供養】 ● 永代供養をする make a donation to a temple or shrine to have services performed in perpetuity for the repose of *somebody*'s soul.

えき【駅】〔鉄道の〕a (railway) station; *a (railroad) depot. ● 次の駅 the next station / 秋葉原の次の駅 the station after Akihabara / 次の次の駅 the station after next; the next station but one / 東京駅 Tokyo Station.

えきがさ【駅傘】 an umbrella [umbrellas] kept at a train station for use by any passenger who needs one; a station umbrella.

えきこん【駅コン】〔駅構内でのコンサート〕a concert held in a station (building).

えきしゃ【易者】 a fortune-teller. ◐易者に見てもらう consult a fortune-teller; have *one*'s fortune told / 易者の身の上知らず. A fortune-teller cannot tell his own fortune.

えきしょう【液晶】 (a) liquid crystal. ◐液晶(カラー)テレビ a liquid-crystal (color) television / 液晶画面 a liquid-crystal (display) screen.

えきでん【駅伝】 1 ＝えきでんきょうそう． 2 〔古代の交通制度〕the post-station system of premodern Japan;〔宿継ぎの馬〕a post horse. ■女子駅伝 a women's「long-distance relay road race [*ekiden*]. 箱根駅伝 the Hakone *ekiden*.

えきでんきょうそう【駅伝競走】 a long-distance relay road race; an *ekiden*.

えきナカ【駅ナカ】〔駅の構内〕the interior of a station;《retail shops》「inside [within] a station. ■駅ナカ店 a retail shop inside a station; an in-station「store [shop]. 駅ナカビジネス (an) in-station business.

えきビル【駅ビル】 a (railway) station which includes a shopping complex.

えきべん【駅弁】 a「packed meal [box lunch, packed lunch] sold on trains or at stations. ■駅弁大学 a minor local college;《口》a little university in the sticks; a small-time [two-bit] university.

えきレンタカー【駅レンタカー】〔JR の〕a car that can be rented from a rental service located near a JR station.

えぐい 1〔あくが強くのどを刺激する〕harsh; acrid; pungent. ◐このタケノコ料理はえぐい. This bamboo-shoot dish tastes harsh [acrid]. / のどがえぐい. My throat feels「raw [irritated]. 2〔思いやりがなく冷酷な〕sharp; biting.

えくぼ【靨】 a dimple. ◐百万ドルのえくぼ a million dollar smile / えくぼができる dimples appear《on *somebody's* cheeks》;《*one*'s cheeks》dimple / 彼は笑うとえくぼができる. His cheeks dimple [Dimples appear] when he smiles.

えこう【回向】〔供養〕a (Buddhist) memorial service《for「a person who has died [the repose of *somebody*'s soul]》; a (Buddhist) prayer for the deceased. ～する hold a memorial service《for *somebody* [for the repose of *somebody*'s soul]》; pray [say prayers] for《a person who has died》. ◐回向を頼む ask for「a memorial service to be held [prayers to be read]. ■回向料 the fee for a Buddhist memorial service.

えことば【絵詞】 an explanation of a scene in a picture scroll; a story in pictures.

エコバッグ 〔ごみになるスーパーのレジ袋の代わりに持参する買い物袋〕 an ecological (shopping) bag; a reusable (cotton or canvas) shopping bag.

えすごろく【絵双六】 picture *sugoroku*; Parcheesi played on a board with pictures that tell a story.

えぞうし【絵双紙・絵草紙】 an illustrated story book (published in the Edo period).

えちごじし【越後獅子】〔越後発祥の獅子頭をつけた子供の曲芸〕 a street performance by itinerant entertainers featuring a tumbling act in which a child performer wears a carved lion's head.

えちぜんくらげ【越前水母】〔ビゼンクラゲ科の大型クラゲ〕 an Echizen jellyfish; a Nomura's jellyfish.

えっちゅうふんどし【越中褌】〔安土桃山時代の細川越中守忠興が始めたものという〕 a stringed loincloth (for men).

えてがみ【絵手紙】 a plain postcard illustrated with a drawing by the sender to which are added a few words.

えと【干支】 the sexagenary cycle; the twelve animals of the Chinese zodiac combined with the five elements (wood, water, earth, metal, and fire); 〔十二支〕 the 12 annual zodiac signs. [⇨ じゅうにし] ◐干支でいうと何の生まれですか[(あなたの)干支は何ですか]. Which year were you born in, in terms of the Oriental zodiac?

えどきりこ【江戸切子】 a type of uncolored cut glass produced in Edo.

えどじだい【江戸時代】 the Edo period (1603–1867).

えどっこ【江戸っ子】 a person born in Edo; 〔今の〕 a Tokyoite; a person born and brought up in Tokyo. ◐生粋の江戸っ子 a Tokyoite heart and soul; a true-born Edo「man [woman] / こちとらちゃきちゃきの江戸っ子だい. I'm a true native of backstreet Tokyo. ■江戸っ子気質(かたぎ) the backstreet Tokyo spirit.

えどま【江戸間】 the standard size for tatami (1.76 × 0.88 meters) in the Kantō region.

えどまえ【江戸前】〔東京湾(産の魚介)〕《fish and shellfish from》Tokyo Bay; 〔江戸風〕 Edo [Tokyo] style. ◐江戸前の魚 fish(es) from inside Tokyo Bay / ネタは全部江戸前です. 〔すし屋で〕 All the ingredients are from Tokyo Bay. ■**江戸前料理** Edo-style ⌈cuisine [food, cooking].

えのきたけ【榎茸】〔担子菌類キシメジ科の食用キノコ〕(an) enoki (mushroom); the winter mushroom; the velvet ⌈stem [foot].

えば【絵羽】■**絵羽羽織** a figured *haori* worn with a stylish kimono. **絵羽模様** designs [patterns] on a *haori*.

えび【海老】〔小型の〕a shrimp;〔中型の〕a prawn;〔大型の〕a lobster;〔イセエビ〕a spiny lobster. ◐ エビで鯛を釣る catch a bream with a shrimp; venture a small fish to catch a great one. ■**干し海老** a dried shrimp. **海老チリソース** (Szechuan style) shrimp in chili sauce. **海老ピラフ** shrimp pilaff. **海老フライ** a fried prawn.

えびす【恵比須】〔七福神の一〕Ebisu; the God of Shipping, Fishing, Commerce (usually depicted carrying a fishing pole and a sea bream).

えびせんべい【海老煎餅】a rice cracker made with dried shrimp.

えびちゃ【葡萄茶・海老茶】(a) reddish brown; (a) (deep) maroon. ◐ えび茶(色)の reddish brown; maroon.

えほう【恵方】〔吉方〕a ⌈direction [compass bearing] deemed to be lucky 《for house moving, traveling, etc.》. ■**恵方参り** a New Year's pilgrimage to a ⌈shrine [temple] that lies in the direction designated as bringing good fortune (in) that year.

えほうまき【恵方巻き】a lucky-direction sushi roll; a thick sushi roll eaten on the night of setsubun while facing the year's lucky direction and making a wish (for health, luck or prosperity).

えぼし【烏帽子】a jet black hat worn by men attending the emperor at court.

えま【絵馬】a votive wooden tablet painted with a picture of a horse offered in prayer or in thanks for a prayer answered. ◐ 願解(がんほど)きの絵馬 a votive horse tablet offered in thanks for a prayer answered. ■**絵馬堂** a gallery of votive horse tablets.

えまき(もの)【絵巻(物)】a picture scroll that unrolls horizontally depicting a sequence of scenes from a historical or fictional narrative. ◐ 平安絵巻さながらの祭りの列 a festival parade right out of a Heian picture scroll / 絵巻を繰り広げる spread out a picture scroll. ■**歴史絵巻** a picture scroll depicting a sequence of scenes from a historical narrative.

えんか【演歌】〔流行歌の一分野〕an *enka*; a variety of Japanese popular song distinguished by its sentimentality and tremolo passages. ■ 演歌歌手 an *enka* singer.

えんかい【宴会】〔社交上の〕a reception; a dinner (party); a feast; a banquet;〔仲間うちの〕a party; a junket. ▶ 宴会に出席する go to a「party [reception]; attend a party;《口》party / 花見の宴会によばれた. I was invited to a cherry-blossom viewing party. ■ 宴会場 a reception hall; a banquet(ing) hall; a function suite; a venue (for a party).

えんがわ【縁側】〔日本家屋の〕a corridor with a plank floor, and usually with sliding glass doors, extending about the other edge of one or more sides of a traditional Japanese house; a veranda(h); a porch.

えんぎ【縁起】〔さいさき〕an omen; a sign of「good [bad] luck [fortune]. 茶柱が立った. 今日は縁起がいいぞ. There's a tea stalk (floating upright in my tea). I'm in for some good luck today. ▶ 縁起のよい lucky; auspicious; of good omen; boding well / 縁起の悪い unlucky; inauspicious; ill-omened; boding ill / 縁起を担ぐ believe in omens; be superstitious. ■ 縁起物 something one hopes will bring good「fortune [luck]; a good luck charm.

えんぎえまき【縁起絵巻】a picture scroll representing the founding of a「temple [shrine].

えんきりでら【縁切り寺】a temple that gives sanctuary to runaway wives; a temple where wives who have left their husbands are given「refuge [shelter].

えんきんりょうようめがね【遠近両用めがね】(a pair of) bifocals; bifocal glasses.

えんこう【援交】=えんじょこうさい.

えんし【遠視】long sight; farsightedness. ▶ 彼は遠視のめがねをかけている. He「wears [is wearing] glasses for farsightedness.

えんじょこうさい【援助交際】the exchange of sexual favors by schoolgirls for money;〔1回の〕a paid-for date. 〜する go on a date in which sexual favors are paid for (school-girl cant).

えんせきがいせん【遠赤外線】far-infrared rays. ▶ 遠赤外線ヒーター[暖房器] a far-infrared heater.

えんそく【遠足】〔徒歩での遠出〕an excursion; a (long) walk; a「hike [tramp];〔日帰り旅行〕an excursion [outing]; a (pleasure) trip. ▶ 学校の遠足〔徒歩の〕a school walk;〔バスなどでの〕a school「excursion [trip, outing] 《by bus》.

えんだん【縁談】 an offer [a proposal] of marriage. ◐ 縁談がある receive「an offer [a proposal] of marriage / その娘にはこれまで降るように縁談があった. That girl has had dozens of offers of marriage.

えんにち【縁日】 a fete day (of a deity); a (temple) festival; a (shrine [temple]) fair. ◐ お不動様の縁日 a fair day「for Fudō. / 縁日の露店 a fair-day street stall; a「fair [festival] booth [stall]. ■ 縁日商人 a「boothkeeper [stallkeeper] (at a fair).

えんのした【縁の下】 the space under the「*engawa* [verandah] of a house;〔床下〕the space under the floor. 縁の下の力持ち a person whose efforts go「unappreciated [unsung, unrewarded, unnoticed]; an unsung hero; a force behind the scenes.

えんぽん【円本】 a book published in the second half of the 1920s and sold for one yen apiece; a one-yen edition; a one-yen book (in a series).

えんま【閻魔】〔冥界の支配神〕Enma;《Skt》Yama; the fifth of the seven judges of the Buddhist realm of the dead, usually regarded as the「Ruler [King, Prince] of Hell. ◐ うそをつくとえんま様に舌を抜かれますよ. Enma will pluck out your tongue if you tell a lie. / えんまの庁 Enma's court of judgment. ■ 閻魔顔 a fearsome look; a frightening face. 閻魔大王 the Great Enma. 閻魔堂 Enma's shrine.

えんまちょう【閻魔帳】 Enma's account book;〔教師の〕a teacher's「mark [grade] book. ◐ そんなことをするとえんま帳に書かれるぞ. If you do that you'll get「put on the blacklist [blacklisted].

えんむすび【縁結び】〔男女の〕matchmaking; bringing a couple together. ◐ 縁結びの神 the god of「marriage [matchmaking]; Hymen; Cupid.

お

おあいそ【お愛想】 1 〔ご機嫌取り・おせじ〕an action done [words spoken] to make *somebody* feel good; an「empty [insincere] compliment; (a piece of) flattery. ◐ お愛想を言う say「nice [flattering, pretty] things 《to *somebody*》; make complimentary remarks; pay *somebody* a compliment. **2** 〔もてなし〕special treatment. ◐ 何のお愛想もできなくてすみません. We have to apologize that we [I'm sorry I] couldn't put out anything special for you. **3** 〔飲食店の勘定〕the bill; *the check. ▶「お愛想」は本来は店の人が使う言葉で，客は使わなかった. ◐ お愛想をする〔店側が〕calculate the bill;〔客が〕pay the bill.

おいえげい【お家芸】 1 〔歌舞伎で，役者の家に伝わる技〕the「specialty [forte] of a school of Kabuki. ◐ 勧進帳は市川家のお家芸だ. *Kanjinchō* is a specialty of the Ichikawa school. **2** 〔固有の得意技〕*one*'s own「specialty [forte]. ◐ 今大会では日本のお家芸であるはずの柔道で金メダルが取れなかった. In this tournament Japan didn't win a single gold medal in judo, a sport that is supposed to be it's forte.

おいずり, おいずる【笈摺】 a kind of *haori* without sleeves that a pilgrim wears to prevent abrasion when carrying a basket on *one*'s back.

おいばら【追い腹】 ◐ 追い腹を切る commit hara-kiri in order to follow *one*'s deceased master to the other world.

おいらん【花魁】 〖日本史〗a courtesan; a licensed prostitute of high class; a high-class prostitute. ■ 花魁道中 a parade of *oiran* in the former Yoshiwara pleasure district of Edo.

おいろなおし【お色直し】 a「bride's [bridegroom's] change of dress during a wedding reception. 〜する change into different clothes (during a wedding reception). ◐ 彼女は 3 回もお色直ししたんだって. I hear she changed (her outfit) three times during the reception! / 新婦にはお色直しのためここでしばらく中座させていただきます. The bride is leaving us for a while now while she changes her dress. / 花嫁はお色直しのあと, 赤い振り袖を着て現れた. After going out to change the bride returned wearing a red kimono with pendant sleeves.

おいわけ【追分】1〔道の分岐点〕a parting of the ways; a point where the road forks.　2〔追分節〕＝おいわけぶし.

おいわけぶし【追分節】a packhorse driver's song.

おうぎ【扇】a fan; a folding fan. ◐日の丸の扇 a Rising Sun folding fan; a folding fan with the Rising Sun on it / 開いた[閉じた]扇 an open [a closed, a folded] fan / 扇のかなめ the pivot of a (folding) fan;〔組織の中心〕a pivot; a linchpin; a key / 野球の捕手は扇のかなめの位置にいる. A catcher in baseball is in 「a pivotal [key] position. / 扇の的 a (folding) fan (set up as a) target.

おうぎおとし【扇落とし】a fan tossing game.

おうぎながし【扇流し】1〔扇を川に流して遊ぶ昔の遊戯〕an entertainment originating in the Muromachi period in which elegant fans are floated on a current.　2〔流水に扇の模様〕a pattern showing a fan floating in a current.

おうしざ【牡牛座】〖天・占星〗the Bull; Taurus (略: Tau). ◐牡牛座生まれの人 a Taurus; a Taurean.

おうだいもの【王代物】a Kabuki play or *jōruri* treating themes of the Heian period.

おうだんほどう【横断歩道】a pedestrian crossing; *a crosswalk (for pedestrians); (白い縞模様をつけた) 「a zebra 「crossing [zone]. ◐押しボタン式横断歩道 a push-button (pedestrian) crossing; 「a pelican crossing (a *p*edestrian *li*ght *cont*rolled crossing から); (白い縞模様のついた) 「a panda crossing ■横断歩道橋 a pedestrian bridge.

おうちょう【王朝】a dynasty;〔天皇政治〕government under direct 「imperial [royal] administration. ◐王朝の dynastic; court / 王朝のみやび court refinement / 王朝の風情を残す儀式 a 「ceremony [solemnity] that retains a courtly 「air [atmosphere]. ■琉球王朝 the Kingdom of the Ryūkyūs.　王朝時代 a dynastic age; a period of monarchic government;〔日本の〕the period of court rule; (特に平安時代) the Heian period.　王朝物〔演劇などの〕a 「court-period [dynasty, monarchy] piece; a Heian-period piece. [⇨ おうだいもの]

おうて【王手】〖将棋〗a check.　〜する check 《the opponent's king》;

put 《the opponent's king》 in check. ◐ 新記録達成に王手がかかる be [come] within one 《step, goal, hit, game, etc.》 of setting a new record / ジャイアンツの優勝に王手がかかった. The Giants have come to within one game of clinching the pennant. ■ **逆王手** a reverse check. **両王手** a double check. **王手飛車(取り)** forking the rook while checking the king.

おうどいろ【黄土色】(yellow) ocher [ochre].

おうばんぶるまい【椀飯振る舞い・大盤振る舞い】**1**〔盛大な宴会〕a ⌈great [sumptuous] feast. **2**〔気前のよいもてなし〕lavish hospitality. 〜する〔盛んにもてなす〕treat [regale] *somebody* lavishly; entertain *somebody* ⌈generously [handsomely];〔気前よく施す〕give ⌈generously [liberally, handsomely].

おうむ【鸚鵡】a parrot.

おうむがえし【鸚鵡返し】repeating another's words; parroting. ◐ おうむ返しに parrot-like / おうむ返しに言う parrot; repeat like a parrot; repeat [echo, regurgitate] another's words (mechanically [uncritically]); parrot ⌈another's words [another]; parrot *something* back.

おうようか【応用花】〔定型を応用して自由に生ける生け花〕a free version of a standard ikebana flower arrangement; free-style ikebana.

おおいちょう【大銀杏】**1**〔大きなイチョウの木〕a ⌈large [giant, big] ginkgo tree. **2**〚相撲〛〔力士の髪型〕a sumo wrestler's topknot (from its resemblance to a gingko leaf). ◐ 大銀杏にはさみを入れる (引退相撲で) cut off a sumo wrestler's topknot (at his retirement ceremony) / 大銀杏を結う〔髪を大銀杏に結う〕dress a sumo wrestler's hair with a gingko-leaf topknot;〔(相撲取りが)十両に出世する〕reach [be promoted to] the rank of jūryō.

おおいりぶくろ【大入り袋】a full-house bonus; a bonus for bumper ⌈sales [crowds]. ◐ 今日は夜の部で大入り袋が出た. We employees got a full-house bonus today for the night ⌈session [performance].

おおおかさばき【大岡裁き】《pass》a wise and humane judgement like those for which Ōoka Echizen (18th-century City Commissioner of Edo) was renowned. ◐ 正に大岡裁きだね. That's a decision worthy of Solomon!

おおおく【大奥】the inner palace; the women's quarters of the shogun's palace (forbidden to men).

おおかみ【狼】**1** a wolf 《*pl.* wolves》. ◐狼の遠ぼえ the「baying [howling] of「wolves [a wolf] / 狼の群れ a pack of wolves; a wolf pack. **2**〔恐ろしい人〕a devil; a fiend. ◐やつは羊の皮をかぶった狼だ. He's a (real) wolf in sheep's clothing.

おおかみしょうねん【狼少年】**1**〔オオカミに育てられた少年〕a wolf child. **2**〔うそばかりつくので信用されなくなった人〕a person who is always crying "Wolf!". ▶『イソップ物語』から.

オーきゃく【O脚】bowlegs; bandy legs. ◐O脚を矯正するためのサンダル sandals for correcting bowlegs.

おおくにぬしのみこと【大国主命】Ōkuninushi 《a Shinto deity worshipped at Izumo Shrine》.

おおごしょ【大御所】**1**〔その道の大家として大きな勢力を持つ人物〕a leading [an outstanding, a powerful] figure [personage] in a certain field; a doyen, a doyenne; a Mr. Big. ◐文壇の大御所 Mr. Big in「the literary world [《Japanese》literary circles] / 財界の大御所 the grand old man of the financial world. **2**〔隠退した将軍〕a retired but still powerful shogun. ◐大御所家康公 the retired and still de facto shogun, Ieyasu.

おおさかずし【大阪鮨】Osaka-style sushi; sushi made the Osaka way.

おおずもう【大相撲】**1**〔興行〕a grand sumo tournament; professional sumo. **2**〔見ごたえのある勝負〕a well-fought bout between evenly matched wrestlers; a long-drawn-out bout; an exciting bout. ■**大相撲地方巡業** a tour of the provinces to hold an exhibition sumo tournament. **大相撲中継** live TV broadcast of a grand sumo tournament; a grand sumo tournament being「broadcast [televised]. **大相撲夏場所** the Summer Grand Sumo Tournament. **大相撲ファン** a sumo fan.

おおだち【大太刀】an extra-long sword.

おおつづみ【大鼓】the big hand drum (used in traditional Japanese music), as opposed to the small hand drum.

おおとろ【大とろ】top-quality tuna, with a high fat-content, from the underbelly of the fish.

おおはらえ【大祓え】the great purification; a Shinto purification rite performed twice a year and also before *daijōsai* (an offering of first fruits by an emperor in the year that he accedes to the throne) and after major disasters. ◐大祓えの詞(ことば) a prayer used at the Shinto great purification rite.

おおばん【大判】 1 〔紙・本などの普通より大きい型〕a large「size [sheet]; (a) folio size.　▷ large-sized; folio(-sized)（形容詞）　2 〔貨幣〕a large oval Japanese gold coin used from the late Muromachi period to the end of the Edo period.

おおふりそで【大振り袖】a kimono with pendant sleeves worn by young women.

おおぶろしき【大風呂敷】1 〔大きなふろしき〕a large-sized「*furoshiki* [cloth wrapper].　2 〔現実に合わない大げさな話や計画〕big [empty] talk; hot air; a pipe dream;《口》bull.　◐ 大風呂敷を広げる〔実現不可能な大きい計画を披露してみせる〕talk big; brag;《口》talk (a lot of) bull.

おおみえ【大見得】〔歌舞伎の所作〕a (dramatic) pose.　◐ 大見得を切る〔歌舞伎で〕strike a pose; pose for dramatic effect;〔自信たっぷりに言う〕state「impressively [confidently, with gravity]; aim to「impress [make an impression on] *somebody* / 彼は独りで必ずできると大見得を切ったよ. He made a show of saying that he could do it by himself.

おおみやびと【大宮人】a courtier at the Imperial Court; a nobleman of the Imperial Court.

おおもり【大盛り】a large「portion [helping, serving].　◐ 焼きそば大盛り3人分 three large orders of pan-fried noodles / 定食のご飯を大盛りにしてくれ. Give me a large rice with today's plate lunch, will you?

おおもん【大門】the main gate《of a castle》.

おおやしま【大八州】the Many Great Islands; the Japanese archipelago.

おかか〔かつおぶし〕dried bonito;〔かつおぶしを削ったもの〕dried bonito「shavings [flakes].　◐ おかかのおむすび a rice ball with a filling of bonito shavings flavored with soy sauce / おかかを削る shave [make shavings of] a dried bonito fillet.

おかげさま【お蔭様】◐ おかげさまでみんな元気です. We are all fit and well.　▶ 特に"thank you"を付け加える必要はない / おかげさまで助かります. That would be a great help, thank you. |〔物をもらって〕Thank you so much for your gift. |〔物を借りて〕Thank you for the loan《of your car, of the money》. |〔応援を仰いで〕Thank you very much for your support.

おがさわらりゅう【小笠原流】the Ogasawara「school [style] of ceremonial etiquette (favored by the Samurai class during the Edo period).

おかしらつき【尾頭付き】a whole fish (with its head and tail).

おかっぱ(あたま)【お河童(頭)】a「pageboy [short bobbed] hairstyle; a short bob. ◐おかっぱにする wear [have] *one*'s hair bobbed; bob *one*'s hair / おかっぱの少女 a girl with「bobbed hair [her hair bobbed].

おかっぴき【岡っ引き】a commoner hired privately by police officials to do menial police work such as searching for and apprehending criminals in the Edo period; a hired thief-catcher.

おかばしょ【岡場所】one of a number of unlicensed「red-light [brothel] districts in the Edo period.

おかぶ【お株】〔得意技〕*one*'s「forte [specialty]; *one*'s favorite「trick [occupation, topic]. ◐お株を取られる be beaten at *one*'s own game; be outdone by *somebody* at *one*'s own「forte [specialty] / お株を奪う beat *somebody* at *his* own game.

おかま【お釜】**1**〔男色〕a gay;《口》a queer; a fag; *《口》a faggot;〔男娼〕a male prostitute. ◐お釜を掘る〔男色を行う〕perform [have] anal sex《with a man》;《卑》bugger《a man》;《卑》give it to《a man》「up [in] the ass / お釜を掘られる〔男色で〕take part in anal sex as the passive partner;《卑》be buggered;《卑》take it up the ass;〔車に乗っていて追突される〕be [get] driven into from behind; be plowed into from behind **2**〔噴火口〕a (volcano) crater.

おかみ[1]【女将】〔旅館や料亭の〕the「proprietress [hostess]《of a Japanese inn》. ◐私がこの宿の女将です. I am the proprietress of this inn. | I「am [have the honor to be] your hostess. ■**若女将** the proprietress-to-be《of an inn》.

おかみ[2]【御上】**1**〔天皇〕the Emperor; His Majesty;〔幕府の将軍〕the shogun. **2**〔政府〕Big Brother; the government;〔当局・役所〕the authorities.

おかみさん【お上さん・お内儀さん】〔奥さん〕(他人の) *somebody*'s wife;《口》*somebody*'s missus;〔庶民的な主婦〕a housewife;〔呼びかけ〕madam; Mrs…;〔商店などの女主人〕the proprietress;〔相撲部屋の〕the wife of a sumo stable master. ◐八百屋のおかみさん the greengrocer's wife / 隣のおかみさん *one*'s neighbor's wife; the woman next door.

おかめ【お亀】〔おたふく〕a round-faced woman with plump cheeks and a flat nose;〔おたふくのお面〕a mask of a plump-faced woman;〔醜女〕a「plain(-looking) [homely] woman. [⇨ おたふく]

おかめそば【お亀蕎麦】buckwheat noodles in soup with slices of boiled fish paste and shiitake mushroom.

おかめはちもく【傍目八目】Onlookers see more of the game than the players do. | The「bystander [outsider] can see what's going on better than the participants can.

おかもち【岡持ち】〔出前おけ〕a wooden carrying box.

おから the edible pulp separated from soybean milk in the production of tofu.

おかわり【お代わり】another [a second] helping [portion];〔飲み物の〕a refill. 〜する ask for [take] a second helping; ask for more; ask for another「portion [serving];〔飲み物を〕ask for a refill. ◐ ご飯を3回お代わりした. He had four「helpings [bowls, bowlfuls] of rice. | He had his rice bowl refilled three times. / コーヒーのお代わり another cup (of coffee); a refill (of *one*'s coffee cup) / 水のお代わりをください. Could I have another glass of water, please? / ビールのお代わりを頼もう. Let's get some more beer(s).

おきあがりこぼし【起き上がり小法師】a self-righting (*daruma*) doll; a doll that rights itself when knocked over.

おきいし【置き石】1〔庭園の〕a stone「placed [set]《in a garden》for scenic effect. 2〚囲碁〛a handicap *go* stone. 3〔線路上の〕a stone placed on a railroad track《as a prank》.

おきがさ【置き傘】a spare umbrella kept at *one*'s place of work. ◐ 駅の置き傘 an umbrella [umbrellas] kept at a train station for use by any passenger who needs one.

おきごたつ【置き炬燵】a movable *kotatsu*.

おきな【翁】an「old [aged] man. ◐ 翁の面 a Noh mask representing an old man.

おきなます【沖膾】finely chopped raw fish meat and vegetables, prepared with vinegar, eaten aboard the boat on which the fish was caught.

おきなわそば【沖縄そば】Okinawan「noodles [vermicelli].

おきや【置屋】a geisha house; an agency with geisha or traditional

dancers on its books for whom it acts as an agent.

おくざしき【奥座敷】 a「Japanese style [tatami]」guest room towards the back of a house; *a back「room [parlor]. ▶秋保(あきう)温泉は仙台の奥座敷といわれている. Akiu Spa is known as「a place of retreat [an oasis (of quiet)]」for (citizens of) Sendai.

おくしゃ【奥社】〔神社の〕an inner「shrine [sanctuary]; a sanctuary to the rear of a main sanctuary, housing the same「deity [deities]」as the main sanctuary.

おくじょちゅう【奥女中】 a maid working in the domestic quarters of a shogun or daimyo.

おくでん【奥伝】〔初伝・中伝に続く, 師匠からの奥義の伝授〕admission to the third of five stages of initiation leading towards mastery of an art. ▶奥伝をいただいた. I was admitted to the third stage of「discipleship [apprenticeship].

おくのいん【奥の院】 an「inner [innermost]」shrine; a sanctuary; a sanctum sanctorum.

おくば【奥歯】 a molar (tooth); a back tooth. ▶奥歯に物が挟まったような言い方をする speak with irritating reserve; talk as if *one* were concealing something; speak as if *one* had something up *one*'s sleeve; be not quite frank 《with *somebody*》.

おぐらアイス【小倉アイス】 ice cream mixed with sweet adzuki bean paste.

おぐらあん【小倉餡】 sweet adzuki bean paste containing both mashed and whole beans.

おぐらひゃくにんいっしゅ【小倉百人一首】⇨ ひゃくにんいっしゅ.

おくりおおかみ【送り狼】 a man who pretends to escort a woman home and then molests her on the way.

おくりがな【送り仮名】 kana added to a「Chinese character [kanji]」to show its「inflection [reading]」in Japanese. ▶送り仮名を送る add kana to a「Chinese character [kanji].

おくりづゆ【送り梅雨】 heavy rain, often accompanied by thunder, towards the end of the rainy season.

おくりび【送り火】 ceremonial fires lit on the evening of the last day of the *Bon* Festival to speed the spirits of the dead on their way.

おくりぼん【送り盆】 the last day of the「*Bon* Festival [festival of the dead], when people see the spirits of their ancestors off. [⇨ むかえぼん]

おくるみ【お包み】a padded coverlet (for swaddling a baby).

おこう【御講】a monthly Buddhist service.

おこさまランチ【お子様ランチ】a special lunch prepared for children at a restaurant; a special menu for「children [kids];《口》a (special) kiddies' lunch.

おこし a millet-and-rice cake.

おこそずきん【御高祖頭巾】(in the late Edo period) a women's headscarf, (a square of cloth used as) a cowl.

おごと【小琴】a small「koto [Japanese harp].

おこのみやき【お好み焼き】*okonomiyaki*; a Japanese-style「pancake (containing vegetables and other ingredients, cooked on a hot plate and served with spicy sauces).

おこもり【お籠り】an overnight prayer visit to [voluntarily staying for a night of prayer in] a shrine or temple.

おこわ【お強】〔強飯(ごうはん)〕steamed rice;〔赤飯〕rice steamed with red beans in it.

おし【御師】a low-ranking Shinto priest.

おしくらまんじゅう【押し競饅頭】a children's game, usually played in winter, in which the children stand in a compact circle with their backs pressed together and push against one another; a game of shove and push.

おしずし【押し鮨】pressed sushi with vinegared slices of fish on it.

おしちや【御七夜】the seventh day after birth;〔お祝い〕celebration on the evening of the 7th day after birth.

おしどり【鴛鴦】〔ガンカモ科の鳥〕a mandarin duck. ◐ おしどり夫婦 a loving couple; a happily married couple (who are always together).

おしぼり【お絞り】a damp washcloth, hot in winter and cold in summer, for cleaning hands before a meal.

おしめ【襁褓】＝おむつ.

おしや【押し屋】〔ラッシュ時の駅の〕a (back) pusher; a pusher-in.

おしゃか【お釈迦】〔作りそこなったもの〕a reject; a defective article;〔こわれて使えなくなったもの〕a broken article; something that cannot be used anymore. ◐ この車はもうお釈迦だ. This car「has had it [has bitten the dust, is ready for the scrap yard].

おしゃく【お酌】**1**〔酌〕pouring sake for each other. ◐お酌をする pour sake for *somebody* / お酌をして回る make the rounds and pour sake / お酌を受ける let *somebody* pour sake for *one* / お酌しましょう. Let me pour. **2**〔酌婦〕a woman who pours.

おしゃぶり〔幼児の〕a「*pacifier [comforter]; a dummy. ◐おしゃぶりをあてがう put a「*pacifier [ǁdummy] into a baby's mouth.

おじゃまむし【お邪魔虫】a nuisance; a pest.

おしょう【和尚】**1**〔高僧〕a (senior) Buddhist priest. **2**〔寺の住職〕a Buddhist priest (in charge of a temple). ◐和尚さん〔呼びかけ語〕Master; Your Reverence.

おしんこ【お新香】pickles; pickled vegetables.

おすべらかし【御垂髪】a traditional coiffure for samurais' wives and Shinto priestesses, with the hair gathered and hanging from the nape of the neck.

おすみつき【御墨付き】〔権威あるものが与えた保証〕a high official's「stamp [seal] of approval; a guarantee; certification. ◐このビルはマグニチュード7の地震でも絶対倒れないという専門家のお墨付きがある. Specialists have guaranteed that this building will be safe even in a magnitude 7 earthquake.

おすわり【お座り】《小児語》〜する sit down / きちんとお座りして食べなさい. Sit (up) properly and eat your food. /〔犬に向かって〕お座り! Sit!

おせおせムード【押せ押せムード】〔調子づいた勢いで相手を圧倒する雰囲気〕being on the「offensive [attack]. ◐後半彼らは押せ押せムードとなった. They「went on the offensive [got into an attacking mood] in the second half.

おせち(りょうり)【御節(料理)】traditional Japanese foods prepared in advance for consumption during the first three days of the New Year.

おそなえ【御供え】an offering (made at a「shrine [temple, household altar]);〔餅〕a *kagamimochi*(; ceremonial *mochi*).

おたいこ【お太鼓】＝たいこむすび.

おたく〔一つのことに深くはまっている人〕an obsessive「fan [devotee]; a freak; an addict / アニメオタク an animation freak / コンピューターオタク a computer「nerd [geek]. ■**オタク族** junkies; freaks.

おたちだい【御立ち台】**1**〔皇居の〕the balcony from which the emperor

and members of the imperial family appear before the public; the Balcony of Appearances.　**2**〔野球場・競技場などの〕a temporary platform for interviewing baseball players or athletes after a game or match; an interview platform; a rostrum.　◐インタビューのためにお立ち台に上った. He mounted the「victor's [winner's] platform for an interview.

おたふく【お多福】〔醜い女〕a plain(-looking) [homely] woman.　[⇨おかめ]

おたふくかぜ〔流行性耳下腺炎〕epidemic parotitis; mumps.

おだまきむし【苧環蒸し】〔料理〕a traditional egg custard dish on a base of *udon* noodles.

おたまじゃくし【お玉杓子・蝌蚪】〔カエルの子〕a tadpole; a polliwog;〔音符〕a (musical) note.

おだわらぢょうちん【小田原提灯】a cylindrical paper lantern; a「collapsible [folding] paper lantern.

おだわらひょうじょう【小田原評定】an inconclusive「conference [debate, discussion]; a long but fruitless debate; a long, empty debate full of nothing (from the hesitance of the defenders of Odawara Castle to decide whether to sue for peace or to join battle with Toyotomi Hideyoshi).

おちあゆ【落ち鮎】an *ayu* [a sweetfish] coming down river (to spawn).

おちえん【落ち縁】a stepped veranda.

おちゃ【お茶】**1**〔飲みもの〕tea;（緑茶）green tea;〔休憩〕a break; a tea break.　◐濃い[薄い]お茶 strong [weak] tea.　**2**〔茶の湯〕the tea ceremony.　◐お茶の会 a tea ceremony／お茶を立てる make tea;〔茶筅(ちゃせん)で〕whisk tea／お茶を習う learn [practice] the tea ceremony.

おちょこ【お猪口】＝ちょく.　◐おちょこに酒をつぐ pour sake into a sake cup／私の傘は風でおちょこになった. The wind blew my umbrella inside out.

おつかれさま【お疲れ様】〔仕事が終わった人をねぎらう言葉〕 Thanks! That's enough for today [Let's call it a day].｜Thanks for all your hard work (today).;〔仕事をしている人へのあいさつ〕Hard at it, I see.　◐今日はお疲れさまでした. All your efforts today are very much appreciated.／お疲れさま(＝さよなら)! またあした. Good-bye! See you tomorrow.／お疲れさまです(＝こんにちは). Good day!

おつくり【お作り】〔刺し身〕 ◐ マグロのお作り (a dish of) sliced raw tuna.

おつけ【お付け】〔みそ汁〕miso「potage [soup].

おつぼねさま【お局さま】〔仕事場でいばっている古参の OL〕a senior female worker in a company who supervises in matronly fashion the behavior of junior employees; a matron (from the fact that the women closest to the emperor had rooms, or *tsubone*, at the palace). [⇨ つぼね]

おつり【お釣り】change;〔余分・余録〕a surplus; something left over. ◐ 千円でお釣りが欲しい. I'd like change for a 1,000-yen bill.

おでき a boil; a swelling. ◐ 顔におできができる have a boil on *one*'s face / おできが痛む. The boil「hurts [is painful].

おでこ 1〔額〕the forehead;《文》the brow. ◐ 彼女はおでこが広い[狭い]. She has a「high [low] forehead. / おでこをさする rub *one's* forehead. **2**〔大きな額〕a beetle brow; a prominent brow; a「jutting [bulging, high] forehead. **3**〘釣り〙〔釣果のないこと〕おでこを食らう go fishing but come home empty-handed.

おてだま【お手玉】beanbags;〔遊び〕a game of beanbags. ～する play beanbags;〘野球〙〔ボールを〕juggle the ball.

おてまえ【お点前】〔茶の湯の作法・様式〕procedures in the tea ceremony. ◐ お点前のしぐさ the movements made when serving tea / お点前を披露する put on a demonstration of tea-serving / けっこうなお点前でございました. The tea ceremony was performed beautifully.

おてもと【お手許】〔料理屋などのはし〕《a pair of》chopsticks.

おてもときん【御手許金・御手元金】 the money used for private purposes by the emperor and the members of his family in the direct line (namely, the empress, empress dowager, crown prince and princess and their children);〔君主の〕the privy purse.

おでん a dish consisting of slices of boiled white radish, cakes of *konnyaku*, small taros, tubes of fish paste, hard-boiled eggs, balls of processed minced fish, etc., heated in a shoyu-based broth. ◐ おでんの屋台 an *oden* street stall / おでんのねた[具] an *oden* ingredient; *oden* ingredients; the makings for *oden*. ■ おでん屋 an *oden* shop.

おてんきや【お天気屋】a「moody [temperamental] person; a「fickle [capricious, changeable] person; a creature of moods. ◐ 彼女はお天気屋だから気をつけたほうがいい. You've got to watch out; she's a moody person.

おてんば【お転婆】tomboyishness. ～な tomboyish. ■お転婆娘 a tomboy.

おとおし【お通し】〖料理〗〔つき出し・前菜〕《F》*hors d'oeuvre*; a relish.

おとぎぞうし【お伽草子】anonyomous fables written in the Muromachi period.

おとぎばなし【お伽話】a fairy tale; a nursery tale. ◐おとぎ話の世界 a fairy-tale world; a never-never land / 子供におとぎ話を聞かせる read a nursery tale to a child.

おとしだま【お年玉】 a gift, usually of money, typically enclosed in a special seasonal envelope, which is presented to a child (by parents or visitors) or to a dependent at New Year's; a New Year「present [gift]. ◐お年玉付き年賀はがき a New Year's lottery「postcard [*postal card]; a New Year's card with a lottery number on it / お年玉をやる give 《*somebody* 5,000 yen》 as a New Year's gift; give *somebody* a New Year's present (of 《￥5,000》) / お年玉をもらう get [receive, be given] 《￥5,000》 as a New Year's gift; get a New Year present (of 《￥5,000》).

おとながい【大人買い】purchasing (of collectibles) by adults.

おとひめ【乙姫】the younger sister of a princess; 〔竜宮の〕the Princess of the Dragon Palace.

おとめざ【乙女座】〖天・占星〗the Virgin; the Maiden; Virgo (略: Vir). ◐乙女座生まれの人 a「Virgo [Virgoan].

おどりぐい【躍り食い】 eating live ice gobies or other small fish after dipping them in a soy-and-vinegar sauce.

おなり【御成り】〔貴人の外出〕the going out 《of an august personage》; 〔訪問〕a visit 《of a high personage》 to a place. ◐御成り道 a road [an avenue] of honor; the road down which persons of high social status traveled. ■御成門 a gate of honor.

おに【鬼】1 〔想像上の怪物〕a troll; an ogre; a demon; a fiend (a creature with a human-like figure, bull's horns, tiger's fangs, superhuman strength, and irascible nature, who carries a club in one hand). ◐怒りに燃えた彼は鬼の形相だった. Fit to be tied, he looked like a raging demon. /〔節分の豆まきで〕鬼は外, 福は内. Out with the devil, in with good fortune. 2 〔無慈悲な人〕a「pitiless [merciless] person;〔気兼ねの相手〕a person in whose presence one feels uncomfortable;〔勇猛な人〕

an intrepid [a fearless] person.　**3**〔精魂傾ける人〕a fiend; a fanatic; 〔異常に執着する人〕a demon; a fiend.　◐仕事の鬼 a demon for work; a work fiend; an indefatigable worker / 勝負の鬼 a person who plays for keeps.　**4**〔遊びの〕it / じゃんけんで鬼を決める decide who will be it by tossing for it [*janken*] / 君が鬼だ. You're it.

鬼に金棒　◐君が選挙参謀になれば彼は鬼に金棒だ. If you become his campaign advisor, it would give him a second string to his bow.

鬼の霍乱(かくらん)　"the devil succumbing to sunstroke"; a rare experience of illness by a person with「an iron constitution.　◐あいつが熱を出したって？鬼の霍乱だね. He's running a fever, you say? Will wonders ever cease!

鬼の目にも涙　Even the hardest heart will sometimes feel pity.

■ 赤[青]鬼 a red [blue] ogre.　鬼軍曹 a tough「drillmaster [drill sergeant].　鬼刑事 a hard-as-nails detective.　鬼検事 a「relentless [fierce] prosecutor.　鬼コーチ a drillmaster; a martinet.　鬼将軍 a「ferocious [stern taskmaster of a] general.

おにうちまめ【鬼打ち豆】roasted soybeans hurled at imaginary ogres on February 3 or 4, the day before the beginning of spring by the solar calendar.

おにがわら【鬼瓦】a ridge-end tile with an ogre's face.　◐鬼がわらみたいな顔の男[女]a「man [woman] of fearsome「countenance [looks].

おにぎり【お握り】a rice ball; a palm-sized triangle, ball, or cylinder of cooked rice usually wrapped in a thin sheet of dried seaweed and stuffed with a pickled plum, some tuna or salmon flakes, fish eggs, spicy vegetables, or other fillings.

おにごっこ【鬼ごっこ】tag; "tig;〔目隠し鬼〕blindman's buff.　◐鬼ごっこの鬼 ⇒ おに 4 / 鬼ごっこをする play「tag ["tig]; play blindman's buff.

おにばば(あ)【鬼婆】〔老女の姿の鬼〕a witch; a hag; a crone; an ogress; 〔無慈悲な老女〕a shrew; a vixen; a harpy.

おのぼりさん【お上りさん】a country bumpkin visiting the big city; a yokel in the big city.

おはぎ【お萩】an oval-shaped sweet made from glutinous rice and covered with「red-bean [adzuki bean] jam, soybean flour, or sesame seeds.

おはぐろ【御歯黒】〔鉄漿(かね)〕black tooth「dye [stain]; tooth black; a liquid for「dyeing [staining]」the teeth black (used by married women in premodern Japan).

おはこ〔得意芸〕*one*'s「forte [specialty, standby]」; *one*'s「favorite [stock] parlor trick [song, etc.]」;〔くせ〕*one*'s mannerism. ◐ そろそろ君のおはこが聞きたいね. I think we'd like to hear your old standby.

おはじき〔遊戯〕a game, similar to marbles, played with shell, stone, or glass discs;〔玉〕the discs used in this game.

おはしょり【お端折り】tucking up the hems of a kimono and holding them in place with a cord;〔はしょった部分〕the portion tucked up and bound in place.

おはらい【御祓い】exorcism; purification. ◐ おはらいをする〔祓ってもらう〕get *one*self「purified [exorcised]」;〔式を行う〕hold a purification ceremony / 神主を呼んで新ビル予定地のおはらいをしてもらった. We had the new building site purified by a Shinto priest.

おはらめ【大原女】a woman peddler in Kyoto selling kindling from Ōhara.

おび【帯】〔和装の〕an obi 《*pl*. ~s》; (女帯) a broad sash worn with a woman's formal kimono; (男帯，あるいは幅の狭い帯) a narrow sash worn with a man's kimono, with a woman's everyday kimono, and with yukata; a waistband; a belt;〔札束の帯封〕a paper band (around a bundle of notes);〔本の帯紙〕a strip of paper around the lower third of a book's dustcover or slipcase, carrying a blurb. ◐ 帯がきつくて苦しいわ. This obi is so tight「it hurts [it's killing me]」. その札束には日本銀行の印を押した帯がかけてあった. Wrapped around the wad of「bills [notes]」was a band of paper bearing the seal of the Bank of Japan. / 帯に短し襷(たすき)に長し. Too short for an obi and too long for a sleeve tie. (＝It's useless.) / 帯に短し襷に長しである be good for neither one thing nor the other / 帯をお太鼓に結ぶ tie the obi into the drum bow / 帯を締める do up [put on] an obi [a sash]; tie「an obi [a sash]」; wear *one*'s obi [sash] 《high, low》/ 帯を解く untie [undo] the「obi [sash, waistband]」;〔女が男と肉体関係を持つ〕give *one*self to a man.

おびあげ【帯揚げ】an obi support (to keep the main bow from slipping down).

おびいた【帯板】〔和装の〕a flat piece of stiff material slipped between the front folds of an obi to give it shape.

おびいわい【帯祝い】a ceremony of wrapping a supportive band of cloth around a four-month pregnant woman's waist, accompanied by prayers for an easy childbirth.

おびじ【帯地】stuff [material, cloth] for an obi; obi material.

おびじめ【帯締め】a cord holding an obi in place; a sash band.

おひたし【お浸し】boiled greens with (a *katsuobushi* and) soy dressing. ▶ホウレンソウをおひたしにして食べた. I had some boiled spinach with (a *katsuobushi* and) soy dressing.

おひつじざ【牡羊座】〚天・占星〛the Ram; Aries (略: Ari). ▶牡羊座生まれの人 an Aries 《*pl.* ~》; an Arien.

おびどめ【帯留め】〔帯締めの飾り〕an ornamental clasp for holding an obi in place.

おびな【男雛】the Emperor doll (in a Girls' Festival display of dolls).

おひねり【お捻り】a monetary gift or gratuity wrapped in paper.

おびひも【帯紐】the obi and cord fasteners used when wearing a kimono. ▶二人は帯ひもを解く仲となった. The two have become intimate.

おびまくら【帯枕】a small oval cushion to keep the obi knot in place.

おひゃくど【御百度】a hundred rounds of worship. ▶御百度を踏む walk back and forth a hundred times before a shrine, offering a prayer each time;〔繰り返し訪ねて依頼する〕visit *somebody* repeatedly to solicit a favor.

おひらき【お開き】a conclusion; a winding up; a close. ▶これをもちましてお開きといたします. This brings our party to a close. | I would like to wind things up now. / お開きにする wind up; bring to a「conclusion [close]; close 《a banquet》/ お開きになる come to「an end [a conclusion]; be closed; wind up; be wound up.

おふだ【お札】a charm (お守り); an amulet (護符); a talisman (まじない札).

おぼろこぶ【朧ろ昆布】kelp [tangle] shaved into thin sheets.

おまじり【お交じり】rice gruel containing a small amount of solid rice.

おまもり【お守り】a good-luck charm; an amulet; a talisman. ▶安産のお守り a good-luck charm for a safe childbirth / 災難よけのお守り an amulet [a good-luck charm] (to ward off calamities).

■ お守り袋 an amulet case.

おみき【御神酒】(a) libation; sake offered to a god.

おみくじ【御神籤】a written oracle / おみくじを引く pick a lot to tell *one*'s fortune.

おみずとり【御水取り】the drawing of sacred water [the ceremony of drawing sacred water] at Nigatsudō of the temple Todaiji on 13 March.

おみやまいり【御宮参り】〔生後 30 日ごろの〕(the custom of) taking *one*'s baby to a shrine (to pray for blessing).

おむすび【お結び】＝おにぎり.

おむつ a diaper; 《口》a nappy; 《文》a (baby's) napkin. ◐ 汚れたおしめ「a wet [messy] diaper; a dirty nappy.

オムライス stir-fried rice wrapped in an omelette; an omelette containing stir-fried rice (as a filling).

おめがね【お眼鏡】〔眼識〕your [*somebody*'s] judgment [discernment]; your [*somebody*'s] critical [discerning] eye. [⇨ めがね 2] ◐ おめがねにかなう find favor《with *somebody*》; catch *somebody*'s fancy; be liked by *somebody*; be [get] in *somebody*'s good books / どうやら彼は社長のおめがねにかなったようだ. He seems to have「got(ten) into the boss's good books [found favor with the boss somehow]. ■ おめがね違い a mistake「in [of] (e)valuation; an error「in [of] judgment. ◐ あの男を後継者と考えておられるようですが, それはおめがね違いというものです. You seem to be considering him as your successor, but that would be an error of judgment.

おめしちりめん【御召し縮緬】silk crepe.

おめでた **1**〔めでたい祝い〕a happy [an auspicious] event; a special occasion; a (matter for)「celebration [congratulation]. **2**〔妊娠〕(a) pregnancy. ◐ おめでたの女性 a pregnant woman; a woman expecting (a baby); a woman with a baby on the way;《口》a woman in the family way.

おもちゃ a toy; a plaything;〔玩弄物〕a「toy [plaything, butt] (of *somebody*). ◐ 子供のおもちゃ a child's toy / 大人のおもちゃ a toy for adults;〔特に性具〕an erotic「aid [device] / おもちゃにする make a「toy [plaything] out of *something* [*somebody*];〔もてあそぶ〕sport [trifle] with *somebody* [*something*]; treat「*somebody* [*something*] like a plaything; (女が男を) play《a man》for a fool; toy with《a man》; turn [twist]《a man》 around *one*'s little finger; (男が女を) trifle with [make sport of] 《a woman》; treat 《a woman》 as a plaything.

おもて【面】〔能面〕⇨ のうめん.

おもてがえ【表替え】〔畳の〕the refacing of tatami mats.

おもてざしき【表座敷】a tatami-floored reception room near the front entrance of a house. ◐熱海は東京の表座敷と呼ばれていた. Atami was called the front parlor of Tokyo.

おもてせんけ【表千家】Omote Senke; the main branch of the Senke school of tea ceremony.

おもならい【重習い】〔謡曲・能〕important passages from Noh songs practiced by students.

おやかた【親方】〔大工などの〕a master 《builder》;〔土木・建築現場の〕a foreman; a supervisor; a boss;〔相撲の〕a stable master;〔呼びかけて〕《口》boss; chief. ◐大工の親方 an independent ⌈builder [carpenter]; a foreman at a building site; a ⌈builder in charge [leader] of a group of builders; a ⌈builders' [carpenters'] boss. ■**親方日の丸** a tendency to laxity among some public employees due to the assurance that the state will never go out of business.

おやこどんぶり【親子丼】a bowl of rice topped with chicken and eggs cooked together.

おやしらず【親知らず】〔知恵歯〕a wisdom tooth. ◐親知らずが生える cut *one*'s wisdom teeth.

おやつ【お八】a snack; between-meals refreshments (by traditional reckoning *yatsu* corresponds to three in the afternoon). ◐おやつにせんべいを食べる have rice crackers for a snack / さあ，おやつにしよう. Let's ⌈have [take] a refreshment break.

おやといがいこくじん【お雇い外国人】〔幕末から明治初期の〕in the Meiji period, a foreign ⌈specialist [technical advisor, expert] in Government ⌈employ [service].

おやぶんはだ【親分肌】～の having the qualities that befit a ⌈boss [leader]. ◐親分肌の男[女] a ⌈big-brother[big-sister] type: a person inclined to look out for others, and who may be relied on in a pinch.

おやま【女形】＝おんながた. ■**立女形** the leading actor for female Kabuki roles.

おやゆび【親指】the thumb; the big finger;〔足の〕the ⌈big [great] toe.

おやゆびぞく

◐ 親指の腹 the ball of the thumb / 親指の指紋 a thumbprint. ■ 親指シフト〘電算〙a keyboard layout assigning "shift" keys to thumbs.

おやゆびぞく【親指族】〔携帯電話などを親指で器用に操作する人〕the thumb tribe, a cell-phonist (who can operate a cell-phone with one hand).

おりがみ【折り紙】 1 〔遊び・細工〕origami; the art of「paper folding [folding paper into figures]; 〔紙〕colored paper used for origami; origami paper. ◐ 折り紙で鶴を折る make [fold] an origami crane; fold origami paper into a crane / 折り紙をする do [make] origami. 2 〔鑑定書〕a note of authentication; a hallmark; a certificate of genuineness. ◐ 折り紙付き ⇨ おりがみつき / この刀は無銘だが正宗作という折り紙が付いている. This sword has no maker's inscription, but it is accompanied by a document certifying it as the work of Masamune. / 折り紙を付ける certify; warrant; guarantee / 彼の技術には安心して折り紙を付けられる. I can vouch for (the excellence of) his craftsmanship.

おりがみつき【折り紙付き】 折り紙付きの certified (as genuine); guaranteed;〔皮肉に〕notorious《bigmouth》; arrant《fool, thief》/ 折り紙付きの品 an「object [item, article] certified as genuine; an article accompanied by a certificate of genuineness / 折り紙付きの腕前 acknowledged「skill [ability] / あいつは折り紙付きの怠け者だ. He's a notorious layabout. | Everybody knows he's a no-account. / 彼女の演説のうまさは折り紙付きだ. We (can)「guarantee [vouch for] her skill at public speaking.

おりく【折り句】 a Japanese acrostic verse; a poem in which each line starts with a syllable of a specified word.

おりづめ【折り詰め】 food packed in a small box made of thin sheets of wood or cardboard. ◐ 鮨[赤飯]の折り詰め a small box of「sushi [rice and adzuki beans]. ■ 折り詰め弁当 a lunch packed in a small box; a packed lunch.

おりづる【折り鶴】《make》「an origami [a folded-paper] crane. [⇨ おりがみ 1] ◐ 折り鶴に願いを込める make an origami crane by way of a prayer《for *somebody*'s recovery》.

おれおれさぎ【オレオレ詐欺】〔高齢者宅に息子や孫を装って電話をかけ金をだまし取る詐欺〕an "it's me" scam; a scam in which a man calls an elderly person and, pretending to be a son or grandson, demands money.

おろし【卸し】1〔すりおろしたもの〕おろし入り焼き肉のたれ a barbecue sauce with grated daikon in it. **2**〔おろし器〕a grater. ■ 大根おろし grated daikon. 紅葉おろし daikon and chili grated together; grated daikon and grated carrot mixed together. 薬味おろし a「spice [condiment] grater. おろししょうが grated ginger. おろしそば soba topped with a mound of grated daikon.

おろしがね, おろしき【卸し金, 卸し器】a grater. ▷ おろし金で大根をおろす grate daikon with a grater.

おろち【大蛇】a monster serpent; a giant snake. ▷ やまたのおろち the eight-headed monster serpent.

おわらい【お笑い】1〔笑わせる芸〕the art of making people laugh;〔落語〕a humorous story. ▷ えー毎度, ばかばかしいお笑いを一席. Here, let me tell you「another [a] crazy story. **2**〔笑うべきこと〕something laughable. ▷ そいつはとんだお笑いだ. That's a big laugh. | What a joke! ■ お笑いぐさ a laugh; a joke; something ridiculous. お笑いタレント a comedian; a comic. お笑い番組 a comedy program.

おんがくはいしん【音楽配信】〔インターネットによる音楽データ販売〕online music「distribution [sales]. ▷ 音楽配信サービス an online music「distribution [sales] service.

おんきゅう¹【恩給】a pension paid to retired public「officials [servants]. ■ 軍人恩給 a soldier's pension.

おんきゅう²【温灸】indirect moxibustion; moxibustion in which the moxa is not applied to the skin directly but through the medium of a moxa holder or other substances such as salt, miso, a slice of garlic, or the leaf of certain plants ▷ 温灸をする apply indirect moxibustion.

おんぎょく【音曲】1〔三味線による俗曲〕a popular old-style Japanese song accompanied by samisen music. **2**〔音楽〕a performance of (Japanese) music. ▷ 歌舞音曲 ⇒ かぶ.

おんせん【温泉】a hot [thermal] spring (spa [bath, facility, resort, inn]). ▷ 伊香保温泉 Ikaho hot springs / 温泉に入る take a hot spring bath; take a bath in a hot spring / 温泉につかる soak in a hot spring bath / 温泉に行く visit [go to] a「hot spring location [spa]. ■ 温泉街 a part of town where hot spring inns or facilities are clustered. 温泉客 a「guest [visitor] at a hot spring 「facility [resort, inn]. **温泉郷** a hot springs 「village [country town]. **温泉水** hot [thermal] spring water(s). **温泉卵** an egg boiled in hot spring waters. **温泉場** a 「location [locale, site, spot] where hot spring baths are available; a hot spring(s) 「spa [resort]; a watering place. **温泉マーク** ♨; the symbol for a hot spring (facility); the hot spring symbol. **温泉町** a hot springs town; a spa (town). **温泉巡り** making the rounds of hot springs; a tour of several hot spring locations. **温泉宿[旅館]** an inn [a hotel] with hot spring bathing facilities; a hot spring 「inn [hotel].

おんち【音痴】1 tone deafness;〚医〛amusia. 〜の tone-deaf. ◐ ひどい音痴 extreme tone deafness;〔人〕a person who is 「extremely [very] tone-deaf. **2**〔あることに関して感覚が鈍いこと〕having no sense 《of *something*》; having no ability 《in *something*》; being hopeless when it comes to *something*. ■**機械音痴** being hopeless 「with [when it comes to] machines;〔人〕a person who is not mechanically inclined. **方向音痴** being hopeless when it comes to (knowing) directions; having no sense of direction;〔人〕a person who has no sense of direction. ◐ 彼はものすごい方向音痴だ. He's unbelievably hopeless when it comes to directions.

おんど【音頭】1〔先頭に立って皆を導くこと〕leading 《others in *doing something*》. ◐ 音頭を取る〔歌などの〕beat time; lead a 「choir [group] in singing;〔作業などの〕take the lead 《in…》; lead / 万歳三唱の音頭を取る lead three cheers / 私が音頭を取りますから皆さん万歳を唱えてください. I'll lead in giving a cheer, so everyone please join in. / 市が音頭を取って健康まつりが開かれた. The city took the lead in organizing a health festival. / 乾杯の音頭を佐藤さんにお願いします. I now ask Mr. Satō to 「lead us in [propose] a toast. **2**〔民謡の一種〕a folk song sung and danced to in a group; a folk dance performed by a group in accompaniment to a folk song. ■**伊勢音頭** the Ise *ondo*.

おんながた【女形】〔歌舞伎の〕a male actor who 「takes female parts [impersonates women, specializes in female roles]; a male player of female roles. [＝おやま] ◐ 女形をする act [play] a female role.

おんなぎだゆう【女義太夫】 a female gidayū reciter.

おんなしょうがつ【女正月】 the women's New Year; January 15 (busy during the new year fortnight, women at last have time to celebrate).

[⇨ こしょうがつ]

おんなもじ【女文字】〔女性の筆跡〕a woman's handwriting. ◐女文字の手紙 a letter「in a woman's handwriting [in a woman's hand, written by a woman].

おんぶ 1〔人を背負うこと〕a piggyback ride. 〜する〔背に負われる〕ride [get] on *somebody*'s shoulders and back; be carried on *somebody*'s back; ride piggyback on *somebody*. ◐赤ちゃんをおぶいひもでおんぶする strap a baby to *one*'s back. **2**〔人に頼ること〕dependence on *somebody* 《to do things for *one*》. 〜する lean [depend] on *somebody*. ◐おんぶにだっこ wholly [heavily] dependent 《on...》.

おんみつ【隠密】**1**〔内密〕secrecy. 〜な secret; clandestine. **2**〔江戸幕府の間諜〕a spy; a secret agent. ◐幕府の隠密 a secret agent of the shogunate.

隠密に〔内密に〕secretly; in「secret [secrecy]; clandestinely. ◐隠密に事を運ぶ do something secretly; act in secrecy / この作戦を成功させるためには,相手側にけどられぬよう隠密に事を運ぶ必要がある. In order to make this strategy succeed, we have to proceed in secrecy so the others don't get wind of it. / 隠密に行動する act in secrecy; carry out covert action. ■隠密行動 covert「action [behavior].

おんよく【温浴】a「warm [hot] bath 〜する take a「hot [warm] bath. ■温浴効果 the (medicinal) effect of a「warm [hot] bath.

か

か【蚊】 a mosquito《*pl.* ～es, ～s》; *《口》a skeeter; ‖a gnat. ◐ 蚊に食われる[さされる] be [get] bitten by a mosquito.

が【蛾】 a moth. ◐ 灯火に群れる蛾 moths (gathering) around a flame / 蛾のまゆ a「moth [moth's] cocoon; the cocoon of a moth.

かい【貝】 a shellfish《*pl.* ～》;〔動〕a mollusk;〔食物〕(a) shellfish;〔貝殻〕a shell ◐ 貝のように口を閉ざす clam up / 貝を拾う gather [collect, hunt for] shellfish / 貝を掘る dig for shellfish; dig [rake] up shellfish.

かいあわせ【貝合わせ】〔平安時代の'神経衰弱'〕a concentration game [Pelmanism] with clamshells; a Heian-period game in which players take turns looking for the mate to each of 180 pairs of clamshells.

かいかどん【開化丼】 a kind of *donburi* introduced in the Meiji period and consisting of meat (typically beef), egg, sugar, onion and soy sauce, placed on top of rice.

かいけん【甲斐犬】 a Kai (dog);〔異称〕a tiger dog.

かいごろし【飼い殺し】〔家畜の〕keeping《a domestic animal》beyond its useful life;〔使用人の〕keeping a superannuated employee on the payroll. ◐ 飼い殺しにする〔使用人を〕keep《an employee》on the payroll without using *his* talents / このまま飼い殺しにされるくらいなら会社を辞めたい. I'd rather quit than be paid to do nothing.

かいし【懐紙】 **1**〔懐中の〕pocket paper; folded paper kept inside the fold of *one*'s kimono. **2**〔詩歌記録用〕paper for writing traditional verse.

かいしゃく【介錯】 assistance (as a second); seconding;〔介錯する人〕a second at ritual hara-kiri. ～する assist [second] *somebody* committing hara-kiri; administer the *coup de grâce* (to *somebody* who has ritually disemboweled himself).

がいしょく【外食】 eating [dining] out. ～する eat [dine] out. ◐ 今晩

は外食してきます. Tonight I'll be eating out. ■**外食券** a meal ˈcoupon [ticket]. **外食産業** the food service industry.

かいすいよく【海水浴】swimming in the ˈsea [ocean]; ‖sea [ocean] bathing. ◐海水浴に行く go for a ˈswim [dip, ‖bathe] in the ocean; go sea bathing; go ˈswimming [bathing] in the ocean / 逗子へ海水浴に行く go for a swim in the ocean at Zushi / 海水浴をする swim in the ˈsea [ocean]; have [take] a ˈswim [dip, ‖bathe] in the ˈsea [ocean] / 鎌倉で海水浴をする have a swim off the beach at Kamakura. ■**海水浴場** a (swimming [bathing]) beach; a seaside swimming area; a ˈbeach [seaside] resort; a public beach for ˈswimming [‖bathing].

かいすうけん【回数券】a coupon ticket; 〔電車の〕a ˈbook [sheet, ‖carnet] of (discounted) tickets;《tear》a ticket from a book of tickets. ◐11枚つづりの回数券 a set of eleven tickets (for the price of ten).

かいせきりょうり[1]【会席料理】a set meal served on individual trays at a traditional Japanese dinner party.

かいせきりょうり[2]【懐石料理】an elegant Japanese meal served in delicate courses.

かいぞくばん【海賊版】a ˈpirated [pirate] edition [version, copy]; 〔CD・レコードなど〕a ˈpirated [pirate, bootleg] CD [record]; a pirate recording. ◐この本は海賊版がたくさん出回っている. There are many pirated editions of this book going around. / 海賊版のコンピューター・ソフト pirated [pirate] computer software.

かいだん【戒壇】the ordination ˈplatform [seat] in a large Buddhist temple. ■**戒壇院** the building that houses the *kaidan*.

かいちゅうでんとう【懐中電灯】*a flashlight; ‖a torch; an electric torch; 〔ペンシル型の〕a pencil ˈ*flashlight [‖torch]. ◐懐中電灯で照らす shine ˈthe [*one's*] *flashlight [‖torch]《on...》; 〔周りを〕shine the *flashlight [‖torch] around / 懐中電灯をつける turn [switch] on the flashlight / 懐中電灯を消す turn [switch] off the flashlight.

かいてん【開店】**1**〔新規に店を開くこと〕the opening of a ˈshop [store]. ～する〔店が〕open (for business); start business; 〔店を〕open [start] a ˈshop [store]. ◐本日開店.〔掲示〕Opening [Business From] Today / 祝開店.〔店頭の掲示〕Newly Opened; Our Opening Day of Business; 〔花輪の掲示〕In Celebration of Your New Venture; 〔祝いの品に記して〕A gift to mark the opening of《the shop》. **2**〔その日の営業を始め

ること〕the opening of a「shop [store] (for the day). ～する〔店が〕open; open for business;〔店を〕open a shop; open up. ◐このデパートは午前10時開店です. The department store opens at 10:00 a.m. ■ **新装開店** the reopening of a「shop [store] after redecoration; (a) post-refurbishment reopening. ◐近日新装開店.〔掲示〕Soon reopening fully redecorated [refurbished]. | Redesigned and opening soon. **開店大売り出し** an opening sale; a (bargain) sale on the opening of a new shop [store]. **開店時間**〔時刻〕(an) opening time;〔営業時間〕opening hours. **開店準備中.**〔掲示〕Closed. | Opening soon. **開店日** an open day; a day when the shop is open.

かいてんずし【回転寿司】 a conveyor belt sushi bar.

かいてんドア【回転ドア[扉]】 a revolving door; revolving doors.

かいとう【解凍】1〔凍っていたものをとかすこと〕defrosting; thawing (out); a thaw. ～する〔物が〕thaw (out); defrost; unfreeze;〔氷や雪が〕melt;〔物を〕thaw; defrost; unfreeze;〔氷や雪を〕melt. ◐冷凍食品を解凍する unfreeze [defrost] frozen food / 電子レンジで解凍する unfreeze [defrost]《food》in a microwave. **2**〚電算〛〔圧縮したデータをもとに戻すこと〕extraction. ～する extract《a file》.

がいとうぼきん【街頭募金】 fundraising in the street; "a street collection.

がいはく【外泊】 spending《two nights》away; staying away from home (overnight); overnighting (in New York). ～する spend《two nights》away; stay away from home; overnight (at a hotel);〔兵士が〕overnight out of barracks;〔入院患者・施設への入所者などが〕go home for the night; spend《two nights》at home. ◐無断で外泊する spend《two nights》「out [away from home] without「permission《from *one*'s parents》/ 外泊の許可を得る get「permission to「stay away from home [spend the night away] / 外泊を許す let *somebody* spend the night「away [out]; give *somebody* permission to stay「out [away] (overnight). ■ **無断外泊** spending《two nights》away from home without「permission [leave].

かいばしら【貝柱】〔閉殻筋〕a shellfish ligament; the adductor (muscle) in a bivalve;〔食品の〕the adductor muscle of certain bivalve shellfish, (used as food). ◐ホタテ貝の貝柱 (a) scallop「ligament [adductor (muscle)] / 干した貝柱 dried shellfish adductor (muscle).

かいまき【掻い巻き】a cotton-stuffed sleeping garment.

かいみょう【戒名】〖仏教〗a posthumous (Buddhist) name. ◐ 戒名をつける give *somebody* a posthumous (Buddhist) name / 戒名をもらう receive [get, be given] a posthumous (Buddhist) name. ■ 戒名料 a fee (payable to a priest [temple]) for a posthumous (Buddhist) name.

かいようしんそうすい【海洋深層水】deep「ocean [sea] water.

かいらんばん【回覧板】《pass on》a circular「notice [bulletin]; 《send round》a circular.

かいわれだいこん【穎割れ大根】white-radish sprouts.

かえで【楓】〔カエデ科カエデ属 Acer 樹木の総称〕a maple tree. ◐ カエデがちょうど紅葉してきている. The maple leaves are just turning (color).

かえる【蛙】a frog; a toad. ◐ カエルが鳴いている. A frog is「croaking [chirping, singing]. / カエルがぴょんぴょんと跳んだ. A frog hopped (along). / カエルの子はカエル. Like breeds like.〖諺〗| Like「father [mother], like「son [daughter]. /〖諺〗その時の彼はヘビににらまれたカエルみたいだった. At that moment he looked like a rabbit (frozen) in a car's headlights.

かえんこうはい【火炎光背】〔仏像の〕a halo of flames adorning a Buddhist image.

かおきき【顔利き】an influential person;《口》a big wheel. ◐ 町内の顔利き a person with local influence.

かおパス【顔パス】◐ おれは顔パスが利く[顔パスだ]. They'll let me in《at the gate》because they know「me [my face]. / 顔パスで(入り口・検問などを)通る use *one*'s influence to「enter [pass through]; enter [pass through] by using *one*'s influence.

かおみせ【顔見せ・顔見世】1【顔見せ】〔大勢の人に顔を見せること〕a public appearance; an appearance before a large number of people;(役者などの初お目見え) *one*'s debut; *one*'s first appearance (on stage). ◐ 顔見せする make *one*'s debut / 顔見せを済ます get through [conclude] *one*'s debut. 2【顔見世】〔歌舞伎で役者全員がそろって挨拶すること〕formal introduction of a (Kabuki) theatrical company in costume;〔顔見世狂言〕an introductory Kabuki performance; a short piece to introduce the players;(京都南座の12月公演) the December performance at the Kyoto Minamiza Theater at which all the well-known actors in the country appear. [⇨ きょうげん]　■**顔見せ興行** a once-a-year all-star run of Kabuki performances.

かおやく【顔役】 an influential man; a man of (wide) influence; a boss.　◐町内[土地]の顔役 a person who is respected in the「neighborhood [district].

かかい【歌会】 a gathering of tanka poets; a tanka poetry reading.

ががく【雅楽】 ceremonial (imperial) court music (and dances) of Japan.　◐雅楽を奏する give a *gagaku* performance.　■**雅楽師** a *gagaku* musician [master].

かかし, かがし【案山子】《put up》a scarecrow; [見掛けだけのもの] a figurehead; a dummy.　◐田んぼの中の一本足のかかし a one-legged scarecrow in a rice field.

かがみ¹【鏡】 1 [姿などを映すもの] a mirror; a (looking) glass.　2 [酒樽のふた] a barrelhead.　◐[祝い事で]鏡を割る break [crack] open a barrelhead.　3 [鏡餅] ⇨ かがみもち.

かがみ²【鑑】 a mirror; a model; a paragon; a shining example.　◐武士の鑑 a paragon of a samurai; a perfect warrior; everything a samurai should be.

かがみびらき【鏡開き】 1 [正月11日鏡餅を割って雑煮などにして食べること] Mirror Opening (Day); the (ceremonial) breaking and eating of *Kagami mochi* on January 11.　2 [お祝いに酒樽のふたを割ること] a barrel-opening ceremony; the splitting open of (the barrelhead of) a sake barrel.

かがみもち【鏡餅】 a mirror-shaped rice cake; three rice cakes of decreasing size piled one on the other and, used as a New Year offering, then broken up and eaten on January 11.　◐鏡餅を供える[飾る] offer up rice cakes (on the altar).

かき¹【柿】 [カキノキ科の落葉高木; 果樹] a (Japanese) persimmon tree; a Chinese persimmon; a kaki (tree); [実] a (Japanese) persimmon; a kaki.　◐柿の種[柿の種子] a persimmon seed; [米菓] a brownish-orange spicy rice cracker made in the shape of a small persimmon seed / 柿のへた a persimmon calyx / 甘[渋]柿 a sweet [an astringent] persimmon.

かき²【牡蠣】〖貝〗an oyster.　◐殻付きのカキ an oyster on the (half) shell / 生食用のカキ an oyster that can be eaten raw / カキのむき身 a shucked oyster.　■**生ガキ** a raw oyster.　**養殖ガキ** a cultivated oyster. **カキ殻**〔1個の〕an oyster shell;〔砕いて粉にしたもの〕(crushed) oyster shell. **カキ床** an oyster bed. **カキ鍋** an oyster「hot pot [fire-pot]. **カキ船** an oyster boat. **カキフライ** fried oysters; oyster fritters; deep-fried crumbed oysters. **カキ飯** rice boiled with oysters. **カキ養殖** oyster farming [culture]. **カキ養殖業者** an oysterman; an oyster farmer. **カキ養殖場** an oyster farm.

かきあげ【掻き揚げ】〚料理〛a (mixed)「vegetable [seafood] tempura. ◐ 小エビのかき揚げ (a) shrimp tempura / 野菜のかき揚げ (a) vegetable tempura.

かきごおり【欠き氷】〔ぶっかき〕shaved ice;〔氷水〕a summer refreshment consisting of a cup or bowl of flavored shaved ice. ◐ かき氷機[器] an ice shaver; an ice-shaving machine.

かきぞめ【書き初め】the first calligraphy of the year; the New Year's calligraphy exercise. ◐ 書き初めの会 the first calligraphy exercise of the year, done in a group / 書き初めをする do calligraphy for the first time in the New Year; do the New Year's calligraphy exercise.

がきだいしょう【餓鬼大将】the leader of a group of「children [kids]; the most domineering child in a group of children;〔弱い者いじめの〕a bully.

かぎっこ【鍵っ子】a latchkey「child [kid].

かきもち【欠き餅】thin「slices [chips] of dried *mochi*. ◐ 欠き餅を焼く toast [grill] *kakimochi* (over an open fire).

かくあんどん【角行燈】a square paper lantern.

かくえき【各駅】each [every] station;〔各駅停車の列車〕a local train; a way train; a train that stops at every station.

かくおび【角帯】a (man's) stiff sash.

かくかい【角界】the sumo world; sumo circles.

かくざとう【角砂糖】cube [lump] sugar. ◐ 角砂糖1個 a [one] lump [cube] of sugar.

がくしゅうさんこうしょ【学習参考書】reference materials for study; a reference book for learners.

かくそで【角袖】1〔着物の袖〕square [bag] sleeves. **2**〔和服の異称〕a kimono 《*pl.* ～s》;〔男物の和装コート〕a Japanese-style men's coat.

がくどうほいく【学童保育】childcare; child-minding; after-school [before-school, out-of-school] care; *a latchkey program;〔その施設〕a childcare center.

かくに【角煮】a ⌈stewed [simmered] cube [chunk] of ⌈meat [fish]. ◐ 豚の角煮 stewed (cubes of) pork (belly); braised pork, Nagasaki-style / カツオの角煮 stewed (cubes of) bonito.

かくべえじし【角兵衛獅子】=えちごじし.

かぐやひめ【かぐや姫】Shining Princess; the central character in the early Heian-period *Taketori monogatari* (*Tale of the Bamboo Cutter*), An old man finds a tiny princess inside a shining stalk of bamboo. When the princess comes of age, she is sought by fine suitors, including the Emperor, but she refuses them all and on the night of the harvest moon returns to the Moon Palace.

かぐら【神楽】*kagura*; (a performance of) sacred (Shinto) music and dancing. ◐ 神楽を奏する play [perform] sacred music / 神楽を舞う dance (a) *kagura*. ■ 神楽歌 a *kagura* ⌈song [chant]; a ⌈song [chant] sung in *kagura*. 神楽師 a *kagura* ⌈performer [dancer]. 神楽殿[堂] a ⌈stage [hall] for *kagura* (performances); the Hall of the Sacred Dances. 神楽囃子 a *kagura* musician.

かくれんぼう【隠れん坊】《play》hide-and-(go-)seek.

がくわり【学割】〔学生割引(証明書)〕a student ⌈discount [rate, reduction]; a student reduction card. ◐ 学割で乗車券を買う buy a train ticket ⌈at the student rate [for the student fare]. ■ 学割料金 a student rate; a special rate for students.

かげうた【陰唄】a song sung behind the scenes in Kabuki.

かけえり【掛け衿】a piece of collar-cloth sewed on a kimono.

かけおち【駆け落ち】running away with a lover; eloping; (an) elopement; 〔結婚〕(an) elopement; a runaway ⌈marriage [match]. 〜する elope; run away 《with *one*'s lover》; run off 《with…》.

かけこみでら【駆け込み寺】a (Buddhist) temple that gave refuge to abused wives in Tokugawa-period Japan. [⇨ えんきりでら]

かけざん【掛け算】multiplication; 〔1回の〕a multiplication. ◐ 掛け算をする multiply; do multiplication.

かけじ【掛け字】〔床の間や壁の〕a calligraphic hanging scroll.

かけじく【掛け軸】a hanging scroll.

かげぜん【陰膳】陰膳を据える set a meal for an absent person (as a prayer for his or her safe return).

かけそば【掛け蕎麦】(plain) *soba* in hot broth; (hot) *soba* without any trimmings.

かけつけさんばい【駆けつけ三杯】requiring a latecomer to drink three cups of sake one after the other.

かけぶとん【掛け布団】the upper of a set of covering and spreading futons;〔ベッドの〕a quilt; an eiderdown.

かけむしろ【掛け筵】a mat curtain of「straw [rushes].

かご【駕籠】a *kago*《*pl.* ~s》; a palanquin (carried on a long pole by two or more men); a sedan (chair).   ◐ 駕籠で行く go by palanquin / 駕籠に乗る ride in a *kago* / 駕籠に乗る人かつぐ人, そのまたわらじを作る人. the butcher, the baker, the candlestick maker. | It takes all sorts to make the world. / 駕籠をかつぐ carry a palanquin on *one*'s shoulders.   ■ 早駕籠 an express palanquin.   駕籠かき a palanquin bearer.

かこう【歌稿】a tanka manuscript; a manuscript draft of tanka poems.

かごめ【籠目】〔かごの編み目〕a crossing of the warp and weft osiers of a basket;〔その形の模様〕the pattern produced by repetition of such crossings; (the eyes of) a basket weave; a「reticulate [reticular] pattern; a basket-weave pattern.   かご目格子 〚物〛 a kagome lattice.   かご目小紋 a fine「basket-weave [reticulate] pattern.   かご目模様 a「reticulate [reticular] pattern; a basket-weave pattern.

かごめかごめ〔遊戯〕bird-in-the-cage; a game in which children sing a song as they circle a child squatting with eyes closed, who has to guess the name of the person directly behind him when all stop as the song ends, in order to fly out of the cage.   ◐ かごめかごめをする play "bird-in-the-cage."

かごや【籠屋】〔かご作り職人〕a basket maker.

かさ【傘】〔雨傘〕an umbrella;〔日傘〕a parasol.   ◐ 携帯用の傘 a portable umbrella / 晴雨兼用の傘 an all-weather umbrella / おちょこになった傘 an umbrella blown inside out《by the wind》/ 女物[男物]の傘 a ladies' [men's] umbrella / 傘をさす put up an umbrella / 傘をさして歩く walk with *one*'s umbrella up / 傘を閉じる close [fold (up)] *one*'s umbrella / 傘を畳む〔長傘を〕furl *one*'s umbrella;〔折り畳み傘を〕fold (up) *one*'s umbrella.   ■ 折り畳み傘 a「folding [telescopic] umbrella;〔二重[三重]折りの〕a bifolding [trifolding] umbrella.   ジャンプ[ワンタッチ]傘 an automatic [a push-button] umbrella.   長傘 a long

(-rib) umbrella.　**傘立て** an umbrella stand.　**傘張り** overlaying an umbrella framework.　**傘屋**〔店〕an umbrella「shop [store]; 〔職人〕an umbrella maker.

かさいほけん【火災保険】fire insurance.　◐その家には一千万円の火災保険がかけてある. The house is insured against fire for ¥10 million. / 火災保険に入る[加入する] take out fire insurance.　■**火災保険会社** a fire insurance company.　**火災保険金** a fire insurance benefit.　**火災保険証書** a fire insurance policy; a certificate of fire insurance.　**火災保険料** a fire insurance premium.

かさがけ【笠懸け】〚日本史〛〔馬上から的の代わりに下げた笠を射る弓技〕mounted archery; target shooting on horseback.

かさぶた a scab; a crust; an incrustation; a slough;〔壊疽(ぇ)・火傷などの〕an eschar.　◐かさぶただらけの covered in scabs; scabby / 傷にかさぶたができた. A scab formed over the「wound [cut]. / かさぶたがとれた. The scab came off. | The dried skin sloughed off.

かさほこ【傘鉾・笠鉾】a large umbrella topped by a pike or artificial flowers and carried on a float in certain festivals.

かしおり【菓子折り】a box of (Japanese) confections often given as an expression of appreciation or thanks.　◐引っ越しの挨拶に菓子折りを持っていく take boxes of confections as gifts on moving into a new neighborhood.

かじき【旗魚】〚魚〛〔メカジキ〕a swordfish;〔マカジキ〕a billfish; a spearfish; a marlin;〔クロカジキ〕a black marlin;〔シロカジキ〕a Pacific blue marlin;〔バショウカジキ〕a sailfish;〔フウライカジキ〕a shortbill spearfish.

かじきとう【加持祈祷】Buddhist「prayers [incantations] to protect against misfortune.　◐加持祈祷を行う perform [chant] incantations; recite healing prayers; practice faith「healing [cures].　**加持祈祷者** a faith healer.

かしぱん【菓子パン】a sweet「bun [roll]; a pastry.

かじゅう【果汁】(a) fruit juice; the juice of a fruit.
　■**天然果汁** natural fruit juice.　**濃縮果汁** concentrated fruit juice.　**果汁入り清涼飲料** a fruit(-flavored) drink (with a fruit-juice content of between 5% and 50%).　**果汁飲料** a fruit(-flavored) drink (with a fruit-juice content of at least 50%).　**果汁100パーセントのジュース**

(a) 100-percent fruit juice.

かしょ【歌書】〔歌論書〕a book on「Japanese poetry [tanka];〔和歌集〕a book of Japanese「poems [poetry]; a collection of tanka.

かしわで【拍手】a「hand clap [clap of the hands] to summon the gods (in front of a Shinto altar).　◐拍手を打つ clap *one*'s hands 《in worship at a Shinto shrine》.

かしわもち【柏餅】a「rice cake [cake of pounded rice] wrapped in an oak leaf and eaten on Children's Day, 5 May.　◐柏餅になって寝る sleep rolled up in a single quilt.

かじん【歌人】a (tanka) poet;〔女性〕a (tanka) poetess.

かすがい【鎹】a clamp; a cramp (iron).　◐子は(夫婦の)かすがい. Children are the bindings that hold a marriage together.

かすじる【粕汁】*kasu* [sake-lees] soup [broth].

かすず【粕酢】*kasu* [sake-lees] vinegar; vinegar made from「*kasu* [sake-lees].

かすづけ【糟漬け】*kasu* pickles; vegetables pickled in sake lees.　◐糟漬けにする pickle [marinate, steep] 《cod》 in「*kasu* [sake-lees].

カステラ〖< Port. *pão de Castella* "bread from Castile"〗(a) sponge cake (learned by the Portuguese from Spanish Castile and transmitted in the 16th century).

ガスぬき【ガス抜き】**1**〔鉱山などで〕gas drainage; gas venting;〔金属やプラスチック加工で〕breathing; degassing; gassing;〔製パンで〕deflating; punching (to deflate the dough);〔スプレー缶の〕releasing the (remaining) gas;〔飛行船の〕deflation.　**2**〔不満などの発散〕letting off steam; giving vent to *one*'s「emotions [frustrations]; calming down; cooling off.　◐双方とも言いたいことを自由に言い合ってガス抜きをすることが必要だ. They both need to let off steam by telling each other exactly what's on their minds.

かずのこ【数の子】(salted, preserved) herring roe.

かすり【絣・飛白】〔模様〕a splashed pattern;〔布地〕*kasuri*; cloth with splashed patterns.　◐絣の着物 a kimono with splashed patterns / 久留米絣 *Kurume-gasuri*; *kasuri* from Kurume (in Kyūshū).

かぜ【風邪】a cold; a chill; an ague; influenza; flu.　◐ひどい風邪 a「bad [nasty, miserable] cold / 軽い風邪 a「slight [mild] cold; the sniffles / 風邪にかかる catch cold; get a cold / 風邪にかかっている have a cold.

■**夏風邪** a「summer [hot weather] cold. **はやり風邪** influenza; flu.

かぜぐすり【風邪薬】 a「remedy [medicine] for a cold; a cold remedy; (a) cold medicine. ■**総合風邪薬** an all-round cold remedy. **非ピリン系風邪薬** a non-pyrine cold remedy.

かぞえどし【数え年】 one's age by the Japanese system [traditional Japanese reckoning] (of one year old at birth, with one year added at every New Year). ◐(年齢を)数え年で数える count *somebody*'s age by the old Japanese system / 数え年で 7 つの時に at [when *one* was] seven by the old Japanese system / 七五三を数え年で祝う celebrate (children reaching the ages of) seven, five and three by the Japanese system / 私は数え年で 60 歳です. I am 60 according to traditional Japanese reckoning.

かた【肩】〔人や動物などの肩〕a shoulder.

肩が凝る[張る]〔肩の筋肉が固くなる〕feel stiff in *one*'s shoulders; have「stiff shoulders [a stiff shoulder];〔気詰まりだ・緊張する〕feel「stiff [tense];〈事が主語〉make *somebody* feel「a strain [tense].

肩で風を切る swagger; strut. ◐肩で風を切って歩く parade about; strut [swagger].

肩を落とす〔落胆する〕drop *one*'s shoulders (in disappointment). ◐がっくり肩を落とす drop *one*'s shoulders in despair.

肩をすくめる〔両肩を上げて身を縮める〕shrug *one*'s shoulders; give a shrug of the shoulders.

肩をたたく〔親しみや祝いの気持ちを込めて,もしくは注意を喚起するために〕pat [clap, slap, tap] *somebody* on the shoulder(s); give *somebody* a pat [clap, slap, tap] on the shoulder(s);〔凝りをほぐすために〕pound *somebody*'s shoulders;〔退職を勧告する〕let *somebody* know that they are not needed at work; urge *somebody* to「resign [quit].

肩を並べる〔横に並ぶ〕line up (shoulder to shoulder);〔対等の位置に立つ〕rank with *somebody*; can compare with *somebody*; be [stand] on a par with *somebody*; equal *somebody* 《in *something*》.

肩を持つ〔味方をする〕side 《with...》; take sides 《with...》; take *somebody*'s side; support; give「assistance [support, aid] 《to...》; stand up for...; take up [espouse] *somebody*'s cause.

かたかな【片仮名】 katakana; the katakana syllabary; the square form of kana. ◐片仮名で外来語を表記する write (foreign) loanwords in katakana; transliterate (foreign) loanwords into katakana.　■ **カタカナ語** a katakana word; a (foreign) loanword transliterated into katakana.

かたぎ【気質】 a character; a spirit; a temperament; a trait; a「turn [frame] of mind.　■ **学生気質** a student temperament; the way students think.　**職人気質** the spirit of a craftsman.　**江戸っ子気質** the (stylish, quarrelsome) temperament of an Edoite.

かたぎぬ【肩衣】 a stiff, sleeveless ceremonial robe (for a samurai in the late Muromachi period); a (stiff) shoulder-piece.

かたぐるま【肩車】 〔人を自分の両肩にまたがらせてかつぐこと〕.　**〜する**〔乗せる〕carry *somebody*「piggyback [on *one*'s shoulders]; give *somebody* a ride on *one*'s shoulders;〔乗る〕ride「piggyback [pickaback]; ride [have a ride] on *somebody*'s shoulders.

かたこり【肩凝り】 a stiff shoulder; stiff shoulders; stiffness「in [of] the shoulders.　◐ 肩凝りから来る頭痛 a headache「from [caused by] stiff shoulders / 肩凝りがする have [get] stiff shoulders / 肩凝りがひどい. I have terribly stiff shoulders.

かたしろ【形代】 **1**〔神体の代わりとする人形(ひとがた)〕 a representation 《in paper, cloth, wood, etc.》of a sacred object of worship.　**2**〔厄払い用の紙人形〕a paper doll used to rub away evil in a Shinto purification rite.

かたたたき【肩叩き】 **1**〔凝りをほぐすために肩をたたくこと〕 pounding the shoulders (lightly)《to relieve stiffness》;〔道具〕a massage device for pounding the back and shoulders.　◐ 祖母の肩叩きをする (gently) pound the shoulders of *one*'s grandmother.　**2**〔退職勧告〕a tap on the shoulder by a superior who is pressuring *one* to take an early retirement.　**〜する** try to pressure *somebody* into「retiring early [(taking) early retirement].　◐ 肩叩きされる, 肩叩きを受ける[にあう] come under pressure to retire early; be pressured into retiring early.

かたつき¹【肩衝】 a square-shouldered tea caddy; a *katatsuki*-type tea canister.

かたつき²【型付き】 a roll of printed kimono cloth.

かたつむり【蝸牛】 a snail.　◐ カタツムリの殻 a snail shell.

かたびら【帷子】〔几帳などに使った薄い布〕the cloth for a hanging screen;〔薄地のひとえ物〕a kimono of light material; (夏向きの) a light kimono for summer.

かため【固め】 **1**〔防備〕defense; fortifying; fortification;〔警護〕guarding. ◐国の固めに意を用いる think of [pay attention to] the defenses of a country / 城の固めを厳重にする tighten the defense(s) of a castle; take the greatest precautions for the defense of a castle. **2** 〔約束・誓い〕a pledge; an engagement. ◐夫婦[親族]固めの杯 the ceremonial exchange of cups of sake at a Shinto wedding that symbolizes「the union of bride and groom [the new relationship of the families of bride and groom] / 固めの杯を交わす〔夫婦の〕exchange ceremonial cups of sake at a wedding.

かたり【語り】(a) narration; a narrative;〔能楽〕a「narrative [narrated] part (in a Noh drama) / ドラマの語りの部分 the narrative of a drama.

かたりて【語り手】〔ドラマなどの〕a narrator; a storyteller;〔義太夫などの〕a reciter 《of *gidayū*》.

かたりもの【語り物】a traditional style of (*gidayū*)「narrative [recitation].

かちゅう【家中】〔家臣〕a retainer; a clansman;〈集合的に〉the retainers of a daimyo; a clan. ◐水戸藩の家中〔1 人〕a retainer of the Mito clan;〈集合的に〉the retainers of the Mito clan.

かつお【鰹】a skipjack tuna; an oceanic bonito 《*pl.* ~(e)s》; a bonito; a victorfish. ◐初がつお ⇨ はつがつお. / かつおのたたき *katsuo* in which the outer surface is lightly grilled, leaving the inner flesh raw, and usually served in slices with onion or other pungent herbs. ■カツオ・マグロ漁業 tuna (and bonito) fishing; the tuna fishing industry.

かつおぶし【鰹節】a dried bonito fillet;〔薄くけずったもの〕dried bonito flakes. ◐かつおぶしを削る shave a dried bonito fillet (to make bonito flakes) / それじゃまるで猫にかつおぶしだね. You might as well ask a cat to look after the cream. ■かつおぶし削り a plane for shaving dried bonito; a dried-bonito plane.

かっこう【郭公】〔ホトトギス科の鳥〕a (common) cuckoo.

がっしょうづくり【合掌造り】〖建〗a traditional style of Japanese architecture distinguished by a steeply canted roof to bear the weight of winter snows. ◐合掌造りの家 a house with a steep thatched roof.

かってぐち【勝手口】a kitchen door; a backdoor; a service entrance; a tradesmen's「door [entrance].

カツどん【カツ丼】a large bowl of rice topped with a breaded fried pork cutlet.

かっぱ【河童】1〔水にすむ想像上の生物〕a *kappa*; a water「spirit [sprite, imp, goblin] haunting, chiefly, mainly rivers;〔水泳のうまい人〕an excellent swimmer;〔水泳をしている子供〕a swimming child. ◐陸(おか)に上がったかっぱ a fish out of water; a person out of his element / かっぱの皿 the concave crown of the mythical *kappa*'s head that holds water, permitting it to be active on land / かっぱの川流れ. Even a *kappa* can be carried away on the current. | Even the best swimmer can drown. | Even a monkey can fall from a tree. / そんなことは屁のかっぱだ. Nothing could be easier. | *《口》It's a cinch. | It's a piece of cake. | It's as easy as pie. **2**〔寿司屋で, キュウリ〕a cucumber. ■ 河童巻き a sushi roll with cucumber inside.

かっぷく【割腹】 disembowelment; hara-kiri. ～する disembowel *one*self; commit hara-kiri. ■ 割腹自殺 suicide by disembowelment.

かっぽう【割烹】 cooking;〔日本料理〕Japanese-style cooking;〔日本料理屋〕a Japanese(-style) restaurant. ■ 割烹着 a cooking apron with sleeves; a smock (apron). 割烹料理 a meal served at a Japanese(-style) restaurant. 割烹料理屋 a Japanese(-style) restaurant. 割烹旅館 a Japanese(-style) restaurant with an attached inn.

かっぽれ a variety of street performance of the late Edo period.

かつら【鬘】 a wig; a false head of hair;〔部分かつら〕a hairpiece; a switch; a toupee. ◐日本髪[ちょんまげ]のかつら a「Japanese female hairdo [topknot] wig / かつらをつける[かぶる] put on a「wig [hairpiece, toupee] / かつらをつけている〔現在の様子〕be wearing a wig;〔習慣〕wear a wig / かつらを取る take off a wig.

かつらむき〚料理〛paring a 5 to 6 cm length of「cucumber [carrot, daikon] into a long, thin band.

かてめし【かて飯】 rice boiled with beans, barley, daikon, or other ingredient.

かどう¹【華道】(the art of) flower arrangement; floral art. ◐華道の先生 a flower arrangement teacher / 華道の流派 a school of flower arrangement. ■ 華道教室 a flower arrangement class.

かどう²【歌道】 the art of composing tanka poetry; the art of Japanese versification.

かどまつ【門松】 *kadomatsu*; a pair of pine and bamboo decorations placed in front of a house as an abode for the New Year gods. ◐門松

かとりせんこう【蚊取り線香】a mosquito coil.

かとんのじゅつ【火遁の術】〔火の中に身を隠す忍術〕a ninja art of concealment, using fire.

かな【仮名】kana; the Japanese syllabaries; hiragana; katakana. ◐仮名で書く write in kana / 仮名をふる write the kana-next to [above, under, on the right of] a kanji to show the reading; give the reading 《of a Chinese character》 in kana / 仮名を漢字に変換する convert kana to kanji; do kana-kanji conversion 《on a word processor》.

かなしばり【金縛り】◐金縛りにあう be「paralyzed [transfixed, petrified, turned to stone, unable to move hand or foot] / 金縛りにあったように動けなくなる be unable to move, as though *one* had been bound hand and foot.

かなづち【金槌】**1**〔道具〕a hammer. ◐金づちで釘を打つ hit a nail with a hammer; hammer a nail「in [home, into 《a board》]; drive「in a nail [a nail into 《a board》]. **2**〔まったく泳げない人〕私は金づちだ. I sink like a stone in (the) water. | I cannot swim a stroke.

かなでほんちゅうしんぐら【仮名手本忠臣蔵】*The Treasury of Loyal Retainers*, a beloved play of the puppet and Kabuki theater.

カナリア【金糸雀】〔アトリ科の鳥〕a canary (bird).

かに【蟹】a crab. ◐カニがはっていた. Crabs were crawling「around [about]. / カニが泡を吹いている. The crab is blowing bubbles. / (形が)カニに似た crab-like; cancroid / カニにはさまれる be「nipped [pinched] by a crab / カニの穴 a crab('s)「hole [burrow] / カニの肉 crab; crab meat / カニのふんどし〔腹節〕an apron / カニ(の)みそ an edible, creamy brown substance inside the shell of a crab, consisting of liver and pancreas; (edible) crab organs / カニの横ばい the sideways movement of a crab. ■**カニ歩き** ◐カニ歩きする move sideways (like a crab). **カニ缶** canned [tinned] crab; a can [tin] of crab (meat). **カニ・サラダ** (a) crab salad; (a) salad with crab. **カニ(風味)かまぼこ, カニかま** steamed fish paste shaped and colored to resemble crab meat; imitation crab sticks. **カニ漁** crab fishing; 《go》 crabbing.

かにざ【蟹座】〘天・占星〙the Crab; Cancer (略: Cnc). ◐かに座生まれの人 a crab; a Cancerian.

がにまた【蟹股】bowlegs; bandy legs. ◐がにまたで歩く walk in a

bandy-legged way; have a bowlegged gait.

かのこ【鹿の子】〔シカの子〕a fawn;〔模様〕a dappled pattern; a pattern with white spots on it. ■鹿の子しぼり[染め] (a) cloth dyed in a dappled pattern; (a) dapple-dyed cloth. 鹿の子餅〔餅菓子〕a kind of rice cake with sweet-boiled beans mixed into it.

かば【河馬】a hippopotamus 《*pl.* ~es, -mi》;《口》a hippo 《*pl.* ~s》; a river horse.

かばやき【蒲焼き】《eel》split, *broiled [ǁgrilled], and basted with a sweet sauce. ◐蒲焼きにする *broil [ǁgrill]《an eel, a loach》with a sweet sauce.

かばん【鞄】〔袋状の〕a bag;(旅行用) a travel(ling) bag; a carryall; a holdall;(小型の手提げ) a handbag; a duffel bag; a satchel;(折り鞄) a Gladstone bag;(ランドセル) a satchel; a backpack;(学生鞄) a (school) bag;〔箱状の〕a suitcase; a case;(旅行用の大型) a trunk;(小型) a valise;(書類用) a briefcase;(紙ばさみ式の) a portfolio.

かばんもち【鞄持ち】《act as》a (private) secretary《to...》; an (unofficial) 「assistant [aide]《to...》; a companion; a 「man [maid] of all work; a flunky; ǁ《口》a (general) dogsbody. ◐僕は卒業後しばらく教授の鞄持ちをしていた. After I graduated I acted as an aide to my professor for a while.

かひ【歌碑】a monument inscribed with a (tanka) poem.

かびん【花瓶】a (flower) vase. ◐花瓶にさす put《a dahlia》in a vase.

かぶ【歌舞】singing and dancing; song and dance. ◐歌舞音曲 a performance of (Japanese) song and dance entertainment.

かぶき【歌舞伎】Kabuki; a traditional form of drama and music performed by a male cast;〔その公演〕a Kabuki performance. ■農村歌舞伎 rural Kabuki. 歌舞伎十八番 the eighteen best plays of the Ichikawa family of Kabuki actors; a repertoire comprising eighteen classical pieces. 歌舞伎者 a dandy; a peacock. 歌舞伎役者 a Kabuki actor.

かぶきもん【冠木門】a type of double-door gate, characteristic of traditional samurai houses, with a heavy extended crossbeam at the top.

かぶと【兜】a (warrior's) helmet; a (warrior's) protective headpiece.

かぶとに【兜煮】〔タイなどの頭を煮たもの〕the boiled head of《a sea bream》.

かぶとむし【兜虫】〔コガネムシ科の昆虫〕a Japanese rhinoceros beetle.

かぶとやき【兜焼き】〔タイなどの頭を焼いたもの〕the broiled head of 《a sea bream》.

かぶらや【鏑矢】an arrow with a device which whistles as the arrow flies.

かふんしょう【花粉症】hay fever; (a) pollen allergy;〚医〛pollinosis; pollenosis. ◐ 花粉症になる develop hay fever / 花粉症に苦しむ suffer from hay fever.　■ スギ花粉症 an allergy to cedar pollen.　花粉症患者 a hay fever sufferer.

かぼちゃ【南瓜】a pumpkin;〔ヒョウタン形の〕*a squash; ǁa vegetable marrow. ◐ カボチャの煮付け pumpkin boiled in seasoned liquid.

かまあげうどん【釜揚げうどん】straight-from-the-pot *udon*; a dish in which hot boiled *udon* is transferred right from the pot to a bowl containing broth, then dipped in sauce and eaten.

かまきり【蟷螂・鎌切】a (praying) mantis 《*pl.* ~es, mantes》; a (praying) mantid.

かまくら¹【鎌倉】鎌倉時代 the Kamakura period (1192–1333).　■ 鎌倉幕府 the Kamakura Shogunate; the Kamakura Bakufu.　鎌倉文化 Kamakura culture; the culture of the Kamakura period.　鎌倉彫り a wooden artifact carved in relief, with an undercoat of black lacquer and an overcoat of red lacquer.

かまくら²〔雪国の行事〕a festival observed in the middle of January in Akita Prefecture, featuring igloo-like snow shelters in which children play house;〔その雪の室(むろ)〕a shelter made of snow.

かます【梭魚・魳】〔ヤマトカマス〕a Japanese barracuda;〔アカカマス〕a brown barracuda;〔オニ[ドク]カマス〕a great barracuda.

かまど【竃】a kitchen stove; a cooking stove;〔所帯〕a household. ◐ 一つ竃の飯を食う eat from the same pot; live under the same roof.

かまとと a pretense of「innocence [ignorance];〔人〕a girl who pretends innocence.

がまのあぶら【蝦蟇の膏】〔むかし香具師(やし)が口上を述べて売った軟膏〕an ointment made from toad secretions mixed with pork grease; toad-oil ointment; "snake oil". ◐ ガマのあぶら売り a street vendor of toad-oil ointment (in premodern Japan).

かまぼこ【蒲鉾】white fish meat made into a seasoned paste, steamed, and typically formed into a semicylindrical shape over a stick;〔指輪〕a semicylindrical ring.　■板付きかまぼこ *kamaboko* molded onto a stick.　笹かまぼこ *kamaboko* shaped like a bamboo leaf.　かまぼこ形[型] a semicylindrical shape.　◐かまぼこ形の semicylindrical ／ かまぼこ型兵舎 a Nissen hut; *a Quonset hut.　かまぼこ天井[屋根] a「semicircular arching [barrel] vault [roof].

かまめし【釜飯】rice boiled with any of a variety of ingredients in a small pot.　■カニ釜飯 rice boiled with crab in a small pot.

かみおむつ【紙おむつ】a disposable *diaper [‖nappy].

かみがき【神垣】a fence around a Shinto shrine.

かみかぜ【神風】a「divine [providential] wind.　■神風タクシー a *kamikaze* [recklessly driven, wildly driven] taxi.

　神風特攻隊 a *kamikaze* corps; a suicide air corps.

かみがた【上方】Kyoto and (its)「neighborhood [vicinity]; the Kyoto-Osaka「area [district].　■上方歌舞伎〔江戸歌舞伎に対して〕Kabuki as performed in the Kyoto-Osaka region; Kamigata Kabuki.　上方芸能〔関西地方の芸能全般〕Kamigata [Kansai] performing arts.　上方言葉〔関西方言〕the Kansai dialect.　上方訛り a Kyoto accent.　上方文化 Kamigata [Kansai] culture.　上方文学〔元禄時代の〕Kamigata literature.　上方舞 a Kyoto dance.

かみきり【紙切り】1〔ナイフ〕a paper knife.　**2**〔寄席の芸〕silhouette cutting; papercutting.　■紙切りばさみ (a pair of) paper scissors.

かみこ【紙子】a (Japanese-)paper「robe [garment].

かみコップ【紙コップ】a paper cup.

かみしばい【紙芝居】〔興行〕storytelling with pictures;〔ひと組の〕a story told with the aid of a series of picture cards illustrating that story.　◐紙芝居のおじさん a picture-card storyteller ／ 紙芝居をする tell a story with picture cards.

かみしも【裃】a *kamishimo*; Edo-period formal dress of the warrior class.　◐今日の彼はまるで裃を着たようだった．He looked very formal today. ／ 今日は裃を脱いで無礼講といこう．Let's dispense with ceremony today.

かみずもう【紙相撲】a game in which two players lean paper cutouts of sumo wrestlers together on a table, which they pound until one paper wrestler falls.　◐紙相撲をする play「paper wrestling [*kamizumō*].

かみだな【神棚】a Shinto home「altar [shrine], usually set on a shelf over a lintel, to honor family guardian gods. ◐神棚に水をあげる[供える] place a glass of water on the *kamidana* as an offering / 神棚に手を合わせる pray in front of the *kamidana*.

かみなり【雷】〔光と音〕a thunderbolt;〔雷鳴〕thunder;〔電光〕lightning; a bolt of lightning;〔激しい叱責〕thundering 《at *somebody*》. ◐雷が鳴った. It thundered. | Thunder「rolled [rumbled, cracked]. ■雷親父 an irascible old man; a thunderer. 雷様〔雷神〕 the god of thunder; Zeus [Jupiter, Thor]. ◐雷様におへそを取られるよ. Cover up or the bogeyman will grab your bellybutton. カミナリ族 a「thunderous lightning [vrooming] motorcycle gang. 雷注意報 a thunderstorm advisory. 雷除け〔避雷針〕a lightning「rod [conductor]; (ラジオなどの) *a lightning arrester;〔護符〕a charm (to protect the wearer) against (being struck by) lightning.

かみのく【上の句】the first three lines of a「*waka* [tanka].

かみひとえ【紙一重】◐紙一重の差 a very slight difference 《between ...》;《by》a paper-[razor-]thin「difference [margin] / 紙一重の差が勝敗を分けた. A paper-[razor-]thin difference separated victory and defeat.

かみやしき【上屋敷】a city residence (of a daimyo).

かむりづけ【冠付け】a literary game of supplying the second and third verses to a given first verse of a haiku poem.

かめ【亀】a chelonian; a turtle;〔陸ガメ〕a tortoise;〔北米産の淡水ガメ〕a terrapin.

かめのこう【亀の甲】〔亀の甲ら〕(a)「tortoise's [turtle's] upper shell; a carapace;〔亀の甲らの模様〕a pattern of conjoined hexagons, as on the carapaces of many species of turtles. ◐亀の甲より年の功. Better than a tortoises shell is the wisdom of its age. | The wisdom that comes from experience is precious.

かめのこだわし【亀の子だわし】a tortoise-shaped scrubbing brush.

かめんうつびょう【仮面鬱病】〚医〛masked depression.

かめんしゅうしょく【仮面就職】taking a job in an easy-to-enter company, really intending to find a better job.

かめんふうふ【仮面夫婦】a couple who only go through the motions of being husband and wife.

かめんろうにん【仮面浪人】a college student who is trying to get into 「another [a better] college.

かも【鴨】 1 a wild duck; (雄) a drake; (雌) a hen; a duck. ◐鴨の群れ a flock of wild ducks. 2 〔だましやすい相手〕《口》a pigeon; a gull; a sitting duck; a fall guy; a pushover; an easy [a soft, a good] mark; a sucker; a patsy; 〘相場〙a lamb. ◐カモが葱(ネ)を背負って来る《a case of》a duck bringing along another ingredient for a hot pot; Everything is falling in place. 〔だまされやすい人が自分の方から近づいてくること〕《a case of》a sucker coming along just at the opportune time; 〔好都合の上にも好都合である〕《this's》doubly convenient; be in double luck / カモにする make a sucker out of *somebody* / カモにされる be taken in; be duped; 《口》be taken for a ride.

かもい【鴨居】 a slotted beam in a Japanese-style room into which the tops of sliding doors, shoji, and fusuma fit.

かもなべ【鴨鍋】 a hot pot with duck meat as one of the ingredients.

かもなんばん【鴨南蛮】 buckwheat vermicelli in soy soup with duck meat and onion added.

かもねぎ【鴨葱】 〘「鴨が葱を背負って来る」の略; ⇨ かも 2〙〔好都合の上にも好都合であること〕something so good one couldn't ask for anything better; a double stroke of good luck. ◐カモネギみたいなそんなうまい話があるものか. だまされるなよ It's too good to be true. Don't get taken in.

かもん【家紋】 the crest of a family; a family crest. ◐実家の家紋の付いた着物 a kimono bearing the crest of *one*'s parents' family / 家紋を入れる put a family crest [have a family crest put] onto 《a gravestone》.

かやく【加薬】 1 〔漢方で補助薬〕an adjuvant. 2 〔薬味〕⇨ やくみ. 3 〔五目飯などに入れる具〕ingredients of fish and vegetables (for mixing with rice to make *gomokumeshi*). ■加薬うどん[そば] an *udon* [a *soba*] dish to which a variety of ingredients are added. 加薬御飯 boiled rice with added ingredients.

かゆ【粥】 rice porridge; watery cooked rice; rice gruel. ◐オートミールのかゆ oatmeal porridge; *oatmeal / トウモロコシのかゆ *cornmeal mush; *mush / 薄いかゆ thin [watery] rice porridge / かゆをすする sip [slurp] rice porridge / かゆを煮る boil rice into porridge; make rice porridge.

からあげ【空揚げ・唐揚げ】 〔薄い衣で揚げること〕deep-frying 「fish

[pieces of chicken] without any coating [after lightly dredging with flour]; 〔その食品〕deep-fried 《flatfish》. ◐鶏のから揚げ deep-fried chicken.

からおり【唐織】〔中国・中国風の〕cloth of Chinese weave;〔絹織物の一種〕silk cloth with a bird-and-flower pattern;〔能の〕a rich brocade used for Noh costumes.

からかさ【唐傘】 a bamboo-and-paper [a waterproofed paper, an oiled paper] umbrella.

からかみ【唐紙】1〔紙〕thick paper, originally imported from China, that is patterned with ground oyster shell and mica powders and now used to cover sliding doors. **2**〔ふすま〕a paper-covered sliding door.

からくりどけい【からくり時計】 a (tower) clock with revolving puppets.

からくりにんぎょう【からくり人形】 a mechanical doll.

からし【芥子・辛子】 mustard.

からしめんたいこ【辛子明太子】 *karashi-mentaiko*; salted cod roe seasoned with salt and hot red pepper.

からすてんぐ【烏天狗】 a legendary ⌈*tengu* [sprite, goblin] with a crow's beak.

からつやき【唐津焼】 Karatsu ware

からて【空手】〔武道〕karate;〔一撃〕a karate ⌈blow [chop]. ◐空手でかわらを5枚割る break five roofing tiles with a single karate chop / 空手の型 the standard ⌈moves [forms] of karate / 空手の突き[蹴り, 打ち] a karate ⌈punch [kick, arm strike] / 私は空手5段です. I have [I am] (a) fifth *dan* at karate. ■**空手チョップ** a karate ⌈blow [chop]. ◐空手チョップを見舞う give *somebody* a karate chop. **空手道** the way of karate; karate.

からみもち【辛み餅】 rice cake served with grated daikon and soy sauce.

がり〔鮨に添える甘酢ショウガ〕slices of ginger pickled in sweetened vinegar.

カリスマせい【カリスマ性】 charisma. ◐現首相にはカリスマ性がある. The present prime minister has charisma. / カリスマ性の強い人 a person with strong charisma / カリスマ性を持つ指導者[政治家] a charismatic ⌈leader [politician].

かりばかま【狩袴】 a long pleated skirt once worn by men over their kimono when they went hunting.

かりんとう【花林糖】a small sugar-coated stick「cookie [biscuit] made from fried dough.

かるかん【軽羹】a steamed sweet bun made from grated yam and rice flour.

かるた〚＜Port. *carta*〛〔遊戯〕a game played with *karuta*;〔札〕*karuta*; any of several different possible sets of cards used in social or gambling games, with each set often composed of cards with texts to be read and corresponding picture cards. ◐かるたの絵札 a picture card in a *karuta* set / かるたの読み札 a text card in a *karuta* set / かるたを取る play *karuta*; have [play] a game of *karuta*. ■かるた遊び playing *karuta*; a game of *karuta*.　かるた会《give, hold》a *karuta* party;〔競技会〕a *karuta* tournament.　かるた取り *karuta* grabbing; a *karuta* grab.

カレー (a) curry. ■インドカレー Indian curry.　カツカレー curry with a (pork) cutlet.　激辛カレー an extremely hot curry.　ドライカレー curried pilaf.　ビーフ[野菜]カレー beef [vegetable] curry.　カレーうどん curry *udon*; *udon* with curry sauce.　カレーパン a curry「bun [doughnut].　カレーライス curry and rice; rice with curry sauce.

かれさんすい【枯山水】a hill-and-stream garden landscape without water; a dry (landscape) garden.

かろう【家老】a chief counselor《of a shogun》; a「principal [chief] retainer《of a feudal lord》.

かろうし【過労死】death from overwork.　～する die「from [of] overwork / 過労死するまで働く work *one*self to death.

かろん【歌論】a「treatise on [theory of] *waka* poetry.

かわうお【川魚】a「river [freshwater] fish. ■川魚料理 freshwater fish cuisine; a freshwater fish dish.

かわきもの【乾き物】dry snacks《such as peanuts and crackers》.

かわのじ【川の字】わが家では親子 3 人川の字になって寝ている．We sleep with our child between us.

かわゆか【川床】〔川面に突き出すように設けた納涼のための桟敷〕a platform built out over a river for enjoying the cool.

かわら【瓦】a tile. ◐瓦で屋根をふく lay tiles on a roof; roof《a house》with tiles; tile a roof.

かわらばん【瓦版】〔読み売り〕commercial newssheets of the Edo period.

かわりきょうげん【替わり狂言】 Kabuki plays that are different from the ones performed in the previous run.

かん【貫】〔尺貫法における重さの単位〕a *kan* 《*pl.* ~》(＝3.75 kg.).

かんおう【観桜】 cherry blossom viewing. ■ 観桜会 a cherry-blossom viewing party.

かんおけ【棺桶】 a coffin. ◐ 遺骸を棺桶に納める put [place] the「body [remains] in a coffin.

がんぎ【雁木】 1〔ギザギザの形のもの〕a zigzag (pattern [line]). ◐ 雁木形に in a zigzag「line [formation]; zigzag. **2**〔桟橋の段々〕the steps「of [down from] a pier. **3**〔防雪用のひさしの下の通路〕a way free of snow beneath the extended eaves on the street side of a row of shops and houses. ■ 雁木棚〔床脇や書院の棚の一種〕a set of three shelves, staggered from upper left to lower right, built into the wall beside a tokonoma alcove. 雁木鋸 a large-toothed saw. 雁木梯子 a wooden ladder, made from a single tree trunk, either by cutting steps in it or by attaching wooden steps.

がんぐろ【がん黒】 a cosmetic vogue for a deeply tanned face, white eyeliner, and false eyelashes. ◐ がん黒の女の子 a girl with blackface makeup made up to look black.

かんげいかい【歓迎会】 a welcome「meeting [party]; a「welcome [welcoming] reception; a reception (dinner). ◐ 歓迎会を開く give [hold] a「reception [dinner, party]「for [in honor of, to welcome]《the ambassador》.

かんけり【缶蹴り】 (the children's game of) kick-the-can. ◐ 缶蹴りの鬼になる be「it [the seeker] in kick-the-can / 缶蹴りをして遊ぶ play (at) kick-the-can.

かんさい【関西】〔地方〕(the) Kansai; the Kansai Region.

かんざけ【燗酒】 warmed [heated, mulled] sake.

かんざし【簪】《wear》an ornamental hairpin.

かんざまし【燗冷まし】 warmed sake that has cooled down.

かんざらし【寒晒し】 1〔寒気にさらすこと〕exposure 《of cloth, of grain》to cold weather. **2**〔白玉粉〕rice flour bleached through exposure to the air in midwinter.

かんじ【漢字】 (a) kanji 《*pl.* ~(s)》; a Chinese「character [ideograph]《used in Japanese writing》. ◐ 漢字で書く write in kanji / 漢字に直す

replace kana with kanji; substitute kanji for kana.

かんじき snowshoes.

がんじつ【元日】New Year's Day; the first day of the year. ◖元日を迎える welcome [greet, see in] the new year.

かんしつぞう【乾漆像】a dry-lacquered image 《of the Buddha》.

かんじん【勧進】**1**〘仏教〙〔仏教を広め人々を教化すること〕(Buddhist) missionary work and education. **2**〔寺社の建築・修理などのために寄付を集めること〕soliciting「contributions [subscriptions] for「pious [religious] purposes. **～する** solicit contributions for「pious [religious] purposes; solicit funds for a「temple [shrine]. ◖勧進して回る travel about 《the provinces》 soliciting contributions for「temple [shrine] improvements and repairs. ■勧進相撲 fund-raising sumo held in aid of a temple or a shrine. 勧進帳 a prospectus for funds solicited by a temple or shrine. 勧進元〔勧進相撲などの興行主〕the「organizer [promoter] of fund-raising held in aid of a temple or shrine;〔発起人・世話人〕a promoter; an organizer; a patron / 勧進元になる promote 《wrestling matches》; act as (a) promoter 《for...》.

かんす【鑵子】〔茶道〕a kettle; a teakettle.

かんぜおん(ぼさつ)【観世音(菩薩)】Kannon; the Bodhisattva of Compassion; the Buddhist deity of mercy. [=かんのん(ぼさつ)]

かんぜりゅう【観世流】the Kanze「school [style] of Noh. ◖観世流六代目家元 the sixth Head of the Kanze School of Noh.

かんチューハイ【缶チューハイ】(a) canned *shōchū* cocktail; a can of *shōchū* mixed with flavored soda water.

かんちゅうみまい【寒中見舞】a winter greeting card; an inquiry [a letter of inquiry] after *somebody*'s health in the cold season. ◖寒中見舞を出す send a winter greeting card (in place of a New Year's greeting card).

かんていりゅう【勘亭流】the Kantei style of calligraphy, characterized by bold, thick strokes and used typically in Kabuki posters and sumo announcements.

かんてん【寒天】**1**〔さむ空〕freezing [cold] weather; a「bleak [cold] wintry sky. **2**〔乾物の食品〕*kanten*; agar(-agar) (made from *tengusa* seaweed); Japanese [Chinese] isinglass [gelatin];〔蜜豆などの材料〕small cubes of cooked「*kanten* [agar]. ◖寒天質[状]の gelatinous; jellylike /

寒天であずきを固めて羊羹をつくる use「*kanten* [agar] to jelly sweetened adzuki-bean paste into *yōkan*.

かんでんち【乾電池】a (dry cell) battery.　■ アルカリ[マンガン]乾電池 an alkaline [a manganese] battery.　充電式乾電池 a rechargeable dry cell battery.　水銀乾電池 a mercury dry cell (battery).　単一[単二, 単三, 単四]乾電池 a size D [C, AA, AAA] battery.　◐ この携帯ラジオには単三乾電池2本が必要です. This pocket radio uses two size AA batteries.　ボタン型乾電池 a「button [disc] battery.

かんとう【関東】〔地方〕(the) Kantō; the Kantō Region.

がんどう【龕灯】〔仏壇の灯明〕a votive light; a light or candle on a Buddhist altar;〔龕灯提灯・強盗提灯〕a cylindrical lantern made of tin or copper with a reflector at one end behind a gyro-swivel candle-stand (enabling one to cast a beam of light).

かんとうだき【関東炊き】〔関西地方で東京風おでんの意〕Kantō-style *oden*.

かんとうに【関東煮】=かんとうだき.

かんどくり【燗徳利】a small「bottle [*tokkuri*] for warming sake.

かんなべ【燗鍋】a pan with a lid and spout for heating [warming] sake.

かんなめさい【神嘗祭】〔伊勢神宮の祭儀〕the offering of the new rice to the imperial ancestors each year in October at Ise Shrine by representatives of the Emperor.

カンニング cheating (in an examination); cribbing.　◐ カンニングをする cheat 《in an examination, on a test》; copy; 《口》crib.　■ カンニングペーパー a cheat sheet: a crib (sheet [note]); a pony.

かんぬし【神主】a Shinto priest.

かんのむし【かんの虫】夜中にかんの虫が起きた[鳴いた]. The baby woke up「with convulsions [crying] in the night. | The baby grew fretful in the middle of the night.

かんのん(ぼさつ)【観音(菩薩)】Kannon; the Bodhisattva of Compassion; the Buddhist deity of mercy.　■ 三十三観音 the thirty-three「manifestations [avatars] of the Kannon.　十一面[千手]観音 (a statue of) the「Eleven-faced [Thousand-armed] Kannon.　馬頭観音 ⇨ ばとうかんのん.　観音経 the Sutra of Avalokiteśvara; the Kannon sutra.　観音講〔法事〕the Kannon sutra-reading rite;〔信者の集団〕a group of Kannon devotees.　観音信仰 Kannon worship.　観音堂 a temple dedicated to Kannon.

かんのんびらき【観音開き】from the double doors of a Kannon altar cabinet. ◐ 観音開きの戸 (hinged) double doors / 観音開きのガラス扉 French「windows [*doors].

かんばい【観梅】*ume*-[apricot-, plum-] blossom viewing. ◐ 観梅に出かける go *plum*-blossom viewing; go to see the *ume* in flower.
■ 観梅列車 a special train for *ume*-blossom viewers.

かんぱい【乾杯】a toast. ◐ 〜する toast *somebody*; drink to *somebody*; drink [give, make] a toast 《to…》/ 人の成功を祈って乾杯する drink to *somebody*'s success; drink success to *somebody* / 新郎新婦に乾杯する toast「a [the] bride and bridegroom.

かんばんむすめ【看板娘】a pretty girl who「stands [sits] at the entrance to attract customers. ◐ 彼女はたばこ屋の看板娘だ. She attracts「custom [customers] at that tobacconist's. | People go to that tobacconist's just to be waited on by her.

かんぴょう【干瓢】dried strips of the flesh of a variety of gourd, used in Japanese cooking, especially sushi rolls. ◐ かんぴょう巻き〔寿司の〕*kanpyō maki*, a kind of rolled sushi that includes *kanpyō*; (a) pickled gourd roll; (a) cooked squash roll.

かんぽう【漢方】〔漢方医学〕traditional Chinese (herbal) medicine.
■ 漢方医 a「doctor [physician, practitioner] of「Chinese [Oriental] medicine. 漢方処方 a prescription for traditional Chinese (herbal) medicine. 漢方薬 a [an] herbal medicine.

かんまいり【寒参り】a midwinter visit to a「shrine [temple]; a midwinter pilgrimage 《to…》.

かんみどころ【甘味処】a sweet parlor.

かんむり【冠】〔漢字の部首〕a crown radical; the crown part of a Chinese character. ■ 雨冠 the rain radical. ウ冠 the kanji roof radical '宀'. ワ冠 the kanji roof radical '冖'.

かんむりたいかい【冠大会[イベント]】a sponsored event.

かんもち【寒餅】a rice cake [*mochi*] made in the middle of the winter; a rice cake preserved in water through the winter.

がんもどき deep-fried bean curd containing bits of various kinds of vegetables.

がんやく【丸薬】a (medicinal) pill; a globule;〔大きい〕a bolus;〔小さい〕

a pellet; a pil(l)ule. ◐ 丸薬入れ a pillbox.

かんれき【還暦】the sixtieth anniversary of *one*'s birth; *one*'s sixtieth birthday. ◐ 還暦の祝い celebration of 「*somebody*'s [*one*'s] sixtieth birthday / 還暦を祝う celebrate *somebody*'s 60th birthday.

かんろに【甘露煮】sweet stewed fish. ◐ ふなの甘露煮 *funa* [crucian carp] simmered slowly in soy sauce, *mirin*, and syrup / 栗の甘露煮 chestnuts 「boiled [stewed] in syrup.

き

きいっぽん【生一本】 1 〔酒などの〕灘の生一本 pure (undiluted) Nada sake; straight Nada sake. ◖生一本の pure; unadulterated; neat; straight; undiluted; sheer 《brandy》. **2** 〔性格の〕～な straightforward; honest.

ぎおんまつり【祇園祭】 the Gion Festival.

きかい【棋界】〔囲碁界〕go circles;〔将棋界〕*shōgi* circles.

きかく【棋客】 a (professional)「go [*shōgi*] player.

ぎがく【伎楽】 an ancient pantomime in which performers wear masks.

きき【記紀】 the *Kojiki* (712) and *Nihonshoki* (720); "Records of Ancient Matters" and "Chronicles of Japan".

ききざけ【利き酒】 sake [wine] tasting. ◖利き酒をする人 a sake taster / 利き酒をする test sake by tasting.

きく【菊】〔キク科の多年草；中国原産の園芸植物〕a chrysanthemum;《俗》a mum. ◖菊の紋 a chrysanthemum crest / 菊の御紋章 the imperial chrysanthemum crest (with sixteen open petals). ■菊人形 a chrysanthemum doll; a doll figure clothed in bunches of chrysanthemum flowers and leaves and representing a famous figure in history. ■菊の節句 the Chrysanthemum Festival. ■菊びより fine autumn weather. ■菊見 chrysanthemum-viewing.

きげんせつ【紀元節】 Empire Day; the Anniversary of the first Japanese emperor Jinmu's Accession (660 B.C.).

きご【季語】〔俳句の〕a season「word [phrase] (used in composing a haiku).

きこう【気功】〔中国に伝わる健康法〕qigong; chigong; the traditional Chinese breathing exercise. ■気功師[士] a qigong「therapist [practitioner, expert, master]. ■気功療法《医》system of deep breathing exercises.

きしめん【きし麺】 noodles made in flat strips.

きじゅ【喜寿】 *one*'s 77th birthday. ◐ 祖父の喜寿の祝いをする celebrate *one*'s grandfather's 77th birthday.

きしゅうけん【紀州犬】 a Kishu (dog).《犬》

きじょうゆ【生醬油】〔熱処理していない〕unboiled [non-heat-treated] soy sauce;〔混ぜ物をしていない〕unadulterated [pure, unmixed] soy sauce.

きしょうよほうし【気象予報士】 a certified「meteorologist [weather forecaster].

きす【鱚】〔シロギス〕a Japanese whiting.

きせい【帰省】 returning to *one*'s hometown (from a distant place of residence) 〜する go [come, return] home; visit [return to] *one*'s native place. ■帰省ラッシュ the homecoming rush 《during holiday seasons》. 帰省列車[バス] a train [bus] for homebound passengers 《during *Bon*》.

きぜわ【生世話】〔歌舞伎の〕a kind of *kyōgen* play depicting the raw realities of the lives of Edo-period characters.

きだい【季題】〔俳句の〕a seasonal topic (in haiku poetry).

きたきりすずめ【着た切り雀】 私は着た切りすずめだ. The only clothes I have to wear are the ones on my back. | I have nothing to wear except the clothes I now「have on [stand in].

きたくこんなんしゃ【帰宅困難者】〔地震による〕a person stranded 《due to failure of the transport system in an earthquake》.

きたまくら【北枕】〔頭を北に向けて寝ること〕北枕にする lie [sleep] with *one*'s head「northward [to the north];〔死者を〕place 《the corpse》 with the head northward.

ぎだゆう【義太夫】 *gidayū(-bushi)*; a style of reciting the dramatic narratives used in the puppet theater. ◐ 義太夫を語る recite [chant] *gidayū*. ■義太夫語り a *gidayū* reciter. ■義太夫本 a *gidayū* recitation text.

きちょう【几帳】 a (curtained) screen; a curtain.

きっか【菊花】 a chrysanthemum (flower). ◐ 菊花の御紋章 the Imperial Crest of the Chrysanthemum. ■菊花展 a chrysanthemum show.

ぎっくりごし【ぎっくり腰】 sharp [acute] lower-back pain; a strained

back;〔椎間板ヘルニア〕a slipped [herniated] disc. ◐ 重い箱を持ち上げようとしてぎっくり腰になった. I strained my back trying to lift a heavy box.

きっさてん【喫茶店】 a teahouse; a tearoom; a coffeehouse; a café; a coffee bar.

きつね【狐】 a fox;〔雌〕a vixen;〔擬人称〕Reynard. ◐ きつねに化かされる[つままれる] be bewitched by a fox / きつねにつかれる be possessed by a fox.

きつねいろ【狐色】 light brown; yellowish [golden] brown; tan; tawny. ◐ きつね色に焦げる be「roasted [cooked] (to a) golden brown / きつね色にこんがり焼く toast 《bread》(to a) golden brown.

きつねうどん【狐饂飩】 wheat noodles in soup, topped with deep-fried tofu.

きつねそば【狐蕎麦】 buckwheat noodles [*soba*] in soup, topped with deep-fried tofu.

きつねつき【狐つき】〔人〕a person possessed by a fox; a victim of fox possession;〔事〕fox possession.

きつねのよめいり【狐の嫁入り】 1〔狐火の行列〕a jack-o'-lantern parade. **2**〔日照り雨〕a light rain while the sun shines; a sun-shower.

きつねび【狐火】 a will-o'-the-wisp; a friar's lantern; a jack-o'-lantern;《L》*ignis fatuus*.

きなこ【黄粉】 (yellowish) soybean flour. ◐ もちにきなこをまぶす dust rice cake with soybean flour. ■黄粉もち rice cake powdered with sweetened soybean flour.

きぬごし【絹漉し】 絹ごしの strained through silk cloth. ◐ 絹漉し豆腐 silk-strained bean curd; fine-grained tofu.

きのこ【茸】 a mushroom;〔有毒な〕a toadstool;〔まだ開かない小さな〕a button; a fungus 《*pl*. -gi》. ◐ きのこが生えていた[出た]. Mushrooms「were growing [came up]. ■毒きのこ a poisonous mushroom; a toadstool. きのこ狩り mushroom picking. ◐ きのこ狩りに行く go mushroom「picking [gathering]; go (out) mushrooming.

きのめあえ【木の芽あえ】〔料理〕a dish dressed with miso and young pepper-tree leaves.

きのめでんがく【木の芽田楽】〔料理〕bean curd [tofu] baked and spread with miso and young pepper-tree leaves.

きふう【棋風】one's「way [style] of playing「go [*shōgi*].

きぶくれ【着膨れ】〔重ね着のために〕bulkiness because of thick (winter) clothing. ◐着ぶくれした bundled up 《people》; padded 《figure》.
　■着膨れラッシュ rush-hour congestion on public transport because people are bundled up in「thick [heavy] winter clothing.

ぎふぢょうちん【岐阜提灯】a Gifu lantern; an「oval [egg-shaped] paper lantern made in Gifu.

きぶつ【木仏】a wooden Buddhist image;〔木石漢〕a callous [an insensitive] person.

きまわし【着回し】the wearing of an item of clothing in many different combinations. ～する ＝きまわす．◐着回しがきく紺のスーツ a navy-blue suit that can be worn in many combinations.

きまわす【着回す】wear in many combinations. ◐インナーを変えたり，アクセサリーを工夫したりして着回す wear 《a suit》in many combinations by wearing different things under it and making clever use of accessories.

きみがよ【君が代】**1**〔天皇の治世〕the imperial reign. **2**〔日本の国歌〕the national anthem of Japan; *Kimigayo*. ◐君が代を歌う[奏する] sing [play] the national anthem of Japan.

きめ【木目・肌理】**1**【肌理】〔肌の〕grain; (skin) texture. ◐彼女の皮膚はきめがなめらかだ．Her skin is of a「velvety [smooth] texture. / きめの粗い coarse 《skin》 / きめの細かい of「fine [delicate] texture; fine in texture; fine 《skin》; smooth 《skin》 **2**【木目】〔木の〕grain; (直線) straight grain; (波状) wavy grain. ◐きめの粗い rough; coarse-[rough-]grained;《stone》of coarse grain; coarse / きめの細かい fine; fine-grained;《marble》of fine grain. **3**〔心くばり〕きめの細かい対策を取る adopt a meticulously thought-out measure.

きめこみにんぎょう【木目込み人形】a *kimekomi* doll; a wooden doll fitted with Japanese costumes made from cloth whose edges are tucked into grooves cut into the wood.

きもすい【肝吸い】〖料理〗clear soup [broth] with eel liver.

きもの【着物】**1**〔和服〕a kimono 《*pl*. ～(s)》; Japanese attire [outer clothing, apparel]. ◐夏の軽い着物 a light kimono for summer wear / 借りた着物 a rented kimono / 着物一重ね a single layer of kimono / 着物姿の少女 a girl in (a) kimono; a kimono-clad girl / 着物美人 a kimono beauty; a woman who looks beautiful in a kimono / 着物の着付けができる have the skill of dressing *somebody* in a kimono / 着物を着る put on a kimono / 着物を着ている wear a kimono; have a kimono on / 手を貸して着物を着せてやる help *somebody* into a kimono / 着物を脱ぐ take off *one*'s kimono / 着物を着た kimono-clad 《Japanese》; kimonoed 《lady》/ 着物を畳む fold (up) a kimono / あの着物を着ると彼女の姿が引き立つ. That kimono sets her (figure) off to advantage. **2** 〔衣服・衣類〕clothes; garments; 〈集合的〉clothing; dress; attire; (wearing) apparel. ◐着物のひだ a pleat [fold, crease] in a garment / 着物を着る dress *one*self / 急いで着物を着る jump into *one*'s clothes; dress in a hurry / 着物を引っかける throw [slip] *one*'s clothes on / 着物を着せる put clothes on *somebody*; clothe 《a child》; 〔手を貸して〕help *somebody* dress himself / 着物を着替える change *one*'s clothes / 着物を脱ぐ take off *one*'s clothes; undress (*one*self); disrobe.

きもん【鬼門】1 〔方角〕the "demon's gate"; the northeastern quarter; an unlucky [a tabooed] quarter. ◐鬼門よけのお札(ふだ) a charm to protect against misfortunes arising from (a house having)「an unlucky [a northeastern] exposure / 鬼門に当たる face northeast / 鬼門を避ける avoid [shun] an unlucky「direction [exposure] / 鬼門をよけて家を建てる build a house so as to avoid an unlucky exposure. **2** 〔苦手〕a weak point; a weakness; a jinx; a hoodoo. ◐数学は鬼門だ. Mathematics is a weak point of mine. ■**裏鬼門** the "back demon's gate"; the southwestern quarter.

ぎゃくぎれ【逆切れ】 a counterblast; a counteroffensive; (a) backlash. ～する snap back 《at *somebody*》. ◐メーカーに電話で苦情を言ったら逆切れした担当者に罵倒された. When I called the manufacturer to register a complaint, the person in charge turned the tables and bawled me out.

ぎゃくたまのこし【逆玉の輿】 marrying into wealth and (social) position. ◐彼は逆玉の輿を狙っている. He's「looking to marry into wealth (and position) [a fortune hunter].

ぎゃくみょう【逆名】生存中に逆名をつけておく assign *somebody* a posthumous Buddhist name while *somebody* is still alive.

キャッチホン 〔割り込み電話サービス〕《a telephone with》call waiting / キャッチホンが入って一時電話を切る temporarily disconnect [put *somebody* on temporary hold] because someone else is ringing / キャッチホンが入った. I've got another call coming in.

キャバクラ a cabaret club; a bar with female companions for male customers.

キャベツ〔アブラナ科の越年草；ヨーロッパ原産の野菜〕a cabbage. ◐ キャベツ1個 a head of cabbage / キャベツの葉 a cabbage leaf / キャベツの千切りをつけ合わせる garnish 《a dish》 with finely chopped cabbage / ロールキャベツ a (stuffed) cabbage roll.

きやり(おんど)【木遣り(音頭)】 a「log-carriers' [lumber-carriers']「chant [song]; a firemen's chant (in a procession).

きゅう【灸】 1〔やいと〕moxa cautery; moxibustion. ◐ 灸をすえる cauterize 《the skin》 with moxa; burn moxa 《on the skin》; give *somebody* moxa treatment / 灸をすえてもらう receive a moxa treatment. **2**〔罰〕chastisement. ◐ 灸をすえる punish [chastise] 《*somebody* for *something*》; scold 《*somebody* for [about] *something*》;《口》haul 《*somebody*》 over the coals.

きゅうこうれっしゃ【急行列車】 an express (train); a fast [rapid] train. ◐ 急行列車で by express (train). ■**特別急行列車**〔特急〕a special express (train); a limited express (train).

きゅうじょう【休場】 1〔劇場の〕closure 《of a theater》. ～する be closed [close down] 《for a month》. **2**〔役者の〕absence (from a performance); nonappearance. ～する do not appear (in a performance). **3**〔力士の〕absence (from a「bout [tournament]). ～する do not「appear [take part] in a「bout [tournament]; sit out a「bout [tournament].

きゅうしょく【給食】 provision of meals; lunch [meal] service; a (provided)「lunch [meal]. ■**学校給食** (provision of) school「lunches [meals]. **給食費** the「charge [cost] for (providing) meals.

きゅうす【急須】 a small teapot (for making green tea). ◐ 急須と湯飲みのセット a set (consisting) of a teapot and teacups / 急須の口 the spout of a teapot.

きゅうどう【弓道】 the Japanese art of archery.

ぎゅうどん【牛丼】 a bowl of steaming rice topped with thinly sliced stewed beef; a beef bowl.

ぎゅうなべ【牛鍋】〔すき焼〕a hot pot in which thin slices of beef are cooked 「*a la Japonaise* [in Japanese style]; 〔鍋〕a pan used for such a hot pot.

ぎゅうにく【牛肉】 beef. ◐ アメリカ[オーストラリア]産牛肉 beef produced in 「the United States [Australia]; American [Australian, Aussie] beef / 牛肉の(輸入)自由化 liberalization of beef (imports) / 牛肉の薄切り thinly sliced beef; thin slices of beef / 牛肉のかたまり a cut of beef. ■霜降り牛肉 (fat-)marbled beef. 輸入牛肉 imported beef. 牛肉屋 a dealer in beef;〔畜殺業を兼ねた〕a butcher who specializes in beef products;〔店〕a beef (butcher's) shop.

ぎゅうにゅう【牛乳】 milk; cow's milk. ◐ しぼりたての牛乳 freshly squeezed milk / 悪くなった牛乳 sour milk; milk that has 「gone off [curdled] / 牛乳をしぼる milk 《a cow》/ 牛乳を沸かす heat [boil] m / 均質[ホモ]牛乳 homogenized milk. ■成分無調整牛乳 nonhomogenized [unhomogenized] milk. 低脂肪牛乳 low-fat milk. 濃縮牛乳 concentrated milk;〔糖分無添加の〕evaporated milk;〔糖分添加の〕condensed milk. 牛乳アレルギー 《a child with》a milk 「allergy [sensitivity]. 牛乳製品 a milk product. 牛乳配達〔事〕milk delivery;〔人〕a milkman; a milk deliverer. 牛乳パック a milk carton. 牛乳瓶 a milk bottle. 牛乳屋〔販売者〕a milk dealer; (搾乳所の) a dairyman;〔配達人〕milkman; a milk deliverer;〔店〕a milk shop.

きゅうぼん【旧盆】 the 「Lantern [*Bon*] Festival according to the lunar calendar.

キューマーク【Qマーク】〔日本における繊維製品の品質保証マーク〕the Q-mark; the Quality mark.

きゅうり【胡瓜】〔ウリ科のつる性1年草; インド・ヒマラヤ原産の野菜〕a cucumber. ■きゅうりもみ sliced cucumbers kneaded with salt (and seasoned with vinegar).

キュレーター〔学芸員〕a curator.

きょうおんな【京女】 a Kyoto woman. ◐ 東男に京女. ⇨ あずまおとこ.

きょうか【狂歌】 a comic tanka; a satirical poem.

きょうく【狂句】 a comic haiku.

きょうげん【狂言】 1〔歌舞伎の芝居〕a Kabuki 「play [drama, performance, piece]. ◐ 今晩の狂言は何ですか. What play will be performed this evening? 2〔能狂言〕a Noh farce; a comic interlude (performed as supplementary entertainment during a Noh program). 3〔作りご

と〕a trick; a sham; a fake; a make-believe; a put-up job. **当たり狂言** a successful play; a hit. **替わり狂言** a 「substitute [replacement]」「play [piece]」. **切り狂言** a curtain closer; the 「final play [last piece]」in a Kabuki program. **前[幕開き]狂言** a curtain-raiser; the first play in a Kabuki program. **狂言強盗**〔行為〕a fake robbery;〔人〕a fake robber. **狂言作者** a Kabuki playwright; a Kabuki dramatist. **狂言師** a Noh comedian. **狂言自殺** a「mock [sham, fake, make-believe, 《口》phon(e)y] suicide. **狂言回し** a subsidiary character (in a Kabuki play) necessary for the development of the plot;〔脇役〕a second fiddle.

ぎょうざ【餃子】a Chinese-style dumpling usually stuffed with ground pork and vegetables and boiled or fried; a pot sticker; a *gyōza*. ■ **揚げ餃子** a deep-fried *gyōza*. **水餃子** a boiled *gyōza*; a *gyōza* served in broth. **蒸し餃子** a steamed *gyōza*. **焼き餃子** a pan-fried *gyōza*; a pot sticker.

ぎょうじ【行司】a sumo wrestling 「referee [umpire]; a *gyōji*. ▶ **行司をする** act as a 「sumo referee [sumo umpire, *gyōji*]; referee [umpire] a sumo bout. ■ **立て行司** the chief「referee [umpire] (at a sumo bout); a top *gyōji*.

きょうじや【経師屋】a person who「frames [mounts] paintings and calligraphic works and「restores [repairs] folding screens and fusuma.

きょうにんぎょう【京人形】a Kyoto doll (of a little child) (for dressing up in traditional clothes).

きょうま【京間】〔江戸間などに対して〕a Kyoto-length tatami (mat).

きょうまい【京舞】Kyoto dancing; a traditional Kyoto dance performed to the accompaniment of the samisen.

きょうやさい【京野菜】Kyoto vegetables; vegetables traditionally grown in and around Kyoto.

ぎょうれつ【行列】〔買い物や劇場の〕a line; "a queue;〔行進〕a procession; a parade; a file; a train; a retinue;〖数〗a matrix. ▶ **行列を作る** stand in [get into] line;〔買い物などの〕form a 「line ["queue]; line ["queue] up.

ぎょえい【御詠】an Imperial poem; a「tanka [short poem] composed by a member of the Imperial family (or any high-ranking person, temporal or spiritual).

ぎょくろ【玉露】refined [highest-quality, top-quality] green tea.

ぎょせい【御製】 an emperor's「poem [tanka]; a poem of imperial composition; a poem by His Majesty.

ぎょたく【魚拓】 《make, take》a fish「print [rubbing];《take》a fish impression.

ぎょでん【魚田】 grilled fish coated with bean paste.

ぎょふ【漁夫】 a fisherman; a fisher.
　漁夫の利 漁夫の利を占める fish in troubled waters; reap what others have sown / 鷸蚌(いつぼう)の争いは漁夫の利となる. A bird and a shellfish locked in a fight are easy game for a fisherman. | While two dogs fight over a bone, a third runs away with it.

きよみず【清水】 ◐清水の舞台から飛び下りる jump off the Kiyomizu Temple stage; take a very decisive step; cross the Rubicon; jump in at the deep end.

きよみずやき【清水焼】 Kiyomizu ware.

きよめ【清め】 purification; cleansing; purgation;〔はらい〕exorcism;〔体の〕ablution. ◐清めの水[塩] purification「water [salt] /〔葬式の〕(お)清めの席で at [in] the purification room. ■(お)清め会場 the purification room; a place [room] where, after a wake or a funeral service, mourners gather to partake of food and drink.

きよもと【清元】 a type of *jōruri* recitation in which voices are pitched higher than usual.

ぎょらん【魚籃】 ＝びく. ◐魚籃観音 a *Kannon* statue bearing a wicker「creel [fish basket].

きらず【雪花菜】 ＝おから.

きり【桐】〔ゴマノハグサ科の落葉高木; 中国原産〕a paulownia; an empress tree; a foxglove tree. ◐桐の下駄 paulownia-wood「geta [clogs]; geta [clogs] made of paulownia (wood) / 桐の花 a paulownia「flower [blossom] / 桐の紋 the imperial crest of the leaf and flower of *Paulownia imperialis*. ■桐材 paulownia wood. 桐たんす a chest of drawers made of paulownia wood; a paulownia chest of drawers. 桐箱 a box (made) of paulownia wood.
　桐一葉 a falling leaf from a paulownia;〔衰えの兆候〕an omen of「declining [waning] fortune; the beginning of the end.

ぎり【義理】〔道理〕justice;〔道義〕morality; moral obligation;〔礼儀〕courtesy; social obligation;〔義務(心)〕(a sense of)「duty [obligation]; a debt of gratitude

きりこ【切子】a facet. ■**切子ガラス** cut glass. **切子細工** cut glassware. **切子灯籠** a *Bon* lantern whose framework suggests a multifaceted object. **切子面**〔切子ガラスの〕a facet.

きりたんぽ〖料理〗mashed rice pressed on a cedar skewer and toasted.

ぎりチョコ【義理チョコ】social「courtesy [obligatory] Valentine chocolates; chocolates that *one* feels obliged to give;《口》just-to-be-nice chocolates.

きりど【切り戸】a narrow low door set within a wide swinging gate;〔能舞台の〕a side entrance.

きりふき【霧吹き】〔行為〕spraying;〔道具〕=霧吹き器. ▶障子を張り替えた後に霧吹きをする. After repapering a paper window, spray the paper (lightly) (with water). ■**霧吹き器** a spray; a sprayer; an atomizer; a vaporizer; a spray gun; a (spray) dampening machine.

きりぼし(だいこん)【切り干し(大根)】dried strips of「daikon [Chinese radish].

きりん【麒麟・騏驎】〖動〗a giraffe;〖画〗〔中国・日本の陶器に描かれた〕a kylin; a mythic Chinese or Japanese animal, painted on ceramic ware, with the body of a deer, the tail of a bull, the hooves of a horse, the brow of a wolf, and a single fleshy horn.

きれいどころ strikingly beautiful women;〔芸者〕geisha girls.

きれなが【切れ長】▶切れ長の目 eyes with extended slits at the corners; long-slitted eyes.

きんいっぷう【金一封】a gift of money in an envelope. ▶金一封を与える grant [give] *somebody* money《in appreciation of his services》; make *somebody* a gift of money.

きんがしんねん【謹賀新年】Best Wishes for a Happy New Year.

きんかん【金柑】〔ミカン科キンカン属植物の総称〕a kumquat.

きんぎょ【金魚】a goldfish ▶金魚のふん goldfish droppings;〔付き従う者〕a「close [slavish] follower. ■**金魚掬(すく)い** a summer entertainment entailing the scooping of goldfish with a fragile wafer-thin dipper. **金魚鉢** a goldfish basin;〔ガラスの〕a goldfish bowl. **金魚藻**〖植物〗hornwort. **金魚屋** a goldfish「seller [vendor].

きんきょく【琴曲】《a piece of》koto music.

きんこんしき【金婚式】〔結婚50周年記念の〕a golden wedding (anniversary). ◯金婚式を祝う celebrate *one*'s golden wedding (anniversary).

ぎんこんしき【銀婚式】〔結婚25周年記念の〕a silver wedding (anniversary). ◯銀婚式を祝う celebrate *one*'s silver wedding (anniversary).

ぎんざ【銀座】〔江戸時代の〕a silver mint of the Tokugawa shogunate;〔繁華街〕the Ginza (district) 《in Tokyo》; a busy shopping street [area].

きんし【近視】〔近眼〕nearsightedness; shortsightedness;〚医〛myopia. ◯強度[軽度]の近視 extreme [mild] nearsightedness; high-[low-]level myopia; high-[mild-]degree myopia ／ 近視の nearsighted; shortsighted; myopic ／ 近視の人 a nearsighted [shortsighted] person; a myope. ■仮性[偽]近視 pseudo(-)myopia; false myopia; myopia spuria. 学校近視 school myopia.

ぎんじょう(しゅ)【吟醸(酒)】〔精米歩合60％以下のもの〕*ginjō* (sake); high-quality sake brewed at low temperatures from rice grains milled to 60 percent of weight or less.

きんたろう【金太郎】*Kintarō*, a baby warrior; a legendary plump, ruddy-faced boy often depicted astride a bear. ■金太郎飴 *Kintarō* candy; a candy bar made so that *Kintarō*'s face appears wherever the bar is cut.

きんつば【金鍔】〔和菓子〕a confection of sweetened beans wrapped in a wheat-flour skin and shaped like the guard on a sword.

きんときまめ【金時豆】red kidney beans.

きんとん a sweetened mixture of boiled and「strained [mashed] chestnuts [beans]. ■栗きんとん ⇨ くりきんとん. 豆きんとん boiled beans mashed and sweetened.

きんなしじ【金梨地】lacquerware with a gold-flecked effect; gold aventurine lacquer.

ぎんなしじ【銀梨地】lacquerware with a silver-flecked effect; silver aventurine lacquer.

ぎんなん【銀杏】〔いちょうの実〕a ginkgo nut;〔いちょうの木〕⇨いちょう.

きんのこと【琴の琴】a seven-stringed koto.

きんのたまご【金の卵】a hard-to-come-by talented young person who shows great promise; a wunderkind; a golden boy; a「product [program] that shows great promise of profitability for an enterprise.

きんばん【勤番】〔交代勤務〕taking turns on duty;〔江戸時代の〕being on

duty in Edo.　◐勤番の藩士 a daimyo's retainer on duty in Edo.

きんびょうぶ【金屏風】a folding screen covered with gold leaf; a 「gold-leaf-covered [gilt] folding screen.

きんぴらごぼう【金平午蒡】chopped burdock root cooked in soy sauce and sugar (sometimes with chopped carrot).

きんぷくりん【金覆輪】gold(en) trimmings.

ぎんぷくりん【銀覆輪】silver trimmings.

ぎんぶら【銀ぶら】a stroll 「on [down, along] the Ginza.　◐銀ぶらをする[に行く] have [go for] a stroll 「on [down, along] the Ginza / 銀ぶらをする人 a stroller 「on [along] the Ginza.

ぎんぷら【銀麩羅】〔衣に卵白を加えた〕tempura that is encased in a batter made from wheat flour and egg white.

きんみずひき【金水引き】〔金色の水引き〕golden paper 「cords [strings] (for decorative tying of a gift package).

きんらん【金襴】gold brocade; brocade with patterns in gold thread.　◐金襴の袈裟(けさ) a surplice of gold brocade.　■**金襴緞子**(どんす) gold-brocade satin damask.

きんらんで【金襴手】*kinrande* porcelain; porcelain with overglaze gold; porcelain with gilt [gold] design(s); "gold brocade" style.

きんろうかんしゃのひ【勤労感謝の日】〔11月23日〕Labor Thanksgiving Day.

く

- **く【句】** 1 〔語句〕a phrase;〔文句〕an expression;〔成句・熟語〕a (set) phrase; a fixed expression. 2 〔詩歌の〕(1 行) a line; (1 節) a verse; (1 連) a stanza;(詩) a poem. ◐〔和歌の〕上[下]の句 the ｢first [last, latter] half of a tanka. 3 〔俳句〕a haiku; a *hokku*. ◐句を作る[詠む] compose [write] a haiku.
- **くいだおれ【食い倒れ】** ruining *one*self by eating extravagantly; wasting *one*'s money on excessive consumption; eating *one*self out of house and home. ◐京の着倒れ, 大阪の食い倒れ. In Kyoto, they spend all their money on clothes, in Osaka on food.
- **ぐいのみ【ぐい飲み】**〔大きく深い杯〕a large sake cup.
- **ぐうじ【宮司】** a chief priest of a Shinto shrine.
- **くかい【句会】** a haiku ｢gathering [meeting].
- **くく【九九】** a multiplication table; the [*one*'s] tables. ◐九九の表〔一般〕a multiplication table;〔9 の欄〕the nine times table / 九九を暗記する learn [memorize, remember] *one*'s tables.
- **くげしょはっと【公家諸法度】** the laws for the Court in the Edo period.
- **くさ【草】**〔芝生や野原の〕grass;〔ハーブ〕a (wild) herb;〔雑草〕a weed; a wild plant;〈集合的に〉(wild) plants; herbage; vegetation. ◐1 本の草 a blade of grass / 背の高い草 high [tall] grass / 一面草だらけである, 草ぼうぼうである be ｢overrun [overgrown, rank] with ｢grass [weeds].
- **くさいち【草市】** a market fair for plants and flowers (as offerings at the *Bon* Festival).
- **くさきぞめ【草木染め】** dyeing with natural dyes of vegetable origin. ◐草木染めの敷物 a vegetable-dyed rug.
- **くさく【句作】** composition of (a) haiku. 〜する compose [write] (a) haiku.
- **くさずもう【草相撲】** an amateur [a local] sumo tournament;〔人〕an

amateur [a local] sumo wrestler.

くさぞうし【草双紙】 an illustrated storybook (in the Edo period); a picture book.

くさだんご【草団子】 a rice-flour dumpling mixed with mugwort (leaves).

くさばのかげ【草葉の蔭】 ◐ 草葉の蔭で under the sod; in the grave / そんなことをするとお父さんが草葉の蔭で泣きますよ. That would be enough to make your father turn (over) in his grave.

くさもち【草餅】 a mugwort rice cake; a (sticky) rice-flour dumpling mixed and flavored with mugwort.

くさや "stinking fish"; a salted, sundried flying fish (that emits a strong smell when cooked whole over an open flame).

くさやきゅう【草野球】 sandlot baseball. ■ 草野球チーム a sandlot team.

くしカツ【串カツ】 deep-fried small pieces of pork (and onion, and leek) on a skewer; fried skewered cutlets; 〔くし揚げ〕a deep-fried kebab.

くしだんご【串団子】 sweet rice「balls [dumplings] on a skewer.

くじゃく【孔雀】 〔雄〕a peacock; 〔雌〕a peahen; 〔雌雄とも〕a peafowl. ◐ 尾を広げたクジャク a peacock in his pride; a peacock with his tail「spread out [displayed].

くしゃみ【嚔】 sneezing; a sneeze; 《医》sternutation; ptarmus. ◐ 昨日 (君のうわさをしていたのだが)くしゃみが出なかったか. Were your ears burning yesterday? / くしゃみをする, くしゃみが出る sneeze; 〔続けざまに〕have a fit of sneezing.

くじら【鯨】 a whale. ◐ 鯨が潮を吹く. A whale blows. | A whale spouts (water). / 鯨が水面におどり出た. A whale「breached [surfaced]. / 鯨の子 a whale calf / 鯨の群れ a「gam [herd, pod, school] of whales / 鯨の肉 whale meat / 鯨の油 whale oil.

くず【葛】〔マメ科のつる性多年草〕a kudzu vine. ■ 葛粉 kudzu starch. 葛湯 kudzu starch gruel.

くずきり【葛切り】 short noodles of kudzu starch, eaten with syrup.

くずざくら【葛桜】 a cherry-leaf-covered kudzu bun filled with bean jam.

くずねり【葛練り】 a sweetened paste of kudzu starch.

くずもち【葛餅】 a confection of steamed「arrowroot [kudzu] flour dipped in molasses and dusted with soybean flour.

くすり【薬】1 〔薬剤〕(a) medicine; a drug; 〔粉薬〕powdered medicine; 〔丸薬〕a pill; 〔水薬〕a liquid medicine; 〔飲み薬〕an ⌈internal [oral] medicine; 〔塗り薬〕an ointment; an unguent; 〔せんじ薬〕a decoction; an infusion; 〔強壮剤〕a restorative; a tonic; 〔薬物〕a medicinal substance; a pharmaceutical; a medicament; medication; 〔化学薬品〕a chemical. ◐ 薬の medicinal / 薬の効能 the ⌈effect [efficacy] of a medicine [drug] / 薬の服用 the taking of a medicine / 薬の副作用 a ⌈secondary [side] effect of a medicine / 薬の乱用 misuse [overuse] of a medicine / 薬を処方する prescribe (a) medicine 《for a patient》/ 薬を調合する compound [prepare] a medicine / 薬を投与する administer a medicine; give 《a patient》medication / 薬をつける[塗る] apply ⌈an ointment [a salve] / 薬を飲む take (a liquid) medicine; take ⌈(powdered) medicine [a pill] with water; take medication; take *one*'s medicine.

ぐそくに【具足煮】 a dish of ⌈crabs [lobster] boiled with their ⌈"armor," or shells, on.

くたにやき【九谷焼】 Kutani ⌈pottery [porcelain, ware].

くちぐるま【口車】 cajolery [wheedling, coaxing]; honeyed words [sweet talk, sweet words, slick talk]; flattery. ◐ 口車に乗る be cajoled; be wheedled; be taken in by *somebody*'s ⌈sweet talk [honeyed words, slick talk]; fall for *somebody*'s ⌈honeyed words [sweet talk, etc.]

くちぶえ【口笛】 a whistle. ◐ …を口笛で呼ぶ whistle for 《a taxi, *one*'s dog》/ 口笛を吹く whistle; give a whistle; 〔指を入れて〕use *one*'s fingers to whistle / 口笛を吹いて合図する signal by whistling.

くちべに【口紅】 〔棒状の〕(a) lipstick; 〔口につける紅〕lip rouge. ◐ 口紅をつける paint *one*'s lips; put 《some》lipstick on *one*'s lips; put on [wear] lipstick / 口紅を直す fix [touch up] *one*'s lipstick.

くちよごし【口汚し】 a 《mere》morsel (of food); 《only》a bite to eat. ◐ これはほんのお口汚しですが. I can only offer you this ⌈morsel [small bite] of food. | I'm sorry I don't have something better to give you.

くどき【口説き】 〔謡曲また浄瑠璃で〕a spoken (rather than sung) portion of a ⌈song [chant]; the words thus spoken; an oral recitation passage.

くないしょう【宮内省】 〔宮内庁の前身〕the Department of the Imperial Household.

くないちょう【宮内庁】 the Imperial Household Agency. ■ **宮内庁御**

用達 a purveyor to the Imperial Household Agency.　宮内庁長官 the Grand Steward of the Imperial Household Agency.

くのえこう【薫衣香】〔練り香〕a potpourri of nine herbs used to scent clothing.

くひ【句碑】a stone「tablet [slab] with a haiku inscribed on it.

くまで【熊手】〔農具〕a rake; a pitchfork;〔竹製の〕a bamboo rake;〔縁起物の〕a charm for raking in good fortune (sold at shrine festivals in November).

くまどり【隈取り】**1**〔色の濃淡をつけること〕shading; gradation.　**2**〔顔の〕*kumadori*; a style of Kabuki makeup used by players of violent roles; bands of red, black, and blue pigment that emphasize passionate feeling.　◐ くま取りした歌舞伎役者 a Kabuki actor wearing *kumadori* makeup.

くも¹【雲】〔空の〕a cloud.　◐ ふわりと浮かんだ雲 a light, fleecy cloud / 軽く刷毛ではいたような雲 a wisp of cloud; a cloud like a thin stroke of whitewash [a thin wash of distemper] / うろこのような雲 a speckling of clouds; mackerel clouds; clouds like fish scales.

くも²【蜘蛛】〘動〙a spider.　◐ クモの糸 a spider's thread;〔空中に漂う〕gossamer / クモの子を散らすように逃げる flee [disperse] in all directions.

くもすけ【雲助】a thuggish「palanquin [sedan-chair] bearer.　■雲助運転手 a「piratical [thievish, dishonest] (cab) driver.　雲助根性 a「predatory [rapacious, thuggish] nature [disposition].

くら【倉・蔵】a warehouse; a storehouse; a godown;〔宝庫〕a treasury;〔情報・資源などの〕a repository;〔穀庫〕a granary; a garner.　◐ 蔵から出す deliver 《goods》 from a warehouse; take 《goods》 out of a godown / あの調子では今に蔵が立つ. At that rate, he'll soon be a millionaire. / 蔵に入れる put 《*one*'s belongings》 in storage; store; warehouse.
■醤油[味噌]蔵〔貯蔵所〕a「soy sauce [miso] warehouse;〔醸造所〕a「soy sauce [miso] brewery.　蔵主 the proprietor of a warehouse.

くらげ【水母】a jellyfish; a sea jelly; a medusa 《*pl.* -sae, ~s》; a medusan.

くりいろ【栗色】a「chestnut [nut-brown] color; chestnut; maroon.　~の chestnut(-colored); maroon; nut-brown; reddish brown.

くりきんとん【栗きんとん】〔クリの実をつぶしてつくったきんとん〕a

sweetened mixture of boiled and mashed chestnuts. [⇨ きんとん]

くりひろい【栗拾い】《go》chestnutting [gathering chestnuts].

くりまんじゅう【栗饅頭】a *manjū* with a bean-and-chestnut paste inside and the top surface toasted a chestnut-brown color.

くりめし【栗飯】rice boiled with chestnuts.

くりようかん【栗羊羹】bean jelly with chestnuts mixed in.

くるまいす【車椅子】a wheelchair. ◐ 車椅子用のスロープ《build, install》a wheelchair ramp / 車椅子バスケットボール[ラグビー] wheelchair「basketball [rugby] / 車椅子マラソン a wheelchair marathon / 車椅子で入れる wheelchair-accessible《bathroom》. ■ 電動車いす《ride in》an electric wheelchair. 車いす利用者 a wheelchair user.

くるまえび【車海老】a prawn.

くるみ【胡桃】〔クルミ科クルミ属 (Juglans) のうち,食用になるものの総称〕a walnut (tree); 〔その実〕a walnut. ◐ クルミの殻 a walnut shell / クルミを割る crack a walnut / クルミを拾いに行く go gathering walnuts / クルミ割り《a pair of》nutcrackers.

くるわ【廓】 1 〔一区域〕a quarter; a district. 2 〔城の〕an area enclosed by earthwork; an enclosure. 3 〔遊廓〕the former licensed quarters; a red-light district. ■ 廓通い ◐ 廓通いをする frequent the「licensed quarters [red-light district]. 廓詞(ことば)・郭言葉 the language peculiar to women of the gay quarters in the Edo period.

くろあえ【黒和え】a dish《of vegetables》in which ground black sesame seeds are used for the dressing.

くろうと【玄人】 1 〔熟練者〕an expert《on [in]…》; a「master [proficient] hand; 〔専門家〕a professional; a specialist《in…》. ◐ くろうと気質(かたぎ) professionalism. 2 〔商売女〕a woman of the demimonde; a demimondaine.

くろうとはだし【玄人跣】surpassing even「an expert [a professional, a master, a specialist]; putting even「an expert [a professional, a master, a specialist] to shame. ◐ くろうとはだしの芸 a performance that would put a professional to shame.

くろおび【黒帯】〔和服の〕a black obi; 〔柔道着などの〕a black belt; 〔柔道・空手の有段者〕a person who is ranked as an expert.

くろこ,くろご【黒子】〖歌舞伎〗a stage assistant dressed in black who assists Kabuki actors during a performance; a *kuroko*.

くろざとう【黒砂糖】muscovado; brown [unrefined] sugar.

くろじゅす【黒繻子】black satin. ◐黒繻子の足袋 black-satin *tabi*.

くろづくり【黒作り】〔イカの塩辛〕the flesh and intestines of a cuttlefish blackened with its ink, salted, and fermented.

くろぶさ【黒房】〖相撲〗the black tassel hanging from the northwest corner of the roof over a sumo ring.

くろまく【黒幕】**1**〔黒い幕〕a black curtain. **2**〔背後で糸を引く人〕a backstage manipulator; an éminence grise; a gray eminence; a kingmaker; *a power broker; a backroom fixer; a string(-)puller; a mastermind; *a wirepuller. ◐あの人が政界の黒幕だ. He's the 「backroom manipulator [gray eminence] who controls the balance of political power (in the Diet).

くろまめ【黒豆】a black soybean.

くろみずひき【黒水引き】black and white strings《on condolence offerings》. ◐黒水引きをかける wrap《a condolence offering》with black and white string.

クロワッサン〔三日月形のパン〕a croissant; a crescent roll.

くわいれしき【鍬入れ式】くわ入れ式を行う hold a groundbreaking ceremony; break the ground《for...》.

くわがた【鍬形】〔かぶとの前立て〕a hoe-shaped helmet crest.

ぐんかんまき【軍艦巻き】"gunboat" wrap; fish roe sushi.

ぐんじょういろ【群青色】ultramarine; azure.

くんせい【薫製】smoking. ◐ニシンの薫製 smoked [kippered] herring;〔丸干し〕a bloater / サケの薫製 smoked salmon / 薫製にする smoke; bloater; kipper; cure with smoke / 薫製の smoked; smoke-dried; bloated. ■薫製肉 smoked meat; smoke-dried[-cured] meat.

ぐんせん【軍扇】a military commander's fan used as a kind of baton.

ぐんばい【軍配】〔武将の〕=ぐんばいうちわ,〔相撲の〕an umpire's fan (in sumo wrestling).

ぐんばいうちわ【軍配団扇】a military leader's fan.

け

けいこ【稽古】〔練習〕practice; training;《口》a practice [training] session;（演技の）a rehearsal;〔学習〕study; learning;〔指導〕a lesson; a class. ～する〔練習する〕practice; train; rehearse;〔指導を受ける〕study; learn; take lessons 《in...》/ お花[お茶]のお稽古 practice in ⌈flower arrangement [the tea ceremony]; a ⌈flower arrangement [tea ceremony] lesson [class] / 琴[三味線, 長唄]の稽古 a koto [samisen, nagauta] lesson / 稽古の虫 a ⌈practice [training] fanatic. ■ぶつかり稽古〔相撲の〕battering practice. 猛稽古 strenuous training. 稽古着 a ⌈practice [training] outfit [suit]; practice [training] wear [‖gear]. 稽古好き[嫌い] a person who ⌈likes [hates] to *practice [‖practise]. 稽古総見〔相撲協会の〕attendance at a final sumo training session, before a tournament, by all Sumo Association directors. 稽古場 a drill hall; a practice area; a training place;〔演技の〕a rehearsal room. 稽古始め the first ⌈lesson [practice (session), training (session)] of a new year.

けいこうとう【蛍光灯】a fluorescent ⌈light [lamp]. ▷蛍光灯がチカチカしている[音をたてている]. The fluorescent light is ⌈blinking [making a noise] / 蛍光灯を取りつける install a fluorescent light / 蛍光灯をつける turn on a fluorescent light.

けいじばん【掲示板】a ⌈notice [bulletin] board;〖電算〗〔ネットワーク上の電子掲示板〕a(n electronic) bulletin board. ▷お知らせを掲示板に張り出す put up [post, tack up] a notice onto a bulletin board /（ネットワーク上の）掲示板にメッセージを書き込む post a message on a bulletin board.

げいしゃ【芸者】a geisha; a woman who can provide professional dance and music entertainment at banquets held in tatami rooms.

けいたいあんていシャツ【形態安定シャツ】a ⌈no-iron [non-iron, crease-resistant, crease-free, wrinkle-free] shirt.

けいたいでんわ【携帯電話】 a cellular phone; a cellphone; a 「mobile [portable, pocket] phone; "a mobile. ▶デジタル方式の携帯電話 a digital cellular phone / ハンドフリーの携帯電話 a hands-free cellular phone / プリペイド方式の携帯電話 a prepaid cellular phone / 携帯電話にかける call *somebody* on his cellular phone / 携帯電話にメッセージを入れておく leave a message on *somebody*'s cellular phone / 携帯電話の着信音 the (call) sound of a cellular phone / 携帯電話の電源を切る turn off *one*'s cellular phone /〔電車内のアナウンスで〕車内での携帯電話のご使用は，他のお客さまの迷惑になりますのでおやめください．To avoid annoying the other passengers, please do not use your cellular phone. | For the comfort and convenience of others, passengers are requested not to use cellular phones in this car. / 携帯電話をマナーモードにする put *one*'s cellular phone on vibration mode. ■**カメラ付き携帯電話** a camera (cellular [mobile]) phone; a (cell) phone cam. **携帯電話会社** a 「mobile [*cellular] phone operator. **携帯電話中毒** phonaholism; (cell) phone addiction;〔人〕a phonaholic; a (cell)phone addict.

けいちつ【啓蟄】〔二十四節気の一〕the day when insects emerge from hibernation underground; around March 6 in the solar calendar.

けいろうのひ【敬老の日】〔9月の第3月曜日(もと9月15日)〕Respect for the Aged Day.

けが【怪我】〔負傷〕an injury; a wound;〔失策〕a mistake. **〜する** injure; hurt / 足[頭, 手]をけがする injure *one*'s leg [head, arm] / けがしなかったかい？ You all right? / ちょっとしたけが a slight 「injury [wound] / 大けが a serious 「injury [wound].

げきから【激辛】 ▶激辛の fiery hot [super-spicy, extra-spicy] 《curry》. ■**激辛食品** super-spicy food. **激辛ブーム** a 「boom [fad] for super-spicy food.

げくう, げぐう【外宮】〔伊勢神宮の〕the Outer Shrine of Ise.

げこ【下戸】 a nondrinker; a person who is allergic to alcohol. ▶下戸のほうだ be not much of a drinking man.

けさ【袈裟】 a *kesa*; a patchwork surplice worn over the robe of a Buddhist priest.

けし【芥子・罌粟】〔ケシ科の越年草；ヨーロッパ東部原産の薬草〕an opium poppy. ▶芥子の実〔食材〕a poppy seed.

げし【夏至】〔二十四節気の一にも数えられる〕the summer solstice; the

solstitial point; the day marking midsummer.

けしゴム【消しゴム】 an eraser; an「India [india] rubber; a rubber. ◐ プラスチックの消しゴム a plastic eraser / 消しゴムで消す erase; rub out 《a pencil mark》with india rubber / 消しゴムのかす eraser leavings.

けしょうひん【化粧品】 cosmetics; makeup; a toilet article; a beauty product. ■ カウンセリング化粧品〔販売員が店頭で相談に応じながら販売する化粧品〕cosmetics for whose use guidance at the time of purchase is mandatory. 男性用化粧品 men's toiletries. 化粧品売り場 a cosmetics「counter [department]; a「beauty [makeup] counter《in a department store》. 化粧品会社[メーカー] a cosmetics「company [maker].

けしょうまわし【化粧回し】〔相撲〕a sumo-wrestler's ceremonial apron.

けずりぶし【削り節】 dried bonito「shavings [flakes].

げた【下駄】〔履物〕a geta 《pl. ~(s)》; a Japanese wooden「clog [sandal].

げたばこ【下駄箱】 a shoe cupboard; a cabinet for outdoor shoes.

けつあつ【血圧】 blood pressure. ◐ 高[低]血圧 high [low] blood pressure / 正常血圧 normal blood pressure; normotension / 血圧を計る take [measure] *somebody*'s blood pressure / 血圧を計ってもらう have [get] *one*'s blood pressure「taken [measured] / 血圧を下げる reduce [control] *one*'s [*somebody*'s] blood pressure / 血圧を高くする[上げる] raise [increase, heighten] *somebody*'s blood pressure. ■ 血圧計 a sphygmomanometer; a blood pressure gauge / (腕に巻く)血圧計のバンド a blood-pressure「cuff [band]. 血圧測定 blood-pressure measurement; sphygmomanometry; a blood-pressure check.

けつえきがた【血液型】 a type of blood; a blood type;〔全体〕a blood group. ◐ 血液型による性格判断 telling *somebody*'s character by their blood group / 血液型の分類(法) blood「typing [grouping] / 血液型の鑑定 a blood group (identification) test / 血液型の確認 blood-type confirmation / 血液型を調べる find out [determine] *somebody*'s blood type.

げっけいかん【月桂冠】 a laurel「crown [chaplet]; a crown of「laurel [honors]; laurels. ◐ 月桂冠を得る〔有名になる〕win [gain, reap, acquire, earn] laurels / 勝利の月桂冠を戴(いただ)く be crowned with the laurels of victory / 月桂冠を戴いた勝者 a laurel-crowned victor.

けっこんきねんび【結婚記念日】 a wedding anniversary. ◐ 25回めの結婚記念日 the 25th wedding anniversary;〔銀婚式〕a silver wedding (anniversary) / 両親の結婚記念日に旅行をプレゼントする give *one*'s parents a trip as a wedding anniversary gift 10回目の結婚記念日を迎える[祝う] reach [celebrate] *one*'s tenth wedding anniversary / 今日は私たちの3回目の結婚記念日だ. Today is our third wedding anniversary.

けっこんさぎ【結婚詐欺】a fraudulent [fake, false] marriage; a matrimonial swindle; a marriage fraud [《口》scam]. ◐結婚詐欺にあう be taken in by a「marriage fraud [matrimonial swindle] / 結婚詐欺に引っかかった人 a person who has been swindled 《out of money》in a marriage fraud [《口》scam]. ■結婚詐欺師 a matrimonial swindler.

けっとうち【血糖値】*one*'s blood sugar level; blood sugar. ◐血糖値が上がる[下がる] the blood sugar level「goes up [goes down, falls].

げっぺい【月餅】a disc-shaped confection of bean paste baked in a skin of wheat-flour dough.

けつろ【結露】dew [water]「condensation; the formation of「condensation [dew]. ～する condense; form dew. ◐壁面の内側が結露する water condenses on the inside of a wall / 結露を防ぐ prevent water condensation.

げばひょう【下馬評】idle rumor [gossipy talk] (by those not in the know). ◐…との下馬評が高い. It is strongly rumored that… / 下馬評では according to the man in the street; according to rumor; rumor [the rumor mill] has it that… / 下馬評では都市部の選挙はかなり野党がリードしそうだ. The rumor mill has it that the party in opposition has a strong lead in elections in urban areas. / 下馬評に上がる[上(のぼ)る] become the subject of a rumor.

けまり【蹴鞠】〔遊戯〕*kemari*; a game played by aristocrats in the Heian period in which several people in a circle try to kick a leather "ball" back and forth among themselves as long as possible without letting it fall to the ground;〔まり〕the leather "ball" used in *kemari*. ◐蹴鞠をする play *kemari*.

けやき【欅】〔ニレ科の落葉大高木〕a keaki; a keyaki; a Japanese zelkova (tree).

けやり【毛槍】a long spear with bunches of feathery ornaments attached to the tip and held upright at the head of a daimyo's procession.

げり【下痢】diarrh(o)ea; loose bowels;〔家畜の〕scours. ～する have loose bowels; have [suffer from] diarrhea. ■水様性下痢 watery diarrhea.　**下痢性の** laxative; diarrhetic.　**下痢止め** an ﹁antidiarrheal [antidiarrhetic]﹂; an obstipant;（小児用の）a paregoric.　**下痢便**《have》watery stools.

けんえん【犬猿】 犬猿の仲[間柄]である be on cat-and-dog terms; be on very bad terms《with…》; hate each other like poison;《口》hate each other's guts.　◐ あの二人は犬猿の仲. They are like cat and dog with each other. | Those two quarrel all the time.

けんかく【剣客】 a master [an expert] in kendo.

げんかん【玄関】〔入口〕the entrance《of a house》; the (front) door《of a house》;〔玄関の間〕the vestibule; the hall(way); the entrance [front] hall; the entry hall.　◐ 玄関前の階段 the front steps / 玄関から入る enter through the front door / 玄関まで送る see *somebody* to the door / ベルが鳴ったので玄関へ出た. The bell rang, and I answered the door.

けんけつ【献血】(a) blood donation; donating blood.　**〜する** donate (*one*'s) blood / 献血を呼びかける appeal for blood donations.

げんごう【元号】 an (imperial) era name.

けんこうしんだん【健康診断】 a medical [physical, health] examination [checkup]; a physical; a checkup;《口》a medical.　◐ 会社[職場]の健康診断 a medical examination ﹁arranged by *one*'s company [conducted at *one*'s workplace].　■**定期健康診断** a ﹁regular [periodic(al)] medical examination [checkup, physical].　**健康診断結果** the results of a medical examination.　**健康診断書** a certificate of health.

けんこうほけん【健康保険】 health insurance.　◐ …は健康保険が適用されません …is not covered by health insurance / 健康保険に入っている be enrolled in a health insurance program / 健康保険組合 a health insurance association / 健康保険証 a health insurance card.

げんこうようし【原稿用紙】 writing paper (on which are printed ﹁columns [rows] of square blocks, one for each writing symbol).　◐ 罫線付きの原稿用紙 lined writing paper / 横書きの[縦書きの]原稿用紙 writing paper ruled with ﹁horizontal [vertical] lines.

けんこうランド【健康ランド】〔大浴場を中心に健康増進や保養のための設備を備えた施設〕a health resort; a health spa with public baths and other health-promoting and recreational facilities.

けんこくきねんのひ【建国記念の日】〔2月11日〕National Foundation Day.

けんざん【剣山】〖生け花〗a pinholder [needle-point holder] used in flower arranging; a frog.

げんじ【源氏】the Genji [Minamoto] family; the Minamotos. ■**源氏名** the assumed [professional] name 《of a nightclub hostess》. **源氏豆** sugar-coated soybeans dyed red or white.

げんじものがたり【「源氏物語」】〔紫式部作の物語〕*The Tale of Genji*.

けんじょ【見所】〔能楽堂の〕the 《audience's》seats.

けんしょう【懸賞】〔事〕a prize competition [contest]; an offer of a prize [reward]; 〔賞〕a prize; a reward. ▶懸賞応募の条件 the conditions of entry for the prize competition 《are given on page 3》／多数の懸賞がかかった取組〖相撲〗a sumo bout for which many prizes are offered／懸賞で賞金を得る win [gain, obtain] prize money in a prize contest [competition]／懸賞に応募する enter a prize contest [competition]／懸賞に当たる win *something* in a prize contest [competition]. ■**懸賞課題[問題]** a task [problem, question] for a prize contest. **懸賞金** prize money; a reward; a price 《on a criminal's head》. **懸賞広告** an advertisement for a prize contest;〔犯人探しの〕an advertisement offering a reward for information leading to the arrest of a criminal. **懸賞小説[論文]** a prize-competition novel [essay]. ▶懸賞小説に応募する enter a prize competition for the best novel. **懸賞付きの** with a prize [reward] offered. ▶懸賞付き写真コンクール a prize photo contest; a photo contest with prizes. **懸賞当選者** a prize winner.

けんしん【検診】(a) medical examination; health screening. ～する examine *somebody*; give *somebody* a health checkup. ▶検診を受ける undergo a medical examination. **一歳児検診** a medical examination for one-year-olds. **がん検診** health screening [a medical examination] for cancer. **歯科検診** a dental examination. **集団検診** a group [mass] examination.

げんだいっこ【現代っ子】a (down-to-earth [practical-minded]) modern child; a child of the times. ▶あの割り切り方はまさに現代っ子だね. That cool practicality is typical of young people today.

けんだま【剣玉】(a) cup and ball; (a) bilboquet. ■**剣玉遊び** ▶けんだま遊びをする play at cup and ball; play a cup-and-ball game; play bilboquet.

けんちん(じる)【けんちん(汁)】Japanese vegetable chowder; a soy-based soup made with fried vegetables.

けんどう【剣道】kendo; (Japanese) fencing; swordsmanship. ◐剣道五段 the fifth *dan* in kendo;〔人〕a fifth-*dan* fencer

けんばん【検番】an assignation office for geisha.

げんぺい【源平】〔源氏と平家〕the Genji and the Heike (clans); the Minamoto and Taira clans;〔争う2組〕two rival「parties [factions]; two opposing sides;〔赤と白〕red and white 《camps》. ◐源平に分ける divide into two rival「groups [parties].

けんべん【検便】a stool「examination [test]; scatoscopy. ◐検便用の便 a stool「specimen [sample]; a sample stool; a specimen of *somebody*'s stool / 検便を行う examine *somebody*'s「stool [feces].

けんぽうきねんび【憲法記念日】〔5月3日〕Constitution (Memorial) Day.

げんまい【玄米】unpolished [unmilled] rice; brown rice. ■**玄米食** a diet of「brown [unpolished] rice;〔主食とすること〕eating「brown [unpolished] rice. **玄米茶** coarse green tea mixed with roasted brown rice. **玄米パン** whole-rice bread.

こ

ご【碁】(the game of) go; a game played with black and white stones on a board, the object being to surround the opponent's stones.

こあげ【小揚げ】〔小型の油揚げ〕small pieces of fried「tofu [bean curd].

こい【鯉】〔コイ科の淡水魚〕a carp 《*pl.* ~s,〈集合的に〉carp》. ◐ 俎(まないた)の上の鯉 ⇨ まないた. / 鯉の滝上り a carp「ascending [swimming up, leaping up] a waterfall;〔比喩的に〕making *one*'s way in the world (in spite of difficulties).

こいこく【鯉こく】carp cooked in「bean [miso] soup.

こいちゃ【濃い茶】1〔濃くいれた茶〕strong tea. **2**〔濃い茶手前用の茶〕powdered green tea for use in the most formal style of tea ceremony.

こいぬ【子犬】a puppy; a pup; a whelp;〔小さい犬〕a「small [little] (type of) dog.

こいのぼり【鯉幟】a carp streamer; large「cloth [paper] carp flown out of doors in early summer, typically to celebrate the traditional Boy's Festival in May. ◐ こいのぼりを立てる put up [raise, erect] a carp banner; fly [float] a carp streamer 《in front of a house》.

-ごう【合】1〔尺貫法における容積の単位〕*gō*《*pl.* ~》(=約 0.18 l);〔尺貫法における面積の単位〕*gō*《*pl.* ~》(=約 0.33 m^2). ◐ 1 合徳利(どくり) a ceramic [an earthenware] sake bottle with a capacity of one *gō* / 1 合升(ます) a one *gō* measuring box / 1 合の酒 a *gō* of sake.

こうあん【公案】〔禅宗の〕a koan; a conundrum for Zen meditation.

こういってん【紅一点】the「sole [one, only] woman in a group of men; a woman in a party of men. ◐ 彼女が正に紅一点であった. She was the (one and) only woman「present [there].

こうおつ【甲乙】1〔甲と乙〕A and B. **2**〔区別〕(a) difference; discrimination;〔優劣〕superiority or inferiority. ◐ その二つは甲乙がない[甲乙つけがたい]. It is difficult to say which (of the two) is better / 甲乙の

ない equal; of equal merit / 甲乙をつける〔差をつける〕distinguish; discriminate; make a distinction 《between...》.

こうがい【公害】〔環境汚染〕(environmental) pollution; pollution 《of the atmosphere》; contamination;〔環境破壊〕environmental destruction. ■**騒音公害** noise pollution.　**排煙公害** exhaust pollution; air pollution caused by exhaust fumes.　**公害反対運動** a campaign against environmental「pollution [disruption]; an anti-pollution「campaign [movement].　**公害紛争** a pollution [an environmental pollution] dispute.　**公害問題** a problem of environmental pollution; a pollution「problem [issue].

こうきょ【皇居】the Imperial Palace.　◖皇居に参内(さんだい)する visit the Imperial Palace.

こうきん【抗菌】～の antimicrobial; antibacterial;〔抗真菌性の〕antifungal.　◖抗菌タイル[マスク, まな板] an antibacterial「tile [mask, chopping board].　■**抗菌グッズ[商品]** antimicrobial [antibacterial, bacteria-resistant] products [merchandise].

こうごう【皇后】an empress; a queen;〔女帝と区別して〕an empress consort; a queen consort.　**皇后陛下** Her (Imperial) Majesty [H(I)M] the Empress.

こうさつ【高札】〔江戸時代の立て札〕a board used for official announcements by the Edo period authorities; an official notice board.

こうさてん【交差点】〔2線の交点〕an intersection (point); a point of intersection; an intersecting point;〔道路の〕an intersection; (a) crossroads; a crossover; a crossing;（高速道路などに合流する）a junction.　◖日比谷交差点 Hibiya「intersection [crossroads] / 銀座4丁目の交差点 the Ginza 4-chōme「intersection [crossroads]; the「intersection [crossroads] at Ginza 4-chōme.

こうじ【麹】*kōji*; a preparation obtained by growing a kind of mold (usually *Aspergillus oryzae*) on boiled rice, barley, soybeans etc., used as a starter for the fermentation in sake and soy-sauce production.

こうしえん【甲子園】1〔甲子園球場〕the Kōshien Stadium.　**2**〔(硬式の)全国高校野球大会〕the National High-School Baseball Tournament.　◖春の甲子園〔選抜高等学校野球大会の通称〕the Spring「Kōshien [High-School Baseball] Tournament / 夏の甲子園〔全国高等学校野球選手権大会の通称〕the Summer「Kōshien [High-School Base-

こうしじま【格子縞】a check (pattern); cross stripes; a checkered pattern; a tartan (design). ◐あらい格子縞のズボン *loud-checkered ["loud check] trousers.

こうしつ【皇室】the (Japanese) Imperial「Family [Household, House]; the reigning line. ◐開かれた皇室 an open Imperial Family.

こうしゅう【口臭】mouth odor; bad [foul] breath. ◐口臭がある have「bad [foul] breath; *one*'s breath smells / 口臭予防 prevention of mouth odor / 口臭予防スプレー a (bad) breath spray.

こうしん【庚申】1〔かのえさる〕the name of one of the divisions of the traditional sixty-year cycle. 2〔青面金剛〕one of the Buddhist demon-gods with a blue face, hair standing on end and grasping a sword; Shōmen Kongō. ■庚申塚 a roadside standing stone dedicated to Shōmen Kongō, usually engraved with three monkeys.

こうすい【香水】(a) perfume; (a) scent; perfumed [scented] water;〔人工の〕a synthetic [an artificial] perfume;〈集合的に〉perfumery;〔男性用の〕cologne. ◐バラの香水 (a) rose perfume / 香水をつける put on (a) perfume;〔習慣的に〕use [wear] perfume / 香水をつけている be wearing scent; have scent on / ハンカチに香水をつける perfume [scent] a handkerchief; put scent on *one*'s handkerchief.

こうせいねんきん【厚生年金】an employee pension; a welfare「annuity [pension]. ◐厚生年金を支給する[受け取る]pay [receive] a welfare「annuity [pension].

こうせいぶっしつ【抗生物質】an antibiotic (substance). ◐抗生物質に対する抵抗力《develop》a resistance to an antibiotic / 抗生物質を投与する administer an antibiotic; use antibiotics.

こうた【小唄】〖邦楽〗kouta; a ballad sung to samisen accompaniment. ◐爪弾(づま)きに合わせて小唄を歌う sing (a ballad) in tune with the plucking of a samisen.

こうたいし【皇太子】the Crown Prince; the Prince Imperial; the Heir Apparent (to the Throne);〔英国の〕the Prince of Wales. ◐皇太子に立てる make somebody the heir apparent (to the throne) [Crown Prince, Prince of Wales]. ■皇太子殿下 His (Imperial) Highness the Crown Prince;〔英国で〕His (Royal) Highness the Prince of Wales. 皇太子妃 the Crown Princess;〔英国の〕the Princess of Wales. 皇太子

妃殿下 Her (Imperial) Highness the Crown Princess; 〔英国で〕Her (Royal) Highness the Princess of Wales.

こうだん【講談】comic [vaudeville] storytelling; the art of public storytelling; 〔話〕a 《battle》 story. ■講談師 a (professional) storyteller [narrator]. 講談本[雑誌] a ⌈book [magazine] of ⌈stories [transcribed oral narratives].

こうちゃ【紅茶】《a cup of》 tea; black tea; 〔砂糖とミルク入りの〕tea with milk and sugar. ◐紅茶にミルクを入れましょうか. Would you like milk in your tea? | Do you take milk (in your tea)? /〔客に〕紅茶にレモンをお付けしましょうか. Would you like some lemon with your tea? / 紅茶のティーバッグ a ⌈tea bag [teabag] / 紅茶の葉 (leaf) tea; tealeaves / 紅茶を淹(い)れる make tea / 私は紅茶党だ. I like [prefer] tea. | I'm a tea person [man, girl]. ■**ブランデー紅茶** tea with (a splash of) brandy. 紅茶茶碗 a teacup.

こうつうじこ【交通事故】a traffic accident;〔自動車などの〕a car accident;〔電車などの〕a ⌈train [railroad] accident. ◐交通事故にあう〔主に歩行者が〕get hit by a car;〔主に運転して〕have [be in] a traffic accident / 交通事故を起こす cause a traffic accident.

こうつうじゅうたい【交通渋滞】a traffic jam; (traffic) congestion;〔完全な麻痺状態〕gridlock. ◐交通渋滞から抜け出す escape from [get out of] a traffic jam / 交通渋滞に巻き込まれる be [get] caught in a traffic jam.

こうつうしんごう【交通信号】a traffic light; a traffic signal. ◐交通信号を守る[無視する] obey [ignore] a traffic signal.

こうでん【香典・香奠】a (monetary) offering made at a funeral to the family of the deceased; an obituary [a condolence] gift; "incense money." ■香典返し a return offering given by the family of the deceased to people who have made a funeral offering. 香典帳 a book in which details of donations made by mourners at a funeral are recorded. 香典袋 a special envelope for ⌈a funeral offering ["incense money"].

こうどう【香道】the incense ceremony; formal aesthetic appreciation of the fragrance of burning aromatic woods; incense-smelling.

ごうとう【強盗】〔犯人〕a robber; a mugger;〔犯罪〕(a) robbery; (a) mugging; a holdup;《口》 a heist. ◐私の家に強盗が押し入った. My house was broken into. | A burglar broke into my house. / 銀行へ強盗に入る rob a bank; carry out a bank robbery; hold up a bank. ■銀行強盗〔犯人〕a bank robber;〔行為〕(a) bank robbery. 緊縛強盗 tying *somebody* up and robbing him. コンビニ強盗〔犯人〕a convenience store robber;〔行為〕a convenience store robbery. ピストル強盗〔犯人〕an armed robber; a「holdup [stickup] man;〔行為〕a「holdup [stickup].

こうねつひ【光熱費】fuel [heat] and lighting expenses [charges, costs]; charges for lighting and fuel.

こうねんき【更年期】a [the, *one*'s] climacteric;《口》the change of life;《reach, go through》the menopause. ◐男性の更年期 a male climacteric;《口》a male menopause ■更年期鬱病〚医〛menopausal depression; involutional melancholia. 更年期後[前]の post-[pre-]menopausal《women》. 更年期愁訴 a「menopausal [climacteric] complaint. 更年期障害〚医〛a climacteric「disturbance [disorder].

こうやどうふ【高野豆腐】freeze-dried tofu; a kind of preserved tofu, supposedly originally made at the temple of Mt. Kōya, traditionally produced by freezing tofu outside in winter and then drying it. It is reconstituted in water before use.

こうよう【紅葉・黄葉】〔秋の変色した葉〕the (colored) leaves of「autumn [*fall]; (colored)「autumnal [autumn] leaves; autumnal foliage; red [crimson, scarlet(-tinged)] leaves; yellow [golden] leaves;〔色の変化〕the「coloring [turning] of the「leaves [foliage] in autumn. ～する turn; change color; turn「red [yellow]; be tinged with「red [yellow]; (come to) look autumnal; take [put] on「autumnal coloring [autumnal tints].

ごえもんぶろ【五右衛門風呂】a bath heated directly on a fire (named after the famous robber Ishikawa Goemon, who was boiled to death in one).

ゴーヤーチャンプルー〔沖縄料理〕*gōyā* [balsam apple] fried with pork, tofu and other vegetables.

こおりざとう【氷砂糖】sugar crystals; crystallized sugar; rock candy; sugar candy.

こおりどうふ【凍り豆腐】=こうやどうふ.

こおりまくら【氷枕】an ice pack; an ice pillow.

こおろぎ【蟋蟀】a cricket. ◐こおろぎが鳴いている. A cricket is「singing [chirping].

こかた【子方】〔能楽〕(an actor of) a child's part 《in a Noh play》.

ごがつにんぎょう【五月人形】martial dolls for the Children's Festival in early May.

ごがつびょう【五月病】May (depression) syndrome; the depression [feeling of letdown] which newcomers experience in May, a month after their admission to college or employment.

こき【古希】seventy (years of age); threescore and ten. ◐古希に達する reach seventy; 《文》attain *one*'s seventieth year / 古希の祝い the celebration of *one*'s [*somebody*'s] 70th birthday.

ごきぶり a cockroach;《口》a roach. ◐ごきぶり捕獲器〔粘着シート式の〕a cockroach trap (making use of a sheet of sticky paper).

こギャル a *kogyaru*; an obsessively trend-conscious teenage girl.

こく【石】〔容積の単位〕a *koku*. 米穀類は 180.39 リットル, 木材は 0.278 立方メートル. ◐米 10 石 10 *koku* of rice / (大名が) 5 万石を領する hold a fief「of [yielding] 50,000 *koku* (of rice).

こくばん【黒板】 a blackboard; a chalkboard;〔緑色の〕a greenboard; a green blackboard / 黒板に書いて説明する explain [demonstrate] 《a theory》on the blackboard; make a blackboard demonstration《of…》/ 黒板にチョークで書く write 《a sentence》on the blackboard「in chalk [with a chalk]; chalk up 《a score》on the board / 黒板をふく wipe the blackboard clean; clean [*clean off] the blackboard. ■**黒板ふき** a blackboard eraser; an eraser; a chalk eraser; a (blackboard) wiper.

こくほう【国宝】a national「treasure [heirloom]. ◐国宝に指定される be designated (as) a national treasure. ■**国宝級** ◐国宝級の絵画 a picture which should be a national treasure; a painting of national-treasure class.

こくみんけんこうほけん【国民健康保険】National Health Insurance; a national health insurance system. ■**国民健康保険組合** a National Health Insurance「association [union]. **国民健康保険証** a National Health Insurance card.

こくみんねんきん【国民年金】〔一般的に〕a national [state] pension; a pension from the government;〔日本の〕the National Pension (System).

こけし a *kokeshi* doll; a wooden doll with a spherical head and a cylindrical body (originally a folkcraft product of the Tohoku region).

ごけにん【御家人】〔鎌倉・室町時代の〕an immediate vassal of the shogun (in the Kamakura and Muromachi periods);〔江戸時代の〕a low-level ｢vassal [retainer] of the Tokugawa shogun.

こけらおとし【柿落とし】the (formal) opening 《of a new theater》. ■ こけら落とし公演 an ｢inaugural [opening] performance.

こころづけ【心付け】〔チップ〕a tip; a gratuity. ◐心付けをする tip; give 《the doorman》 a tip; remember.

ごさんけ【御三家】〔徳川家の尾張・紀伊・水戸の三家〕the three branch families of the Tokugawa House;〔ある分野での有力な三者〕the ｢big [top] three.

ごさんのきり【五三の桐】a family crest consisting of paulownia flowers superimposed on three paulownia leaves.

こしぎんちゃく【腰巾着】a [*somebody*'s] shadow; a hanger-on 《*pl.* hangers-on, hanger-ons》; a person who is glued to *somebody* as if he were the very purse at his waist. ◐その子はお母さんの腰巾着だ. The child follows his mother around everywhere.

こしだかしょうじ【腰高障子】a sliding paper screen with waist high paneling.

こしたんたんと【虎視眈々と】ready to pounce; ready for a chance to attack. ◐虎視眈々と反撃の機会をうかがう be watching eagerly for a chance to counterattack.

ごじっぽひゃっぽ【五十歩百歩】両者は五十歩百歩だ. There is ｢little [not much] difference between the two. | There is little to choose between them. | It is six of one and half a dozen of the other. | One is as bad as the other. | One is not much better than the other.

こしびょうぶ【腰屏風】a ｢low [waist-high] folding screen.

ごじゅうおん【五十音】the Japanese syllabary (organized according to a standard order).

ごじゅうのとう【五重の塔】a five-storied [-storeyed] pagoda.

こしょう【胡椒】〔コショウ科の常緑つる性木本； インド南部原産の香辛料植物〕pepper;〔果実〕(未熟果実) a black peppercorn; (果皮を除いた成熟果実) a white peppercorn;〔調味料〕pepper; (粒胡椒) a peppercorn; unground pepper; (粗挽き胡椒) a grain of pepper; ground pepper. ◐

(料理が)こしょうがきいている be peppery; taste of pepper.

こしょうがつ【小正月】January 15, or January 14 to 16 by the lunar calendar.

ごしょぐるま【御所車】a kind of elegant ox-drawn court carriage used chiefly by the nobility of the Heian period.

ごしょにんぎょう【御所人形】a naked clay doll baby, whitened with chalk and with a large round head, produced in Kyoto in the Edo period.

ごぜんさま【午前様】coming home「after midnight [in the small hours];〔人〕a night revel(l)er (who doesn't return until early morning).

ごぜんじるこ【御膳汁粉】〔こしあんの汁粉〕(a) sweet soup of strained adzuki beans with *mochi* in it.

こそで【小袖】a kimono with short sleeves worn as underclothing by the upper classes and as an overgarment by ordinary people during the Heian period; it is the origin of today's kimono;〔絹の綿入れ〕a (wadded silk) kimono.

こたつ【炬燵】a *kotatsu*; a low table over a heat source (now usually electric, but formerly a charcoal brazier) and the whole covered with a quilt to warm the legs of people who sit at the table;〔置き炬燵〕a (portable) *kotatsu*; an electric *kotatsu*;〔掘り炬燵〕a sunken *kotatsu*.

こだて【戸建て】a (detached) house; a free-standing house; a single-family house.

ごちそうさま【御馳走様】◐〔食後に〕ごちそうさま. Thank you. That was delicious. | Thank you very much (for a wonderful meal). / ごちそうさましていい? May I leave the table? /〔食べ物をもらって〕ごちそうさまです. Thank you. It looks delicious. / おやおや, ごちそうさま.〔のろけ話を聞いて〕Yes, yes! We know「she's [he's] wonderful. |〔男女の仲の良いところを見せつけられて〕That'll do! Wait till「later [you're at home]. | *《俗》Get a room!

こづつみ【小包】〔小さな包み〕a (small) parcel; a packet; a package; a pack. ◐ 小包にする wrap 《books》 (in a small parcel); make (up) a parcel of 《books》; do 《them》 up in a「parcel [package].

こっとう(ひん)【骨董(品)】an antique; a curio 《*pl.* ~s》; objects [articles] of virtu;〔古いだけで無価値の物〕bric-a-brac. ■ **骨董趣味** a「taste [liking] for antiques. **骨董商**〔店〕an antique shop; a curiosity shop; a curio shop; 〔人〕a dealer in「antiques [curios]; an antique(s) dealer; an antiquary.　骨董(品)市 an antique fair.

こて【籠手・小手】〔弓道の〕(腕甲) a bracer;〔よろいの〕a bracelet;〔剣道の防具〕a (fencing) glove; a gauntlet;〔前腕〕a forearm;〔前腕部への剣道の決まり手〕a hit「on [to] the forearm; a stroke to the wrist.

こと【琴】a koto; a zither-like Japanese musical instrument about 180 cms long and 30 cms wide with thirteen strings, it is played wearing plectrums on the fingers of the right hand.

こどものつかい【子供の使い】〔要領を得ず，役に立たない使い〕a hopeless [a useless, an incompetent] messenger.　◐〔借金取りなどが〕子供の使いじゃあるまいし，手ぶらで帰るわけにはいかないんだよ．This isn't child's play. So, don't expect me to leave empty-handed.

こどものひ【こどもの日】〔5月5日〕Children's Day.

ごにんばやし【五人囃子】dolls representing five musicians, displayed at the Girls' Festival (March 3).

ごねどく【ごね得】getting more by「holding out [grousing].　◐あいつのごね得に終わった．In the end, he made so much trouble that he got what he wanted.

こはくいろ【琥珀色】amber (color).

こはだ【小鰭】〘魚〙a medium-sized Konoshiro gizzard shad.

こばら【小腹】◐小腹が立つ[を立てる] be slightly「annoyed [angry, offended] / 小腹が減った．I'm「slightly [a little] hungry.｜〝《口》I'm a bit peckish. / 小腹を満たす stave off (*one*'s) hunger.

こばん【小判】a *koban*(*g*); an oval Japanese gold coin of the Edo period.　◐慶長小判 a *koban*(*g*) minted in the Keichō era.

こばんざめ【小判鮫】〘魚〙a remora; a shark sucker; a sucking fish; a suckfish; a pegador.　◐こばんざめ商法 (a) parasite business.

こぶちゃ【昆布茶】a kind of tea made from powdered and seasoned kelp.　■梅昆布茶 *ume*-flavored kelp tea.

こぶまき【昆布巻き】a kelp roll; rolled tang with (dried) fish in it.　◐ニシンの昆布巻き herring rolled in kelp.

ごへいもち【御幣餅[五平]餅】a skewered rice-cake with sesame, miso or soy sauce.

ごぼう【牛蒡】〔キク科の越年草; ユーラシア大陸原産の食用植物〕a great burdock; an edible burdock;〔食材〕a burdock root.

ごぼうぬき【牛蒡抜き】 ◐警官隊は座り込んでいる学生たちをごぼう抜きにして護送車にほうり込んだ. The police squad hauled away the sit-in student demonstrators and tossed them into the paddy wagons. / ゴール寸前 5 人をごぼう抜きにして優勝した. In the home stretch she outstripped five rivals to win going away.

こま【独楽】 a spinning top. ◐こまを回す spin a top.

ごま【胡麻】〔ゴマ科の 1 年草; アフリカ原産の食用植物〕(Oriental) sesame; a gingili;〔種子〕a sesame seed. ◐ごまをする pound sesame seeds;〔へつらう〕flatter; toady; fawn upon…; curry favor with 《one's superior》; play the sycophant / ごまを炒(い)る parch [roast, toast] sesame seeds. ■黒[白]ごま black [white] sesame. すりごま ground sesame seeds. 練りごま sesame (seed) paste. ごま和(あ)え vegetables dressed with ground sesame. ごま油 sesame oil; gingili. ごま酢 sesame vinegar. ◐ごま酢和え boiled spinach or other vegetables seasoned with a dressing of ground sesame and vinegar. ごまだれ sesame sauce; a sauce made with ground sesame. ごま豆腐 sesame tofu. ごま味噌 miso [soy bean paste] with ground sesame and sweetened sake.

こまいぬ【狛犬】 a pair of (stone-carved) guardian dogs 《at the gate of a Shinto shrine》.

こまげた【駒下駄】 low clogs.

ごますり【胡麻擂り】〔へつらい〕apple-polishing; brown-nosing; sycophancy; toadying;〔へつらう人〕an apple-polisher; a brown-noser; a flatterer; a sycophant; a toady.

こまち【小町】 神田小町と呼ばれたものだ. She used to be called the "「Belle [Rose] of Kanda." ■小町娘 a girl of exceeding loveliness.

こむそう【虚無僧】 a mendicant Zen priest of the Fuke sect, wearing a sedge hood and playing a *shakuhachi*.

こめ【米】 rice.

こも【菰・薦】1【菰】〔イネ科の大型多年草; 湿地植物〕Manchurian wild rice;〔菰〕a rush mat. **2【薦】**〔藁むしろ〕straw matting;〔1 枚〕a「straw [rush] mat. ◐こもで包む wrap *something* in a straw mat.

ごもく【五目】 ■五目寿司 vinegared rice mixed with vegetables, fish, and other ingredients. 五目そば Chinese noodles with various vegetables, seafood and meat. 五目飯 boiled rice cooked with fish, meat, and vegetables; a Japanese-style pilaf.　**五目焼きそば** noodles stir-fried with vegetables, pork, shrimp, and other ingredients, often topped with quail eggs.

こもり【子守】〔乳幼児の世話〕nursing; tending a baby;〔世話する人〕a person who looks after a baby; a (dry) nurse; a nursemaid;(留守を頼まれる) a baby-sitter.　◐ 子守をする nurse [tend, care for, look after] a baby; baby-sit.

こもりうた【子守歌】a nursery song; a lullaby; a cradlesong.　◐ 子守歌を歌って子供を寝かしつける lullaby [sing] a baby to sleep; sing a lullaby to put a child to sleep.

こもん【小紋】a fine pattern.　◐ 小紋の fine-patterned / 小紋のちりめん thin silk crepe with a fine pattern.　■ **江戸小紋** finely detailed dye-work of the Edo period, used for *kami-shimo* ceremonial clothing.

こやすじぞう【子安地蔵】a *Jizō* (statue [image]) worshipped for easy childbirth.

ごようたし【御用達】a purveyor to the Government.　◐ 英王室御用達 a purveyor to the British Royal Household / 芸能人御用達のレストラン a restaurant that caters to celebrities; a celebrity watering hole.　■ **宮内庁御用達** a purveyor to the Imperial Household.

ごりむちゅう【五里霧中】五里霧中である be (lost) in a fog; be at a loss; be at sea《in regard to...》; be tossed on an ocean of doubts.　◐ 仕事について最初の1か月間はまったく五里霧中だった． During my first month in my new job, I was completely at sea.

ころもがえ【衣替え】〔衣服の〕a seasonal change of clothing.

こんがすり【紺絣】a kind of tie-dye textile with a white pattern on an indigo-blue ground.　◐ 紺絣の着物 an indigo-blue kimono with a pattern of white (splashes) on it.

こんにゃく【蒟蒻】〔サトイモ科の多年草; コンニャク原料植物〕a konjak (u); a devil's tongue;〔食品〕paste made from the starch of the konjak.

こんぴら【金比羅】〚Skt〛*Kumbhīra*; the guardian deity of seafarers; the Japanese Neptune.

こんぺいとう【金平糖】〚<Port〛confeitos pointed sugar candy balls.

こんよく【混浴】mixed bathing.　～する bathe together.

さ

さいおうがうま【塞翁が馬】the ceaseless ironies of fate.　◐ 人間(じんかん)万事塞翁が馬.〚諺〛 | In human affairs, every turn of fortune, good or bad, anticipates its reversal.

さいきょう【西京】〔京都〕the Western Capital; Kyoto.　■ **西京漬け**《a pomfret or other fish》pickled in sweet Kyoto-style miso.　**西京味噌** sweet white miso made in Kyoto.

さいせいし【再生紙】recycled paper.　◐ この名刺は再生紙を利用しています. This business card is made of recycled paper. / このトイレットペーパーは 100 パーセント再生紙です. This toilet paper is 100-percent recycled paper.

さいせんばこ【賽銭箱】an offertory「box [chest].

さいばし【菜箸】long chopsticks for「cooking [serving].

さいふ【財布】a wallet; a purse;〔がま口〕a coin purse; a pouch;〔札入れ〕a billfold; a pocketbook;〔硬貨と紙幣を分けて入れる型〕a wallet.　◐ **革の財布** a leather billfold; wallet.　**財布の紐** purse strings.　◐ 彼女は財布の紐が固い. She keeps a tight hold on the purse strings. / 財布の紐を締める tighten the purse strings; tighten *one*'s belt / 財布の紐をゆるめる loosen the purse strings / 財布の紐を握っている hold [control] the purse strings《of...》.

さおだけ【竿竹】a bamboo pole.

さおもの【棹物】〔棒状の和菓子〕*saomono*; traditional sweets, such as yōkan, that are cut in bite-sized pieces from long blocks.

さかき【榊】〚植〛a species of camellia with thick, dark-green leaves《branches of *sakaki* are used in Shinto observances》.

さかずき【杯】a sake cup; (足付きの) a sake goblet.

さかな【肴】a side dish (to go with sake).　◐ 酒とさかな sake and「side dishes [hors d'oeuvres] / 酒のさかなが何もない. There is nothing to go with the sake. / 人をさかなにする have a good「time [laugh] at somebody's expense.

さかむし【酒蒸し】steeping in sake and steaming. ▶アサリの酒蒸し sake-steamed clams.

さくっと〔手早く; 短時間で〕quickly; snappily; with alacrity / この仕事はさくっと済ませちゃいましょうよ。Let's snap to it and finish the job「quickly [lickety-split].

さくら¹【桜】**1**〔バラ科サクラ亜属の植物の総称〕a Japanese cherry; a Japanese flowering cherry;〔木〕a cherry tree;〔花〕cherry「blossoms [flowers];〔桜色〕(a) light pink. ▶桜の名所 a place famous for its cherry blossoms. ■桜並木 a row [rows] of cherry trees《lining the street》. 桜吹雪 a blizzard of falling cherry blossom petals.

さくら²〔大道商人の〕a decoy; a dummy purchaser;《俗》a shill; a capper;〔競売の〕a by-bidder;〔劇場の〕a plant; a claqueur;〈集合的に〉a claque.

さくらえび【桜海老】〔サクラエビ科のエビ〕a「spotted [sakura] shrimp.

さくらにく【桜肉】horseflesh; horsemeat.

さくらもち【桜餅】a rice cake filled with sweet bean paste and wrapped in a pickled cherry leaf.

さくらゆ【桜湯】a drink made from a hot infusion of salted cherry blossoms.

さくらんぼ【桜んぼ】a cherry; (茎でつながった) a cherry bob. ▶桜んぼの種 a cherry「stone [pit]. ■さくらんぼ狩り cherry picking.

ささ【笹】〔イネ科のササ属の総称〕bamboo grass. ▶笹の葉 a bamboo grass leaf. ■笹舟 a bamboo-leaf boat.

さざえ【栄螺】a「turban [wreath] shell; a turbo《pl. turbines, ~s》; a horned turban. ▶サザエの壺焼き a turbo cooked in its own shell.

ささみ【笹身】〔鶏の〕white [breast] meat《of chicken》.

さしいれ【差し入れ】**1**〔中に入れること〕insertion. ▶書類の差し入れが楽なファイル a folder for slipping documents into. **2**〔受刑者などに物品を届けること〕giving [sending] things to a prisoner from the outside;〔その物品〕goods brough to a prisoner from the outside. **3**〔陣中見舞い〕a supply of「provisions [food, refreshments]《to a person occupied with some task》. ▶私たちは一休みして差し入れのお菓子をいただいた。We took a break from work to eat the「snacks [refreshments] that had been provided for us.

ざしき【座敷】〔部屋〕a ｢Japanese-style [tatami] room; 〔客間〕a ｢drawing [reception] room; a parlor.

ざしきわらし【座敷童】〔座敷に住む妖怪〕the protective deity [genius loci] of a home in the Tōhoku region of Japan.

さしみ【刺身】sashimi; (sliced [slices of]) raw fish [meat]. ◐ マグロの刺身 tuna sashimi; (sliced [slices of]) raw tuna / 刺身のつま a garnish served with raw fish.

ざぜん【坐禅】Zen meditation; seated ｢meditation [contemplation] (as practiced in the Zen sect).

さそりざ【蝎座】〖天・占星〗the Scorpion; Scorpio (略: Sco). ◐ さそり座生まれの人 a Scorpio 《*pl.* ~s》; a Scorpionic.

さだいじん【左大臣】*sadaijin*, or minister of the left, a court office in pre-modern Japan; superior in rank to an *udaijin*, or minister of the right.

さつき【五月・皐月】the fifth month of the lunar calendar; May.

さつまあげ【薩摩揚げ】a (deep-)fried cake of ground fish; fried surimi.

さつまいも【薩摩芋】a sweet potato.

さつまげた【薩摩下駄】Satsuma ｢geta [clogs] (made of cedar and with a broad platform).

さといも【里芋】〔サトイモ科の多年草; 熱帯アジア原産の食用作物〕a taro; a coco-yam; a dasheen.

さとう【砂糖】sugar. ◐ 砂糖で固めた sugared; candied 《fruits》/ 砂糖で甘くした sugared; sweetened with sugar / 錠剤を砂糖でくるむ sugar a pill / 砂糖を入れる put in sugar; sugar; sweeten with sugar.
■ 赤砂糖 brown sugar. 角砂糖 ⇨ かくざとう. 黒[粗製]砂糖 raw [unrefined] sugar; muscovado. 氷砂糖 ⇨ こおりざとう. 粉砂糖 powdered [castor] sugar. 白[精製]砂糖 refined sugar. 砂糖入れ〔食卓用の〕a sugar ｢bowl [‖basin].

さどう【茶道】(the) tea ceremony.

さとがえり【里帰り】〔実家への一時帰宅〕a visit (to *one*'s parents') home; 〔新婦の〕a bride's first visit to her ｢old [parents'] home.

さとかぐら【里神楽】a country kagura (performed in a Shinto shrine, as against a Court kagura). [⇨ かぐら]

さとみや【里宮】a branch shrine in the foothills of a mountain on whose summit the main shrine is situated.

さば【鯖】〔総称〕a mackerel 《*pl.* ~, ~s》; a scombroid; 〔マサバ〕a chub mackerel; 〔ゴマサバ〕a spotted chub mackerel; a blue mackerel.

さばずし【鯖寿司】(pickled, marinated) mackerel sushi.

さび¹【寂】〔枯淡・幽雅〕subdued refinement; elegant [quiet] simplicity. ◐ 芭蕉俳諧のさび the elegant simplicity of Bashō's *haikai* poetry.

さび²〔ワサビの略〕wasabi. ◐ さびを利かせる include plenty of wasabi;〔引きしまった感じにする〕spice up 《*one*'s lecture》. ■ さび抜き 《sushi》without wasabi.

さび³〔曲の聞かせ所〕the catchy part of a song; (ポピュラー音楽の主要部) the chorus.

ざぶとん【座布団】a square floor cushion for「kneeling [sitting (cross-legged)] on.

サボる〔仕事を〕absent *one*self from work; loaf on the job;《口》lie down on the job;《俗》(仕事するふりをして) soldier on the job;〔学校を〕absent *one*self from [cut, skip] school; play「truant [*《口》hooky] from school;〔講義を〕cut a「class [lecture] / 掃除の当番をサボる do not「show up [appear] when it「is *one*'s turn to do the cleaning / 授業を 2 時間サボる cut two hours of「lessons [classes].

さみだれ【五月雨】early summer rain. ◐ 五月雨がしとしと降っている. An early summer rain is gently falling.

さむえ【作務衣】*samue*; a Buddhist priest's work clothes.

さむらい【侍】a samurai; a warrior.

さめ【鮫】a shark. ◐ 鮫肝油 shark liver oil. [=鮫油] / 鮫(の)皮 shark-skin; shagreen / 鮫油 shark oil.

さめはだ【鮫肌】rough skin;〔病気〕fishskin disease; ichthyosis.

さゆ【白湯】(plain) hot [warm, boiled] water. ◐ (薬を)さゆで飲む take 《medicine》with「hot [warm] water.

ざゆうのめい【座右の銘】*one*'s motto; a maxim; an adage; a pet saying.

さら【皿】〔平たい食器〕a plate; a dish; (大皿) a 《meat》platter; (受け皿) a saucer; (スープなどを入れる) a soup「dish [bowl]. ◐ 皿を洗う wash (the)「dishes [plates]; do the dishes; (強くこすって) scrub 《the egg off》 a「dish [plate]. ■ 大皿 a large「dish [plate]; a platter. 角皿 a「square [rectangular] dish [plate]. 飾り皿 an ornamental dish. 菓子皿 a *candy ["sweets] plate. ケーキ皿 a cake plate. 小皿 a small「dish [plate]. 耐熱皿 a heat-resistant「dish [plate]. 取り皿 an individual plate.

サラきん【サラ金】〔高利貸し〕a loan shark (targeting salary earners).

さらさ【更紗】〖＜Port *saraça*〗printed cotton; chintz; *(printed) calico; ‖print. ■インド更紗 Indian cotton; chintz; Indian print. 古代更紗 antique print cotton. ジャワ更紗 (Javanese) batik. 木綿更紗 cotton print; chintz; *calico.

サラダ a salad. ▷サラダを作る make [mix] a salad. ハム[フルーツ, 野菜]サラダ a ham [fruit, vegetable] salad. サラダオイル[油] salad oil. サラダ・ドレッシング salad dressing. サラダ菜 lettuce; salad greens. サラダ・バー a salad bar. サラダ・ボール a salad bowl.

ざりがに【蝲蛄】a crawfish; ‖a crayfish.

さる¹【申】〔十二支の〕the Monkey, *one* of the twelve animals of the「Oriental [Chinese] zodiac ▷申の日 the Day of the Monkey / 申の刻(こく) the Hour of the Monkey(; 3-5 p.m.) / 申の方(かた)〔西南西〕the Direction of the Monkey(; west-southwest).

さる²【猿】a monkey; (類人猿) an ape. ▷尻尾のない[短い]猿 a「tailless [short-tailed] ape / 芸をする猿 a performing monkey / 猿も木から落ちる. Even a monkey sometimes falls from a tree. | Homer sometimes nods.〖諺〗| Accidents happen to the best of us. ■雄[雌]猿 a「male [female] monkey. 子猿 a baby monkey. ボス猿 a boss monkey. 猿山〔動物園の〕Monkey Mountain; Monkey Island.

さるがく【猿楽】〔狂言の本流〕*sarugaku* as the prototype of the *kyōgen* farce; a medieval Noh farce;〔能楽の本流〕*sarugaku* as the prototype of the Noh play.

ざるそば【笊蕎麦】buckwheat noodles [*soba*] topped with sliced dried seaweed, served on a「woven [latticed] bamboo tray.

さるまわし【猿回し】a variety of street performance using monkeys;〔人〕a person who puts on「monkey performances [a monkey show]; a monkey trainer.

さわがに【沢蟹】a Japanese river crab.

さわら【鰆】〖魚〗a Japanese Spanish mackerel.

さんが【参賀】a visit to the Imperial Palace to congratulate the Imperial Family (on a happy occasion, and in particular at New Year's).

さんかいき【三回忌】the second anniversary of *somebody*'s death.

さんかくけい【三角形】a triangle. ■二等辺[直角, 球面]三角形 an isosceles [a right, a spherical] triangle.

さんきょく【三曲】a trio of musical instruments (usually, koto, samisen, and Chinese fiddle, or *kokyū*).

さんきんこうたい【参勤交代】a daimyo's alternate-year residence in Edo (a practice initiated in 1635).

さんげん【三絃】a three-stringed instrument;〔三味線〕a samisen.

さんさい【山菜】an edible wild plant. ◐山菜料理 a meal prepared from edible wild plants.

さんさんくど【三々九度】三々九度の杯をする perform the ceremony of the three-times-three exchange of nuptial cups; exchange nuptial cups.

さんさんごご【三々五々】by twos and threes; in groups (of twos and threes); in small groups; in knots. ◐三々五々連れだって来る come「by twos and threes [in small groups].

さんさんななびょうし【三三七拍子】a three-three-seven beat.

さんじゃく(おび)【三尺帯】a short kimono waistband (used by artisans and children).

さんじゅうさんしょ【三十三所】the thirty-three temples in Kansai sacred to「Kannon [the Buddhist deity of Mercy].

さんしゅのじんぎ【三種の神器】the three sacred emblems of sovereign rule; the Three Sacred「Treasures [Regalia] of the Imperial Family; the three divine symbols of the Japanese imperial throne.

さんしょう【山椒】〔ミカン科の落葉低木〕a Japan pepper tree; a Japanese prickly ash;〔香辛料〕Japanese pepper;〘生薬〙〔果皮〕zanthoxylum fruit. ◐山椒は小粒でもぴりりと辛い. A grain of pepper may be tiny but it still is sharp on the tongue. | Piquant though small.

さんにんづかい【三人遣い】〔文楽で〕manipulation of a Bunraku puppet jointly by three operators.

さんばそう【三番叟】the「customary [traditional] prelude 《to a theatrical program》.

さんぽ【散歩】a walk; a stroll; a lounge; an outing; an airing; a promenade; a turn;《口》(健康のための) a constitutional. ～する promenade; take a「walk [stroll]; have an outing; take the air; take a turn; (のんびりと) stroll; ramble (about); saunter / 散歩に行く go for a walk / 散歩に出かける go out for a walk.

さんぼんじめ【三本締め】a threefold repetition of *ippon-jime*.　[⇨ いっぽんじめ]

さんま【秋刀魚】a Pacific saury.

さんまい【三枚】三枚におろす〔魚を〕fillet 《a sea bream》.　◐三枚おろし filleting a fish.

-ざんまい【-三昧】〔あることにふけること〕読書ざんまい　◐読書ざんまいである be absorbed in reading; be immersed in *one*'s book / 読書ざんまいに暮らす pass (the) hours poring over *one*'s books.

　道楽ざんまい　◐道楽ざんまいに日を送る pursue a life of pleasure and gaiety.

さんやく【三役】**1**〚相撲〛the sumo wrestlers of the three ranks komusubi, sekiwake, and ozeki.　**2**〔会社・政党などの〕the three「key [top-ranking] officials 《of the party》.　■**三役揃い踏み**〚相撲〛the ritual on the last day of a tournament in which sumo wrestlers of *sanyaku* rank, three from the east and three from the west, enter the ring and stamp in unison.

し

しあつ【指圧】 a digital compression.　■**指圧痕** 〖医〗 digital「marking [impression].　**指圧療法** 〖医〗 shiatsu; digital compression [finger-pressure] therapy [cure]; manual therapeutics; acupressure;〔特に脊柱の〕chiropractic; chiropraxis.　◐指圧療法を行う practice [perform] shiatsu [acupressure] / 指圧療法師 a shiatsu practitioner; an acupressurist;〔特に脊柱の〕a chiropractor.

しいたけ【椎茸】〔担子菌類キシメジ科の食用キノコ〕a shiitake mushroom.

じうた【地唄】 a genre of traditional songs with samisen accompaniment, popularized in Western Japan in the Tokugawa period.

じうたい【地謡】 a chorus in *utai* singing.

しお【塩】〔調味料の〕salt;〖化〗salt.　◐地の塩〖聖〗the salt of the earth / ひとつまみ[ひとさじ]の塩 a「pinch [spoonful] of salt / 塩でもむ rub with salt / 塩で味をつける season with salt / 塩で清める purify with salt.

しおから【塩辛】 salted and fermented「meat [internal organs, eggs] of「fish [squid, shellfish, etc.].　◐カツオの塩辛 the salted and fermented internal organs of bonito / イカの塩辛 salted, fermented strips of squid.

しおづけ【塩漬け】〔塩に漬けること〕pickling with salt [in brine];〔食べ物〕food「preserved [pickled, soused] with salt [in brine]; salted food.　◐塩漬けにする pickle [preserve] 《vegetables》 with salt; salt [souse] 《meat》;〔未使用のままにしておく〕leave unused; put [keep] in mothballs; mothball / 白菜を塩漬けにする pickle Chinese cabbage in brine.

しおばらい【塩払い】 sprinkling of salt on a person who has just returned from a funeral.

しおひがり【潮干狩】 shellfish gathering (at low「tide [water]).　◐潮干

狩に行く go gathering shellfish 《at Enoshima》/ 潮干狩をする gather ⌈shellfish [live shells] (at low ⌈tide [water]).

しおやき【塩焼き】1〔海水を煮詰めて塩を作ること〕extracting salt by boiling seawater. **2**〔魚に塩をふりかけて焼くこと〕サンマの塩焼き a Pacific saury that has been sprinkled with salt and ⌈broiled [grilled].

しか【鹿】〔一般に〕a deer 《pl. ~》;(雄鹿) a stag; a buck; a hart;(雌鹿) a doe; a hind;〔日本鹿〕a Japanese deer; a sika;〔子〕a fawn.

しがいせん【紫外線】 ultraviolet rays. ◯ 極紫外線〚物〛extreme ultraviolet rays. 紫外線カットガラス[カットフィルム]〔自動車などの〕UV-blocking[-filtering] glass [film]. 紫外線写真 an ultraviolet photograph. 紫外線情報 an ultraviolet forecast. 紫外線治療 (an) ultraviolet treatment.

じかたび【地下足袋】 split-toed and rubber-soled cloth work shoes.

じかんたいおとどけ【時間帯お届け】〔宅配便・郵便などの〕time-period delivery; delivery 《of a parcel》during a specified time period. ◯ 時間帯お届けサービス a time-period delivery service.

じかんたいわりびき【時間帯割引】 an off-peak time discount.

しきさんば【式三番】 the three celebratory Noh plays.

しきねん【式年】 an anniversary year (in memory of a late emperor, in which the third, fifth, tenth, twentieth, thirtieth, and fiftieth year after the death of an emperor are commemorated).

しきのう【式能】 the ceremonial performance of a Noh play.

しきぶとん【敷き布団】 a fold-up mattress for spreading on a tatami floor; a sleeping mat.

しきまつば【敷(き)松葉】 a covering of pine needles laid over the surface of a garden (against the frost, for aesthetic effect).

じきゃく【次客】〔茶道で正客(しょうきゃく)(the guest of honor) の次の客〕the second guest of honor.

しきりじかん【仕切り時間】〔相撲〕the (allotted) time for the warming-up ritual before sumo wrestlers must grapple.

しぎん【詩吟】 recitation [chanting] of a Chinese poem. ◯ 詩吟を吟ずる recite [chant] a Chinese poem.

しぐれ【時雨】 a shower (of rain) in late autumn or early winter; a late-autumn or early-winter rain; a (light) shower. ◯ 時雨が通りすぎた. The shower has passed.

しぐれに【時雨煮】boiling 《shellfish》 in soy sauce with ⌈*mirin* [sweet sake] and ginger. ◐ ハマグリの時雨煮 boiled clams; clams boiled in soy sauce.

しこ【四股】〖相撲〗*shiko*; (a wrestler's) ritual stamping of the sumo ring with his right and then his left foot. ◐ 四股を踏む ritually stamp the surface of the wrestling ring.

しこうろくみん【四公六民】〔江戸時代の年貢制度〕an Edo period taxation system under which a farmer had to give 40% of the year's crops to the government and could retain the rest.

じごくみみ【地獄耳】〔すばやく聞きつけること〕《have》 big [sharp] ears; (人) a person who is quick to learn secrets;〔一度聞いたことを忘れないこと〕《have》 a fabulous memory; (人) a person who never forgets what he has heard. ◐ あの男は地獄耳だから気をつけなさい. Take care; that guy has sharp ears.

しごとおさめ【仕事納め】the last business day of the year. ◐ 通例会社の年末の仕事納めは 12 月 28 日である. In most cases, December 28 is the last business day of the year at offices.

しごとはじめ【仕事始め】the opening of business for the year; the first business day of the year. ◐ 官公庁の仕事始め the opening of government offices at the beginning of the year.

じざいかぎ【自在鉤】a pot hanger; an adjustable pothook; a pothook.

じざけ【地酒】the sake of the ⌈place [district]; (sake of) local brew; (a) ⌈locally brewed [boutique] sake.

しし【獅子】a lion; (雌) a lioness;〔異名〕the king of the beasts (百獣の王). ◐ 子獅子 a lion cub / 獅子身中の虫 a snake in *one*'s bosom; a treacherous confidant / 獅子奮迅の勢いで ⇨ ししふんじん / 獅子のような leonine; lionlike.

ししおどし【鹿威し】a length of bamboo, attached near its midpoint to a furlcrum above a stone (basin); the bamboo fills with water from a rivulet until it overbalances, the water spills out, and the bamboo rebounds, striking the stone with a loud report.

ししざ【獅子座】〖天・占星〗the Lion; Leo. ◐ 獅子座生まれの人 a Leo; a Leonian.

ししとう(がらし)【獅子唐(辛子)】a *shishito* pepper; a sweet Japanese ⌈chile [chilli] pepper.

じしばい【地芝居】a local Kabuki or marionette performance (by amateur players).

ししふんじん【獅子奮迅】獅子奮迅の勢いで with irresistible force; with furious energy;《口》like fury /獅子奮迅の活躍を見せる put on a display of「furious [frenzied] activity.

ししまい【獅子舞】a ritual dance at a shrine festival or at New Year's by a performer wearing a lion's mask; the Lion Dance.

しじみ【蜆】〚貝〛a corbicula clam.　■シジミ汁 a miso soup with corbicula.

じしゃく【磁石】a magnet;〔羅針盤〕a compass.　■棒磁石 a bar magnet.

じしゃぶぎょう【寺社奉行】a magistrate of shrines and temples (in the Edo period).

ししゃも【柳葉魚】〚魚〛a smelt.　◐子持ちししゃも a smelt with roe.

しじゅうくにち【四十九日】the forty-ninth day (after *somebody*'s death). ◐亡夫の四十九日の法要を営む hold a memorial service on the forty-ninth day after the death of *one*'s husband.

しじゅうしちし【四十七士】the forty-seven *rōnin* in the domain of Akō who in 1703 avenged their lord's death.

しじゅうはって【四十八手】1〔相撲の手〕the forty-eight techniques in the art of (sumo) wrestling;〔一般的に〕《know》all the tricks《of...》. 2〔人をあやつる法〕social tact; maneuvers; savoir-faire.

しじゅほうしょう【紫綬褒章】the Medal with Purple Ribbon (for academic or artistic excellence).

じしんばん【自身番】an Edo-period police「box [station].

じせいのうた【辞世の歌】a (31-syllable) death poem; a poem composed on *one*'s deathbed; a「farewell [deathbed] poem [tanka].

しそ【紫蘇】〔シソ科の 1 年草; 中国原産の食用植物〕(同属の総称) perilla; a beefsteak plant.　◐シソの実〔食材〕perilla [beefsteak] seeds / シソ (の)葉 (a)「perilla [beefsteak] leaf.

じぞう【地蔵】〚仏教〛〔地蔵菩薩〕*Jizō*; the Guardian Deity of Travelers and Children;〚Skt〛*Ksitigarbha*(-*bodhisattva*);〔石像〕a small stone statue, often wearing a red bib, representing *Jizō*.　■石地蔵 a stone statue of *Jizō*.　笠地蔵 a *Jizō* statue with a conical straw hat to protect it from rain and snow.　子安地蔵 *Jizō* the Patron of Pregnant Women.

六地蔵 *Jizō* of the Six States of Existence.　地蔵眉 a long,「curving [arched]」eyebrow tapering at the end.

じぞうがお【地蔵顔】a「plump [round]」cheerful face; a cheerful face.

しぞく【士族】a descendant of a samurai; a member of the samurai class.

じだいげき【時代劇】a costume play; a period adventure「drama [film]」; a period film.

じだいまつり【時代祭り】the Festival of the Ages; a festival presented by the Heian Shrine in Kyoto, in which a procession marches around the city, representing each of the historical periods of Japan.

したきりすずめ【舌切り雀】The「Tongueless [Tongue-Cut]」Sparrow; a Japanese folktale in which a sparrow whose tongue has been cut out punishes a dishonest old woman and rewards an honest old man.

じだこ【字凧】a kite with kanji or kana (written) on it.

しだし【仕出し】〔出前〕catering; delivering meals to order.　◐仕出しをする supply meals to order; cater 《for a large banquet》 / 仕出しを頼む[取る] order a meal (to be sent by a caterer); order catering 《for a party》 / 出前仕出つかまつります.〔掲示〕Dishes delivered (to order). ■仕出し弁当 a lunch delivered by a caterer.　仕出し屋[人] a caterer; 〔店〕a caterer's shop.　仕出し料理 food prepared by a caterer; catered food.

したまえ【下前】one half of the front of the kimono lapped under the other.

したまち【下町】a low-lying area of a city with small family-run shops and factories, particularly the area of eastern Tokyo near Tokyo Bay; the *shitamachi*.　▶「下町」に相当する英語は見当たらない. たとえば "downtown" と訳すことはできない.「下町育ちです」というようなことを述べるとすれば, I was brought up in the backstreets of Asakusa [Ueno, Tsukiji, etc.] のように言ってから, 説明をするよりない.　■下町言葉 the language spoken in the *shitamachi* area of Tokyo.　下町情緒 the friendly atmosphere of the *shitamachi* areas (of a city).　下町育ち a *shitamachi* bred person.　下町風 《in》 the *shitamachi*「style [fashion]」.

しちごさん【七五三】〔七五三の祝い〕a gala day for children of three, five and seven years of age, who dress up in traditional kimono and visit the local shrine.

しちごちょう【七五調】 the seven-five-syllabic meter characteristic of certain kinds of Japanese poetry. ◐ 七五調の詩 a「poem [verse] in 7-5 meter.

しちさん【七三】〔7と3の割合〕(a proportion of) seven to three;《split》seventy-thirty. ◐ 髪を七三に分ける part *one*'s hair at the side; wear *one*'s hair parted at the side.

しちてんばっとう【七転八倒】 ◐ 七転八倒の痛み《endure》terrible agony; (an) excruciating pain; (a) pain that makes *one* writhe in agony / 七転八倒の苦しみをする, 七転八倒して苦しむ writhe [throw *one*self about] in agony.

しちなんはっく【七難八苦】 all kinds of troubles; endless [a sea of] troubles.

しちふくじん【七福神】 the Seven「Deities [Gods] of Good Fortune; seven deities drawn from Buddhist, Shinto and Taoist traditions, typically shown on board a *takarabune* [" treasure ship"]. ▶ 恵比須, 寿老人, 大黒天, 毘沙門天, 福禄寿, 弁財天, 布袋(ほてい).

しちみとうがらし【七味唐辛子】 a mixture of red cayenne pepper and other spices, used to sprinkle over *udon* or *soba*, etc.

しちりん【七輪】 a small round charcoal stove made of clay or earthenware.

じちんさい【地鎮祭】 the ceremony of purifying a building site; a Shinto ground-breaking ceremony to pacify the local guardian spirits.

じついん【実印】 *one*'s「registered [legal] seal.

しっき【漆器】 lacquer (ware); lacquer (ed) [japan] ware; lacquer (work).

しっしん【湿疹】 eczema; humid [moist] tetter. ◐ 湿疹が出る eczema [a rash] breaks out.

じって【十手】 a short metal truncheon carried by low-ranking Edo-period police officials (*okappiki*) who arrested criminals.

しっぽうやき【七宝焼】 *cloisonné* ware. ◐ 七宝焼の花瓶 a *cloisonné* vase.

しっぽく【卓袱】 a Chinese table; a Chinese tablecloth. ◐ 卓袱料理 a Japanized Chinese dish served on large plates from which diners help themselves.

して【仕手】【シテ】〚能〛 the *shite*; the leading character in a Noh play; a

Noh protagonist.

しで【幣】〔神道でしめなわなどに下げる細長くした白い紙〕a zigzag chain cut from folded white paper and suspended from the straw rope marking off a sacred area (of a Shinto shrine).

じてんしゃ【自転車】a bicycle; a cycle;《口》a bike;〔motorcycle に対して〕"a「push-bike [push (bi)cycle]. ◐ 26 インチの自転車 a bicycle with 26-inch wheels / 自転車に乗る〔またがる〕get on [《文》mount] a bicycle;〔乗って走る〕ride a bicycle. ■**貸し自転車** a rental bicycle; bicycles for hire. **子供用自転車** a「child's [children's] bicycle. **電動ハイブリッド自転車**〔アシスト付き自転車〕a pedal-cycle with an auxiliary electric motor. **二人乗り用自転車** a tandem (bicycle). **補助輪付き自転車** a bicycle with training wheels. **自転車置き場** a bicycle park; a bicycle parking「place [area, lot, shed]; a parking place for bicycles. **自転車通学[通勤]** bicycling to「school [work]; commuting by bicycle. **自転車店[屋]** a bicycle shop. **自転車泥棒**〔盗むこと〕bicycle theft;〔盗む人〕a bicycle thief.

じてんしゃそうぎょう【自転車操業】precarious day-to-day management《of a shop [factory]》; surviving from one day to the next; barely getting by; scraping by on insufficient cash flow. ◐ この一年自転車操業でやってきた. We have just managed to stay afloat (by desperate measures) this year. | We have just managed to survive this year.

じどうぎゃくたい【児童虐待】child abuse; child-battering. ■**児童虐待者** a person who「abuses [batters] children.

じどうしゃ【自動車】a car; a motorcar; a motor vehicle; *an automobile; an auto《pl. ~s》;《口》a machine. ■**営業用自動車** a car for business (use);〔社用車〕a company car; a trade car. **貸し自動車** a rental car. **貨物自動車** a truck; a lorry. **電気自動車** an electric car. **乗合自動車** a bus; a motorbus; an autobus. **ボロ自動車**《口》a jalopy; a banger.

じどうしゃきょうしゅうじょ【自動車教習所】a driving school.

じどうはんばいき【自動販売機】a vending machine; an automat; a slot machine. ◐ たばこの自動販売機 a cigarette (vending) machine.

じどうポルノ【児童ポルノ】child pornography.

じどり【地鳥・地鶏】locally produced poultry.

しない【竹刀】a bamboo sword《for practcing the martial art kendo》.

しにくち【死に口】 the summoning by a (female) medium or shaman of the spirits of the dead.

しにせ【老舗】 an old [a long-established] store [shop]; a ⌈store [shop] with a tradition of long standing; an old establishment. ◐ 7代続いた老舗 an establishment which has been in the family for seven generations.

しにめ【死に目】 the moment of death. ◐ 死に目に会う be with *somebody* when he dies; be present at *somebody*'s death; attend *somebody*'s deathbed; close the eyes of 《*one*'s mother》 / 海外出張中で残念にも父の死に目に会えなかった. Sadly, I was unable to ⌈with my father when he died [at my father's deathbed] because I was abroad on business.

しのぎ【鎬】 the ridges on the sides of a sword blade. ◐ しのぎを削る compete ⌈viciously [ruthlessly]《with…》; vie《with… to do [for…]》 / 航空各社はいま顧客獲得でしのぎを削っている. There is cutthroat competition among the airlines for customers. | Airlines are competing ruthlessly for customers.

しばいぬ【柴犬】 a Shiba (Inu [dog]); a (little) brushwood dog.

しばえび【芝蝦】 a Shiba shrimp.

しばづけ【柴漬け】 assorted vegetables sliced up and pickled in salt with red *shiso*.

じビール【地ビール】 local [locally brewed] beer.

じびか【耳鼻科】〔耳鼻科学〕otorhinology;〔病院の〕the ear, nose, and throat department.

しびれ numbness;《get, have》pins and needles;〔病気の〕palsy; paralysis. ◐ 足にしびれが切れた. My legs have gone to sleep. | I've lost all sensation in my legs. | I have pins and needles in my legs. / しびれを切らす〔足に〕get pins and needles in *one*'s legs; *one*'s legs ⌈go to sleep [go numb];〔待ちあぐんでいらいらする〕cannot wait (any longer); run out of patience; lose (*one*'s) patience; grow impatient

しふく【仕服・仕覆】〔茶道〕a pouch used in the tea ceremony, usually of silk brocade or some other elegant material, for holding a tea caddy.

しぶん【士分】 the status of samurai;〔武士〕the samurai class.

しへい【紙幣】 paper money; (a) paper currency; a banknote; *a bill; ⁑a note. ◐ 1,000円紙幣 a thousand-yen ⌈*bill [⁑note] / 1,000円紙幣100枚 a hundred thousand-yen bills; a hundred bills of a thousand yen (each).

ジベタリアン〔地面に直接すわる若者を指す語〕a 「teenager [youngster] who sits or squats on the ground in a group with others.

しまあじ【縞鯵】〖魚〗a yellow jack.

しまうま【縞馬】〖動〗a zebra.

しまだ【島田】the *shimada* coiffure; an elaborate pompadour「hairstyle [coiffure]; originating in the Edo-period demimonde, it was later taken by unmarried women.

しまながし【島流し】exile「on [to] an island; banishment to an island. ● 島流しにする exile [banish]《a criminal》to an island; send《a political opponent》to「a prison island [an island prison colony] / 島流しになる be「exiled [banished] to an island.

しまもよう【縞模様】a striped pattern. ● 赤と白の縞模様 a pattern of red and white stripes / 縞模様のある striped; with a pattern of stripes / 縞模様のネクタイ a striped「tie [*necktie] / 派手な縞模様のシャツ a loud, striped shirt.

しまんろくせんにち【四万六千日】the festival day of *Kannon* on July 10th (when visiting a temple is thought to be as effective as visiting it on forty-six thousand other days).

しめかざり【注連飾り】a sacred rice-straw festoon with various auspicious symbols attached to it, typically hung over entrances or from Shinto household altars at the New Year.

しめさば【締め鯖・〆鯖】〖料理〗(pieces of) salted and vinegared mackerel.

しものく【下の句】the final two lines of a「waka [tanka].

しもふり【霜降り】● 霜降りの〔服地・髪〕pepper-and-salt / 霜降りの服 a pepper-and-salt suit. ■ 霜降り肉 marbled beef.

しもやけ【霜焼け】chilblains; frostbite. ● しもやけができる, しもやけになる〈局部が主語〉be affected with chilblains; be frostbitten;〈人が主語〉have chilblains《on *one*'s hands》/ 足指のしもやけがかゆい. The chilblains on my toes are itching.

しもやしき【下屋敷】a (daimyo's)「villa [suburban residence].

しもん【指紋】a fingerprint; a print; a (finger) mark; a dactylogram;〔親指の〕a thumb print.

じゃがいも〔ナス科の多年草; 南米アンデス高地原産の食用植物〕a potato

《*pl.* ~es》; a white [an Irish] potato. ◐ ゆでたてのじゃがいも freshly boiled potatoes / 新じゃがいも a new potato.

しゃく¹【勺】〔尺貫法における面積の単位〕a *shaku* 《*pl.* ~》 (=約 0.033 m²);〔尺貫法における容積の単位〕a *shaku* 《*pl.* ~》 (=18 cc).

しゃく²【尺】〔尺貫法における長さの単位〕a *shaku* 《*pl.* ~》 (=約 30.3 cm);〔尺度〕a measure; a rule; a scale;〔長さ〕length.

しゃくはち【尺八】〔縦笛〕a *shakuhachi*; a Japanese vertical bamboo flute with five or seven finger holes.

しゃけん【車検】〔自動車の車体検査〕(an official, a regular) vehicle inspection;〔日本の〕a *shaken*; a Japanese Car Inspection (略: JCI). ◐ 車を車検に出す take a car in for its inspection. ■車検証 a vehicle inspection ["an MOT] certificate;〔車体に貼る〕a vehicle inspection sticker.

しゃこ【蝦蛄】〖動〗a squilla 《*pl.* ~s, -lae》; a mantis「crab [shrimp].

じゃこう【麝香】musk. ◐ じゃこうのにおいがする be musky; be scented with musk; smell「of [like] musk.

しゃし【社司】a Shinto priest; the chief priest of a Shinto shrine.

しゃじょうあらし【車上荒らし】〔行為〕theft from a vehicle;〔人〕a vehicle thief (who steals the contents of a vehicle).

しゃちほこ【鯱】a fabled fish with a lionlike head, dragonlike sharp scales along the back, and an arched tail that points skyward (used as a castle roof decoration).

しゃちゅう【社中】〔結社の仲間〕a clique; a coterie;〔芸人の〕a troupe; a company.

しゃっくり a hiccup; a hiccough. ~する hiccup; hiccough; have the hiccups. ◐ しゃっくりを止める stop *one*'s hiccups / しゃっくりをしながら言う say between hiccups.

しゃでん【社殿】(the main building of) a Shinto shrine; a sanctuary.

じゃのめ【蛇の目】〔太い輪の形〕a double ring; a bull's eye;〔蛇の目がさ〕an oiled paper umbrella with a bull's-eye design.

しゃふ【車夫】a ricksha(w)「man [puller].

しゃぶしゃぶ〖料理〗*shabu-shabu*; a hot-pot dish paper-thin slices of beef or pork swished in boiling broth (hence the onomatopoeic "shabu-shabu") then dipped in sauce and eaten.

シャボンだま【シャボン玉】a soap bubble. ◐ シャボン玉がこわれた.

The soap bubble「burst [popped]. / シャボン玉を飛ばす[吹く] blow (soap) bubbles / シャボン玉を突いて割る prick [burst] a bubble.

しゃみせん【三味線】a three-stringed musical instrument with a long neck and a sound box covered with cat skin; a samisen.

しゃれぼん【洒落本】a novel, written in dialogue form, whose subject is the demimonde of the late Edo period.

じゃんけん rock-paper-scissors; janken; a finger game in which rock (a fist) loses to paper (five fingers) but beats scissors (two fingers) while scissors tops paper.

しゅうか【秀歌】an excellent [a superb] tanka; a gem among tankas.

しゅうぎ【祝儀】**1**〔祝いごと〕(a) celebration; festivities;〔婚礼〕a marriage ceremony; a wedding. ◐祝儀不(ﾌ)祝儀すべての場合に on all occasions, joyous or mournful.　**2**〔祝い物〕a (congratulatory) gift《of money》; a present.　**3**〔心付け〕a tip; a gratuity; a consideration. ◐祝儀をやる[あげる, 出す] give *somebody* a tip [gratuity]; tip《a waiter》/ ご祝儀をいただく[もらう] receive a「tip [gratuity] / 祝儀を包む wrap up a gift of money《for *somebody*》; give a gift of money《to *somebody*》/ 祝儀をはずむ give a huge tip; be a big tipper.　■祝儀袋 an envelope「containing [for] a gift of money.

しゅうく【秀句】〔優れた俳句〕an excellent haiku.

じゅうごや【十五夜】**1**〔陰暦15日の夜〕the night of the full moon. ◐十五夜の月 a full moon (on the fifteenth night);〔秋分ごろの〕the harvest moon.　**2**〔陰暦8月15日の夜〕the 15th night of the eighth lunar month.

しゅうじ【習字】penmanship; calligraphy. ◐習字がじょうず[へた]だ be a「good [poor] calligrapher; have「good [poor] handwriting.　■英習字 English penmanship.

じゅうしょく【住職】the「chief [head] priest [incumbent]《of a Buddhist temple》; the superior《of a temple》.

しゅうでん【終電】the last train (of the day). ◐終電に乗り遅れる miss the last train (of the day).

じゅうでん【充電】a charge; charging; recharging.　～する〔蓄電池に〕charge《an accumulator》(with electricity); give a charge of electricity to《a storage battery》.　■充電器 a (battery) charger.　充電式の rechargeable. ◐充電式シェーバー a rechargeable shaver.

じゅうどう【柔道】judo. ■柔道家 a judo「expert [wrestler, competitor]; a *jūdōka* 《*pl.* ~》. 柔道着 a judo「uniform [outfit, suit]; *one*'s *jūdōgi*. 柔道場 a judo「hall [dojo].

じゅうにし【十二支】the twelve「signs [symbols, branches, animals] of the Chinese zodiac.
十二支は次のとおり:
子(ね) the Rat; 丑(うし) the Ox; 寅(とら) the Tiger; 卯(う) the Rabbit, the Hare; 辰(たつ) the Dragon; 巳(み) the Snake; 午(うま) the Horse; 未(ひつじ) the Sheep; 申(さる) the Monkey; 酉(とり) the Cock, the Rooster; 戌(いぬ) the Dog; 亥(い) the Boar.

じゅうにひとえ【十二単】〔装束〕a layered kimono (worn by a court lady in the Heian period).

じゅうはちばん【十八番】〔第十八番目〕the eighteenth; No. 18;〔十八篇〕eighteen pieces;〔歌舞伎十八番〕a repertoire of eighteen classical pieces; a Kabuki drawing card;〔おはこ〕*one*'s「specialty [forte]; *one*'s「favorite [best] trick [performance]. ◐十八番をやる show off *one*'s specialty / あれはあの人の十八番です. That's his forte. |〔歌など〕That's his favorite 《karaoke》song. / それなら私の十八番だ. That's my「specialty [favorite].

しゅうぶんのひ【秋分の日】〔9月22日か23日〕 Autumnal Equinox Day.

じゅうみんきほんだいちょうカード【住民基本台帳カード】a Basic Resident Registration Card; a Jūki Card.

じゅうみんひょう【住民票】a certificate of residence. ◐住民票を移す move [transfer] *one*'s certificate of residence.

しゅこう【酒肴】〔酒と肴〕food and「alcohol [drinks]; wine and food;〔酒の肴〕an accompaniment to「a drink [alcohol]; something to go with a drink.

じゅず【数珠】a (Buddhist) rosary; (a string of) Buddhist prayer beads.

しゅっさん【出産】giving birth; having a baby; childbirth; (a) birth; (a) delivery; (a) confinement. ~する have a baby; give birth to 《a child》; 《文》be delivered of 《a baby》; be brought to bed (of a child). ■出産予定日 an expected date of「confinement [birth, delivery]; a [*one*'s] due date; the date a baby is due. ◐出産予定日は3月6日です. My baby is due on March 6.

しゅっちょう【出張】a business ˹trip; an official trip [tour]. ～する make ˹a business [an official] trip 《to...》; go [travel] 《to...》 on (official) business. ■**海外出張** an overseas business trip; a business trip abroad. **短期出張** a ˹short [brief] business trip. **長期出張** a long [an extended] business trip. **日帰り出張** a one-day business trip.

じゅどうきつえん【受動喫煙】passive smoking.

しゅふ¹【主夫】a househusband;〔子がいる〕a stay-at-home [an at-home] dad; *《口》(a) Mr. Mom.

しゅふ²【主婦】〔家庭の〕a housewife; a homemaker;〔客に対し〕the hostess. ◐働く主婦 a working housewife; a housewife with a job outside the house. ■**専業主婦** a full-time housewife. **主婦業** ◐主婦業に専念する be a full-time housewife; dedicate oneself wholly to being a housewife.

しゅみだん【須弥壇】a dais for a Buddhist image.

しゅらもの【修羅物】the Noh play genre in which the ghost of a samurai general sings of battles as he dances.

しゅんが【春画】an erotic picture;〈集合的に〉pornography.

しゅんぎく【春菊】〔キク科の1年草；地中海地方原産の食用・観賞植物〕a garland chrysanthemum.

じゅんきゅう【準急】a local express (train).

しゅんぶんのひ【春分の日】〔3月20日か21日〕Vernal Equinox Day.

じゅんまい【純米】■**純米吟醸酒** *ginjō* sake with no added alcohol. **純米酒**〔醸造アルコールを含まず，米・米こうじのみから造る〕*junmai* sake; sake in which the only ingredients are rice and yeast. ■**純米大吟醸酒** *daiginjō* sake with no added alcohol.

しょいん【書院】〔書斎〕a study;〔客間〕a drawing room. ■**書院造り** a feature of Edo-period residential architecture that includes a tokonoma alcove.

しょう¹【升】〔尺貫法における容積の単位〕a *shō* 《*pl.* ～》(＝約 1.8 l). ◐ 米3升 three *shō* of rice.

しょう²【笙】a type of reed instrument with 17 bamboo pipes; introduced from China in the Nara period, it is played both by exhaling and inhaling.

しょう³【簫】a *shō no fue*; a traditional Chinese and Japanese wind instrument resembling a panpipe.

じょう【丈】〔尺貫法における長さの単位〕a *jō* 《*pl.* ~》(=約 3.03 m); 〔長さ・丈(ﾀｹ)〕(the) length; (the) measure.

しょいちい【正一位】under the ritsuryō system the first rank in the hierarchy of the government as well as the highest rank given to a shrine.

しょうエネ(ルギー)【省エネ(ルギー)】energy「conservation [saving]; saving (of) energy; conservation of energy. ■ **省エネ(ルギー)住宅** an energy-efficient[-saving] house.

しょうが【生姜】〔ショウガ科の多年草; 熱帯アジア原産の香辛料植物〕ginger;〔香辛料〕ginger. ○ しょうが色の gingery; ginger-colored. ■ **おろし生姜** grated ginger.

しょうがつ【正月】〔一月〕January (略: Jan.);〔新年〕the New Year; the first few days of January when the New Year's holiday is celebrated. ■ **正月休み** the New Year holidays. **正月料理** (special) New Year's dishes.

しょうかどうべんとう【松花堂弁当】a Shōkadō lunch box; a lunch box divided into four square compartments (said to have been favored by an early Edo-period priest of that name).

じょうかまち【城下町】a castle town; the capital (town) of a daimyo's fief; the seat of a daimyo's government. ○ 金沢は前田藩の城下町です. Kanazawa is the castle town of the Maeda clan.

しょうがやき【生姜焼き】〔豚肉の〕pork fried with ginger and soy sauce; ginger-fried pork.

しょうがゆ【生姜湯】(hot) ginger tea.

しょうき【鍾馗】Shōki the Plague-Queller; a legendary figure with big eyes, a thick beard, a black hat, and knee-high boots reputed to have the power of driving away the God of Plague.

しょうぎ【将棋】*shōgi*; a board game resembling chess that was introduced to Japan in the Nara period.

しょうぎだおし【将棋倒し】○ 将棋倒しになる fall down one upon another; fall [be knocked] over like「dominoes [ninepins] / 衝突と同時に通路の乗客は将棋倒しになった. When the crash occurred, people in the aisles knocked each other down like so many dominoes.

しょうきゃく【正客】a guest of honor.

しょうぐん【将軍】〔大将〕a general;〔武家時代の〕a shogun; a generalissimo 《*pl.* ~s》.

しょうけいもじ【象形文字】a hieroglyph; a hieroglyphic (character); 〈集合的に〉hieroglyphics.

じょうご【上戸】1 〔酒飲み〕a drinker; a tippler; a sot; a boozer; a bacchant; a votary of Bacchus; a wet.　◐ 君は上戸か下戸か. Are you a drinker or a nondrinker?　2 〔酒の上でのくせ〕泣き上戸 a crying drink.

しょうこう【焼香】incense burning; burning powdered incense at a Buddhist funeral or memorial service.　~する burn [offer] incense 《for the repose of a departed soul》.　■焼香壇[机, 台] a censer [an incense-burner] stand.

しょうこんしゃ【招魂社】one of many Shinto shrines dedicated to the spirits of the war dead (in 1939 they were renamed Gokoku-Jinja).

しょうじ【障子】a shoji 《*pl.* ~(s)》; a sliding paper「door [screen] (with translucent white paper pasted on to a lattice frame).

しょうしか【少子化】a「smaller number of [trend toward having fewer] children; a「declining [falling, decreasing, dwindling] birthrate [fertility rate, population of children]; a drop in the birthrate; a baby shortage; a lack of children.　◐ 猛烈な勢いで高齢化と少子化が進んでいる. The population is aging and the birthrate declining precipitately.　■少子化社会 a society with「fewer children [a declining birthrate].　少子化対策 measures to counteract the falling birthrate.

じょうしきまく【定式幕】〔歌舞伎の引き幕の一種〕the principal (draw) curtain for a Kabuki stage.

しょうじんあげ【精進揚げ】deep-fried vegetables; vegetable tempura.

しょうじんりょうり【精進料理】a vegetable dish; vegetarian food; 〔菜食〕a vegetarian diet.

じょうだい【城代】1 〔城を守護する者〕a keeper of a castle; a castle warden; a deputy representing a「castellan [governor of a castle] in his absence.　2 〔江戸幕府〕the keeper of the shogunal castle at Osaka or Sumpu.

じょうだいがろう【城代家老】an elder councilor charged with responsibility for a daimyo's castle when his lord is absent in Edo. [⇨ さんきんこうたい]

しょうちくばい【松竹梅】a pine, a bamboo, and「an apricot [a plum] tree; the three trees that bring good fortune; 〔料理などの3つの等級〕

the「upper [top],「medium [middle], and「lower [lesser] grades; first, second, and third class.

しょうちゅう【焼酎】*shōchū*; (Japanese) spirits distilled from sweet potatoes, rice, etc; distilled「liquor [spirits]. ◐ 焼酎のお湯割り *shōchū* (mixed) with hot water.

しょうでん【昇殿】昇殿を許される〔神社〕be granted the privilege of stepping into the「holy of holies [sanctum sanctorum] of a Shinto shrine;〔宮廷〕be admitted to Court (granted to aristocrats of fifth rank or lower).

じょうとうしき【上棟式】the ceremony of putting up the ridge beam [ridgepole]; celebration of the completion of the framework 《of a house》. ◐ 昨日上棟式が行われた. The ceremonial raising of the roof beam took place yesterday.

しょうにん【上人・聖人】a saint; a holy person; a high priest. ◐ 日蓮上人 The Venerable Nichiren.

しょうひぜい【消費税】a consumption tax [duty]; an excise tax; (a) sales tax; (a) value added tax (略: VAT).

しょうぶ【菖蒲】〔サトイモ科の多年草〕sweet flag; sweet sedge; a calamus 《*pl.* -mi》. ■菖蒲湯 bathing in bath water scented with *shōbu* leaves often done on 5 May as a ritual purification.

しょうぶふく【勝負服】〖競馬〗silks;〔ここ一番というときに着る服〕*one*'s lucky「clothes [outfit, suit, etc.].

しょうへい【障屏】sliding doors, screens or other partitions (in a Japanese house). ■障屏画 paintings on sliding doors or screens or on single- or multi-panel free-standing screens.

しょうゆ【醤油】soy (sauce); shoyu. ■醤油入れ a small 《fish-shaped, bottle-shaped》 soy sauce container (accompanying a box lunch). 醤油差し[つぎ] a soy (sauce) pot [cruet]. 醤油樽 a soy keg. 醤油だれ a soy-based sauce 《for dipping *shabu-shabu* into》.

しょうりょうながし【精霊流し】launching a paper lantern or votive offerings in a straw boat on the water to see off the spirits of *one*'s ancestors on the last day of the *Bon* Festival.

じょうるり【浄瑠璃】(a) *Jōruri*; a type of dramatic recitation, accompanied by a samisen, that is associated with the Japanese puppet theater.

しょうわじだい【昭和時代】the Shōwa period (1926–1989).

しょきばらい【暑気払い】forgetting [《口》beating] the summer heat. ▶暑気払いに to forget [《口》beat] the summer heat.

じょきん【除菌】disinfection; 〖医〗sterile filtration. ～する disinfect. ■除菌イオン antimicrobial ions. ▶除菌イオン発生装置 an antimicrobial-ion generator.

しょく【初句】〔和歌・俳句の最初の五音〕the first five syllables 《of a tanka》; 〔詩の第一句〕the first line 《of a poem》.

しょくもう【植毛】〔毛髪を植えつけること〕hair implantation.

しょくもつせんい【食物繊維】dietary fiber. ▶食物繊維飲料 a fiber drink.

しょだん【初段】the first dan; the lowest grade of the senior class 《in judo, etc.》.

しょちゅうみまい【暑中見舞】an inquiry [a letter of inquiry] after *somebody*'s health in the hot season; 〔状〕a summer greeting card.

しょっつる【塩汁】a sauce made in Akita from salted and fermented fish meat. ■しょっつる鍋 〖料理〗a pot of fish, vegetables, and tofu prepared in a *shottsuru*-based soup.

しょどう【書道】calligraphy; the art of writing with a brush.

しょなのか, しょなぬか【初七日】the seventh day after *somebody*'s death (counting the day of death as well); a memorial service held on the sixth day after death. ▶初七日の法要を営む hold a memorial service on the sixth day after *somebody*'s death.

じょのくち【序の口】1 〖相撲〗*jonokuchi*, the lowest rank on the「*banzuke* [official listing of sumo ranks]. 2 〔はじまり〕the beginning; the start; the「first [initial] stage. ▶これで驚いちゃだめだよ、まだほんの序の口なんだから. Don't let this surprise you, it's still only the beginning!

じょや【除夜】New Year's Eve. ▶除夜の鐘 the New Year's Eve bells; the bells「speeding [ringing out] the old year / 除夜の鐘を鳴らす[打つ] ring out the old year.

しらあえ【白和え】a salad dressed with white sesame, tofu, and white miso.

しらが【白髪】(a)「gray [white, hoary] hair. ▶白髪交じりの髪 grizzled [grizzly] hair; hair「shot [streaked] with gray / 白髪の老人 a「gray-haired [white-headed] old「man [woman] / 白髪を抜く pull out a white hair / 白髪を染める〔自分で〕dye *one*'s「gray [white] hair《black》;〔染めてもらう〕have *one*'s (gray) hair dyed《black》.

しらこ【白子】1〔タラ・フグ・アンコウなどの魚類の精巣で食用〕 milt《of fish》; soft roe.   ◐白子を持った魚 a soft-roed fish. **2**〔人間〕an albino《*pl.* ~s》;〔病気〕albinism.

しらす【白子】a young sardine; a whitebait《pl. ~》. ■**白子ぼし** dried young sardines.

しらたき【白滝】〔糸状に加工した白いこんにゃく〕noodles made from konjak starch, often used in sukiyaki.

しらたま【白玉】〔だんご〕rice-flour dumplings. ■**白玉粉** refined rice flour.

しらは【白羽】a white feather. ■**白羽の矢** a white-feathered arrow. ◐…に白羽の矢を立てる single *somebody* out for《a post》; mark *somebody* out for《a position, a mission》/ 白羽の矢が立つ be「singled [marked] out / 新社長のいすには北原氏に白羽の矢が立った. For the company's new president the choice has fallen on Mr. Kitahara.

しらみつぶし【虱潰し】◐しらみつぶしに one by one; thoroughly; exhaustively / しらみつぶしに調べる comb《a place for weapons》; go over《a house》with a fine-tooth comb《looking for *something*》/ 一軒一軒しらみつぶしに回る go from house to house《in search of *somebody*》.

しりとり【尻取り】しりとり(遊び)をする play a game in which one responds to a word with another that begins with the same syllable as *one*'s opponent's ends.

しりょく【視力】sight; eyesight; vision; visual「power [acuity]. ◐視力が弱い have「bad [weak, poor] eyesight; be weak-sighted / 視力が普通だ have normal「vision [eyesight] / 視力を失う lose *one*'s eyesight; lose the use of *one*'s eyes / 視力を回復する recover *one*'s sight / 視力を検査する test *somebody*'s eyesight / 左目の視力が弱くなってきた. My eyesight in my left eye has grown weaker.

しるこ【汁粉】a sweet porridge of adzuki-bean paste thinned with water; eaten hot with rice-flour dumplings. ■**田舎汁粉** country-style *shiruko* (in which the beans are only roughly crushed). **汁粉屋** a *shiruko* shop.

しろ【城】a castle;〔城砦〕a citadel; a stronghold; a fortress.

しろあり【白蟻】a white ant; a termite.

しろがすり【白飛白】a white kimono with splash patterns.

しろくま【白熊】a「white [polar] bear.

しろざけ【白酒】white sake (made from sake and rice malt, and served on 3 March at the Doll Festival).

しろじ【白地】a white (back)ground.

しろたえ【白妙】〔白布〕white cloth;〔白色〕white. ◐白妙の富士 snow-mantled[-capped] Mt. Fuji.

しろたび【白足袋】《a pair of》white tabi.

しろぶさ【白房】〖相撲〗the white tassel hanging from the southwest corner of the roof over a sumo ring.

しろみ【白身】〔木材の〕sapwood;〔卵の〕the (egg) white; albumen;〔鶏肉などの〕white meat;〔豚肉の〕fat. ◐卵の白身 the white of an egg;(食材) egg white. ■**白身魚** a white-[light-]meat fish.

しろみそ【白味噌】white miso.

しろむく【白無垢】an all-white kimono; a pure-white dress. ◐白無垢の花嫁 a bride in white.

しわ【皺】〔皮膚などの〕wrinkles; lines; furrows / 目じりのしわ wrinkles at the corners of *one*'s eyes; crow's-feet / 目元の小じわ fine wrinkles around *one*'s eyes / 眉間にしわを寄せる knit *one*'s brows.

しんうち【真打】〔寄席などで最後に演じる人〕the star; the「star [lead] attraction; *the headliner, ‖the topliner.

しんえん【神苑】a garden attached to a Shinto shrine; a sacred garden.

じんがね【陣鐘】an alarm bell [a gong] sounded as a call to arms to encamped warriors.

しんかん【神官】a Shinto「priest [ritualist].

しんかんせん【新幹線】the Shinkansen; the Bullet Train. ◐東海道[上越]新幹線 the「Tokaido [Joetsu] Shinkansen.

じんぎ【神祇】the「gods [deities] of heaven and earth.

しんきゅう【鍼灸・針灸】acupuncture and moxibustion. ■**鍼灸マッサージ** acupuncture, moxibustion and massage. ◐鍼灸マッサージ師 an acupuncture, moxibustion, and massage therapist.

じんぐう【神宮】〔やしろ〕a Shinto shrine. ◐明治神宮 Meiji Shrine.

しんくうパック【真空パック】〔食品などの〕vacuum packing; gas flushing;〔袋〕a vacuum pack; a gas flushed package.

しんこ【新香】pickled vegetables; vegetables pickled in brine.

しんじいけ【心字池】a lake in a traditional Japanese garden, shaped like the kanji character for "heart".

しんしき【神式】Shinto rites.

しんしきけっこん【神式結婚】a Shinto-style wedding.

じんじゃ【神社】a Shinto「shrine [temple]. ◐ 靖国神社 Yasukuni Shrine.

しんじゅう【心中】〔一家の〕(a) family suicide;〔恋人同士の〕(a) lovers' suicide; (a) double suicide. 〜する die together 《for love》; commit double suicide. ■一家心中 (a)(collective) family suicide. 親子心中 (a) parent-child suicide. 無理心中 a murder-suicide. 心中未遂 an attempted double suicide.

しんじゅうもの【心中物】a love suicide「drama [story]; a *Jōruri* or Kabuki double suicide drama.

しんじょ【糁薯・真薯】〖料理〗a kind of fish-cake made from ground fish or prawn combined with grated yam, flavored and steamed or boiled; *shinjo*. ■海老しんじょ shrimp [prawn, lobster] *shinjo*.

しんしょく【神職】a Shinto priest; Shinto priesthood.

しんたい【神体】a *shintai* 《*pl*. 〜(s)》; an object of worship in a Shinto shrine which a deity is believed to inhabit.

じんだいこ【陣太鼓】a war drum.

しんちくいわい【新築祝い】a gathering to celebrate the completion of a new house; a housewarming (party).

しんちゃ【新茶】the first tea of the season; newly picked (spring) tea.

じんちゅうみまい【陣中見舞】a「visit to [gift for]《an active-duty soldier, a student studying for exams》. ◐ 選挙事務所への陣中見舞 a「visit [gift] to an election campaign headquarters to offer support.

しんてん【親展】〔封筒の表書き〕Confidential. ◐「親展」と書かれている手紙 a letter marked "Confidential" / 親展の confidential; personal; private. ■親展書 a「confidential [personal] letter.

しんでんづくり【寝殿造り】the architectural type of a Heian period aristocratic mansion.

しんとう¹【神灯】〔神前の〕a「sacred [shrine] lantern;〔祭礼の〕a festival lantern.

しんとう²【神道】Shinto; Shintoism; the traditional polytheistic religion of Japan.

しんないぶし【新内節】〔浄瑠璃の一派〕the Shinnai style of *Jōruri* chanting.

じんばおり【陣羽織】a surcoat worn over armor 《in feudal Japan》.

しんぷ【新婦】a bride. ◐新婦のお色直し a bride's change of dress during a wedding reception.

しんぶつこんこう【神仏混淆】the syncretism of Shinto with Buddhism.

じんべえ【甚兵衛】men's summer wear consisting of knee-length shorts and short-sleeved jacket, often worn at festivals.

しんまい【新米】**1**〔米〕new rice; the first rice of the year. **2**〔新入り〕a beginner; a「new [green, raw] hand; a novice; a fledgling; *a tenderfoot; a freshman; ʺa fresher; *《口》a greenhorn; a rookie;《文》a neophyte;〔工員〕a「new [green] hand; a new [the latest] recruit;〔新参者〕a newcomer.

しんやスーパー【深夜スーパー】a late-night supermarket.

じんりきしゃ【人力車】a jinrikisha; a rickshaw. ■人力車引き〔人〕a rickshaw「man [puller].

しんりんよく【森林浴】walking in the「woods [forest(s)] for therapeutic purposes [as therapy, to soothe the spirit]. ◐森林浴をする walk in the「woods [forest] for therapeutic purposes; go for a walk in the woods《to treat stress》.

しんろう【新郎】a bridegroom. ■新郎新婦 the bride and「bridegroom [groom]; a bridal pair;(結婚式後の)the happy couple.

す

す【酢】 vinegar. ◐ サバを酢で締める pickle [marinate] mackerel in vinegar. ■米酢 rice vinegar. りんご酢 cider vinegar. 酢和え〔事〕dressing《vegetables》with vinegar;〔物〕vegetables dressed with vinegar.

すいか【西瓜】 a watermelon. ◐ すいかを割る split open a watermelon.

すいきんくつ【水琴窟】 a device employing running water from a garden basin which drips into an urn buried upside down, producing a sound similar to that of a koto.

すいしょう【水晶】〖鉱〗〔石英〕(rock) crystal. ◐ 水晶のような crystalline; crystal《stream》. ■水晶占い〔事〕crystal gazing;〔人〕a crystal gazer. 水晶時計 a「crystal [quartz] clock [chronometer]; a quartz watch.

すいせん【水仙】〖植〗a narcissus 《*pl.* narcissuses, narcissi》; a daffodil (ラッパズイセン); a jonquil (キズイセン).

すいぼくが【水墨画】 a painting in「*sumi* [India ink]; an Indian ink painting.

すいみんやく【睡眠薬】 hypnotics; sleeping pills.

すいもの【吸い物】 broth; soup. ◐ 鯛(たい)の吸い物 sea-bream soup / 吸い物を吸う eat soup / 吸い物椀 a soup bowl.

すえぜん【据え膳】 a meal set before one; what others have arranged for one. ◐ 据え膳食わぬは男の恥. Shameful is he who spurns a woman's invitation [advances].

すがたづくり【姿造り】〖料理〗sashimi arranged in the shape of the fish from which it was cut.

すがたり【素語り】 a *Jōruri* recital without samisen accompaniment.

すぎ【杉】〔スギ科の常緑高木; 日本固有〕a「Japanese cedar [red cedar, cryptomeria]; a *sugi* 《*pl.* -(s)》.

すぎあや【杉綾】 ■杉綾縫い (a)「herringbone [catch] stitch. **杉綾模様** a herringbone pattern.

すぎかふん【杉花粉】《be allergic to》*sugi* [cedar] pollen. ■**杉花粉症** *sugi* [cedar] pollen allergy; hay fever.

すきや【数寄屋】〔茶室〕a tea-ceremony「room [hut];〔茶室作りの建物〕a house built in the style of a tea-ceremony hut. ■**数寄屋造り** the *sukiya* style of construction.

すきやき【鋤焼き】 sukiyaki; a meal, cooked in a pot at table, of sliced beef, toasted tofu, and vegetables, flavored with soy sauce, and dipped in raw, beaten egg.

すけべい, すけべ【助平】〔好色〕lechery; lewdness;〔好色家〕a「lecherous [lewd] person; a lecher; a satyr. ◐ **～な** bawdy; lecherous; lewd; lustful; lascivious; *《俗》horny. ■**ど助平**〔きわめて好色な人〕a lecher; a sex fiend; a pervert;《口》a perv. ◐ **ど助平な** filthy; perverted. **助平根性**〔好色〕lechery; lewdness;〔気が多く貪欲なこと〕greed.

すごろく【双六】 *sugoroku*; a traditional board game in which pieces are advanced by throwing dice; a Japanese backgammon / **すごろくをする** play *sugoroku*. ■**絵すごろく** ⇨ えすごろく.

すさのおのみこと【素戔嗚尊・須佐之男命】★Susanoo-no-mikoto; the son of Izanagi-no-mikoto and Izanami-no-mikoto, and younger brother to Amaterasu-oomikami, the Sun Goddess.

すし【鮨・寿司】 sushi; (raw) fish on vinegared rice. ■**鮨種** (seafood used in) sushi toppings. **鮨飯** sushi rice. **鮨屋** a sushi「shop [bar].

すじこ【筋子】 salmon roe.

すしづめ【鮨詰め】 鮨詰めになっている〈人などが主語〉be packed like sardines;〈場所が主語〉be jam-packed《with…》. ◐ **すし詰めの電車** a jam-packed train; a train「crammed [jammed] with passengers.

すすき【薄】〔イネ科の多年草〕miscanthus; (Japanese) silver grass. ■**枯れすすき** withered miscanthus.

すずき【鱸】〖魚〗a Japanese sea bass.

すずむし【鈴虫】 a bell cricket.

すずめ【雀】 a (Japanese) sparrow; a tree sparrow. ◐ **雀が鳴いていた.** Sparrows were「chirping [twittering]. **雀の涙ほどの** only a tiny amount of…; a mere particle of…; a modicum of…; an atom of….

すずめばち【雀蜂】〔スズメバチ科のハチ〕a wasp; a (yellow) hornet; a yellow jacket.

すずらん【鈴蘭】〔ユリ科の多年草〕(同属の総称) a lily-of-the-valley 《*pl.* lilies-of-the-valley》.

すずり【硯】an inkstone; an ink slab. ■硯石 an inkstone. 硯箱 an inkstone case.

すそまわし【裾回し】the lower lining of a kimono.

すそわた【裾綿】cotton padding inserted at the hem of the main panels of a kimono.

すだれ【簾】a reed「screen [portière]; a「rattan [bamboo] blind. ■すだれ頭〔バーコード・ヘア〕a combover.

ずつう【頭痛】(a) headache; (an) ache in *one*'s head; a pain in the head. ◐割れるような頭痛 a「splitting [racking] headache. ■頭痛薬 (a) headache medicine;〔錠剤〕a headache pill.

すっぽん【鼈】〘動〙a Chinese softshell turtle. ■月とすっぽん ◐両者は月とすっぽんだ[月とすっぽんほど違う] The two are as different as「day and night [ⁿchalk and cheese]. | They are completely different. | There is a world of difference between the two. すっぽん料理 a turtle dish.

すなかぶり【砂被り】〘相撲〙a ringside seat 《where a spectator might be sprinkled with sand kicked up by the sumo wrestlers》.

すなどけい【砂時計】an hourglass; a sandglass.

すなば【砂場】a sandbox; a sandpile;〔砂掘り場〕a sandpit. ◐砂場で遊ぶ play in a sandbox.

すね【脛】the leg; the shank;〔向こう脛〕the shin. ◐すねに傷を持つ have「a guilty [something on *one*'s] conscience; have a stain on *one*'s past; have a skeleton in *one*'s closet.

すねかじり【脛嚙り】a sponger; a hanger-on 《*pl.* hangers-on》. ◐あいつは親のすねかじりだ. He「sponges [lives] on his parents.

すのもの【酢の物】a vinegared dish.

すべりだい【滑り台】**1**〔進水式の〕a launching platform; sliding [launching] ways. **2**〔子供の遊び台〕a (playground) slide. ◐滑り台で滑る slide [play] on a slide.

スポこん【スポ根】〔スポーツ根性〕fighting spirit 《in sports》. ■スポ根物 a sports-hero story.

すましじる【澄まし汁】clear soup.
すみ【墨】〔汁〕*sumi*; black ink; India(n) [Chinese, China, Japan] ink;〔固形〕an ink stick. ▶墨を磨(ｽ)る rub an ink stick in water to make ink; prepare liquid ink from an ink stick, an inkstone, and water.
すみえ【墨絵】an India(n)-ink drawing; an ink [a *sumi*] painting. ▶墨絵の山水 a landscape brushed in「*sumi* [India ink]. ■墨絵画家 a *sumi-e* painter; a chiaroscurist in India ink.
すみそ【酢味噌】vinegared「miso [bean paste]. ■酢味噌あえ dressing 《vegetables》with vinegared miso.
すみれ【菫】〔スミレ科の多年草〕(スミレ属植物の総称) a violet. ■三色すみれ a pansy. すみれ色 a violet color; violet.
すめし【酢飯】vinegared rice.
すもう【相撲】〔競技〕sumo (wrestling);〔力士〕⇨ 相撲取り. ■相撲取り，お相撲さん〔力士〕a sumo wrestler. 相撲番付 a sumo ranking chart. ▶上から幕内・十両・幕下・三段目・序二段・序の口 に分かれる．幕内には上から 横綱・大関・関脇・小結・前頭 がある．The six grades of sumo wrestlers are, from the top: Makunouchi, Jŭryō, Makushita, Sandanme, Jonidan, Jonokuchi.　The five rankings of Makunouchi wrestlers are, from the top, Yokozuna, Ōzeki, Sekiwake, Komusubi, and Maegashira.　相撲部屋 a sumo stable.
すもも【李】〔バラ科の落葉小高木；中国原産の果樹〕a Japanese plum;〔実〕a plum.
するめ【鯣】dried squid.
スロー・ライフ (a) slow life. ▶スロー・ライフを送る live a slow life.
すん【寸】〔尺貫法における長さの単位〕a *sun* 《*pl.* ~》(＝約 3.03 cm).
すんし【寸志】a token of *one*'s「gratitude [appreciation, esteem]; a small present. ▶寸志．〔包みの上書き〕With compliments.

せ

せいがいは【青海波】〔衣服の文様〕a dye pattern of imbricated waves.

せいかつしゅうかんびょう【生活習慣病】a lifestyle-related illness. ▶成人病の新しい呼び名.

せいかんせんしょう【性感染症】a sexually transmitted disease (略: STD).

せいがんのかまえ【正眼の構え】〚剣道〛the "aiming-at-the-eye" posture.

せいこううどく【晴耕雨読】～する work in the fields in fine weather and read at home in wet weather (an image of an idyillic pastoral life).

ぜいこみ【税込み】～の[で] before tax; pretax. ◐税込み40万円の月給 pretax monthly pay of ￥400,000; a salary of ￥400,000, before (deduction of) tax. ■税込み価格 the posttax price 《of cigarettes》; the price「after [including] tax.

せいざ【正座】the formal posture when sitting; sitting on *one*'s heels with *one*'s back straight; kneeling on the floor in the formal (*seiza*) position; *seiza*. ～する sit on *one*'s heels.

せいじ【青磁】celadon (porcelain); celadon ware. ■青磁色 celadon (green); soft blueish green.

せいじんのひ【成人の日】〔1月の第2月曜日〕Adult's Day; Coming-of-Age Day; a national holiday in Japan held on the second Monday of January for people who became twenty years old in the course of the previous year.

せいてん【青天】the「blue [azure] sky; the blue heavens.
　青天の霹靂(へきれき) a bolt「from [out of] the blue; a thunderbolt from a clear　sky. ◐その報道は商業界にとっては青天の霹靂だった. The news hit the commercial world like a bolt from the blue.

せいでんき【静電気】static electricity. ◐車のドアに触れたとき静電気

[157]

がバチッときた. I got a shock from static electricity when I touched the car door. ■静電気除去[防止] elimination [prevention] of static electricity; static electricity「elimination [prevention].

ぜいにく【贅肉】〔体についた余分の肉〕superfluous [waste] flesh;〔脂肪〕fat; flab;〔比喩的に余計な部分〕a superfluity.　◐腰の回りに贅肉がつく fat builds up around the waist;〈人が主語〉build up fat around the waist.

ぜいびき【税引き】◐税引きの[で] after「taxes [deductions] / 税引きの手取り the amount left (to *one*) after taxes.

せいぼ【歳暮】〔年末の進物〕a year-end「present [gift]; a gift sent in December (typically from a department store, to express gratitude for favors received during the year);〔年末〕the「end [close] of the year; year-end.　■**歳暮売出し** a year-end sale.

せいめいほけん【生命保険】life「insurance [assurance].　◐彼には 5,000 万円の生命保険がかけられている. He has life insurance「for [amounting to] ¥50 million. | His life is insured for ¥50 million.

せいりつう【生理痛】menstrual pain; menstrual cramps; period pains.

せいりょう【清涼】～な cool; refreshing.　■**清涼飲料(水)** a soft drink; a「cooling [refreshing] drink; a beverage;〔炭酸飲料〕a carbonated drink.

せがき【施餓鬼】〚仏教〛the *Bon* rites of offering food to relieve the suffering of the hungry ghosts in hell.

せき【咳】a cough; coughing;〚医〛a tussis.　◐たんのからんだ咳 a cough with (stubborn) phlegm; an obstructive cough;《have difficulty》coughing up phlegm / 湿っぽい咳 a「moist [wet, damp] cough / 乾いた咳 a dry cough / 強い咳 a loud cough; a racking cough; a「convulsive [spasmodic] cough / 喘息(ぜんそく)の咳 an asthmatic cough / 咳が出る have a cough; be coughing; cough / 咳がなおる get over [get rid of] a cough.

せきがはら【関ケ原】〔大決戦〕an absolutely critical battle;〔歴史を決する戦い〕a battle which changes the course of history.　◐関ケ原の戦い the Battle of Sekigahara《fought in 1600 between Ishida Mitsunari and Tokugawa Ieyasu for suzerainty over all Japan》/ 次の試合が関ケ原だ. The next game will decide our fate.

せきしょ【関所】〚史〛a barrier (station);〔検問所〕a checking station; a checkpoint.　◐君には就職試験という関所が控えている. You have a way station to pass through in the form of an employment exam. / 関所を越える pass a barrier station; pass through a checkpoint / 関所を破る break through a barrier (station).　■関所手形 a permit to pass barrier stations; a travel pass.　関所破り unlawful passage through a barrier station.

せきてい【石庭】a rock garden (in Japanese style).

せきはん【赤飯】white glutinous rice steamed with red adzuki beans for eating on celebratory occasions; auspicious white rice with red beans.

セクハラ〔性的いやがらせ〕sexual harassment.　◐職場でのセクハラ sexual harassment「in [at] the「office [workplace] / 職場におけるセクハラ事例 a sexual harassment case「in [at] the workplace / セクハラで人を訴える sue *somebody* for sexual harassment / セクハラで訴えられる be「sued for [accused of] sexual harassment / セクハラの被害者 a victim of sexual harassment / セクハラの加害者 a sexual harasser / セクハラを受ける be sexually harassed.　■環境型セクハラ hostile environment sexual harassment.　対価型セクハラ quid pro quo sexual harassment.　セクハラ・ガイドライン sexual harassment guidelines.　セクハラ裁判 a sexual harassment trial.

せけんてい【世間体】decency; appearances.　◐世間体がよい look「good [all right, acceptable, decent]; be respectable / 世間体が悪い look bad; not look「good [right]; be disreputable; be discreditable.

せけんばなし【世間話】small talk; gossip; 《have》a chat.　◐30分ほどは世間話で過ごした. We spent about half an hour chatting about everyday things. / 世間話をする chat [have a chat]《with *somebody*》(about things in general).

せしゅ【施主】1〔葬式などの〕a chief mourner; the「person [member of the family of the deceased] who organizes and pays for「a funeral [a Buddhist (memorial) service].　**2**〔施し人〕a donor; a donator; a benefactor.　**3**〔工事の〕a client; a customer; an owner.

せせりばし【せせり箸】poking at *one*'s meal with *one*'s chopsticks (a breach of good manners).

せたい【世帯】a household.　■核家族世帯 a nuclear household.　高齢者単独世帯 a household consisting of a single elderly person.　高齢夫婦世帯 a household consisting of an elderly couple.　単身世帯 a one-person household.　独居老人世帯 ＝高齢者単独世帯.　二[三]世代同居

世帯 a household consisting of「two [three] generations living together; a「two [three]-generation household. 世帯員 a member of a household. 世帯主 the head of a「household [family]; a householder.

せっく【節句】a seasonal festival Doll Day (3 March), Boy's Day (5 May), Tanabata (7 July) , etc.

せった【雪駄】(Japanese) sandals with leather soles.

せっぷく【切腹】seppuku; hara-kiri; suicide by disembowelment; self-disembowelment.

せつぶん【節分】the last day of winter in the traditional lunar calendar, usually February 3 or 4; (the day of) the bean-scattering ceremony (to drive out devils and attract good fortune).

せとぎわ【瀬戸際】a critical moment; a crisis; the brink [threshold, edge]《of...》. ◐ 瀬戸際になって at the last moment; at the eleventh hour / ...の瀬戸際にある be on the「brink [verge, point] of....

せともの【瀬戸物】china; pottery; porcelain; earthenware;〈集合的に〉crockery. ■瀬戸物屋 a china「store [shop]. 瀬戸物類 china; earthenware.

せみ【蟬】a cicada《*pl.* ~s, -dae》; *a cicala; *a harvest fly; *a balm cricket; *a locust. ◐ 蟬が鳴いている. A cicada is [The cicadas are] singing. / 蟬の抜け殻 the cast-off「skin [shell] of a cicada; the「molt [cast] of a cicada. ■蟬取り cicada catching.

せみしぐれ【蟬時雨】a chorus of cicadas; the singing of (the) cicadas.

せん【銭】a sen (＝1/100 yen).

せんぐう【遷宮】the temporary removal of the object of worship from the shrine during its rebuilding.

せんこう【線香】a stick of incense; a joss [an incense] stick.

せんこうはなび【線香花火】small sparklers; small fireworks which resemble incense sticks. ◐ この住民運動を線香花火に終わらせてはならない. We can't let this residents' campaign「be just a flash in the pan [just fizzle out]. / 線香花火のように消える fizzle out; flicker and go out; be (just) a flash in the pan.

せんごくぶね【千石船】a junk with a capacity for one thousand *koku* of rice; a large junk.

せんざ【遷座】the transfer of a Shinto shrine《to a new site》.

ぜんざい【善哉】〔汁粉の一種〕a thick, sweet soup, made of crushed-bean paste in western Japan and strained-bean paste in eastern Japan.

せんじゃふだ【千社札】a votive ⌈card [slip, sticker]; a worshiper's name-card ⌈left [attached to a pillar] at a shrine (as a prayer).

ぜんしゅう【禅宗】Zen (Buddhism); the Zen sect. ● 禅宗の寺 a Zen temple / 禅宗の僧侶 a Zen ⌈priest [monk].

せんしゅうらく【千秋楽】the closing [last, concluding] day [night, evening] 《of a show》; the last day of a sumo tournament; a close; an end; the finish.

ぜんじょう【禅杖】a stick used to chastise dozing zazen meditators.

せんす【扇子】a (folding) fan. ● 扇子の骨[要(かなめ)] the ⌈ribs [pivot] of a fan / 扇子をぱちんと閉じる snap a fan shut / 扇子をたたむ close [shut, fold] a fan / 扇子を開く open [unfold] a fan.

ぜんそく【喘息】〖医〗asthma. ■ アトピー性喘息 atopic asthma. 気管支喘息 bronchial asthma. 小児喘息 infantile asthma.

せんたくき【洗濯機】a washing machine; a washer. ● 洗濯機で洗濯する wash the clothes [do the washing] in [with] a washing machine. ■ 全自動洗濯機 a fully automatic washing machine. 電気洗濯機 an electric washing machine. 二槽式洗濯機 a twin-tub ⌈washing machine [washer]. 無洗剤洗濯機 a detergent-free washing machine.

せんたくや【洗濯屋】〔店〕a laundry; a cleaner's; 〔人〕(男性) a laundryman; a washerman; a launderer; (女性) a laundrywoman; a washerwoman; *a washwoman; a laundress.

せんちゃ【煎茶】green (leaf) tea; ordinary [nonpowdered] green tea.

せんとう【銭湯】〔公衆浴場〕a public bath; a bathhouse.

せんにちまいり【千日参り】going to pray at a shrine or temple for a thousand days in succession.

せんにん【仙人】1 〔神仙〕a Taoist or (in Japan) Buddhist ascetic who has obtained magical powers and immortality through ascetic practices in the mountains. 2 〔山中の修行者・隠者〕a wizardlike unworldly man; a hermit.

せんにんばり【千人針】a cotton belt with a thousand 《red》 stitches, each sewn by a different woman, worn by soldiers as a protective charm; a "thousand-stitch belt."

せんばつこうとうがっこうやきゅうたいかい【選抜高等学校野球大会】the National Invitational High-School Baseball Tournament.

せんばづる【千羽鶴】a thousand 「origami [folded-paper] cranes tied together on a string and often assembled as a prayer for good health;〔模様〕a design of a thousand cranes.

せんべい【煎餅】a Japanese cracker made from glutinous rice and soy, sesame, or other savory flavoring; a rice cracker;〔軽焼の〕a cracknel (of wheat flour). ■ 揚げせんべい a fried rice cracker.　手焼きせんべい a hand-made rice cracker.　煎餅布団 thinly stuffed bedding; a thin, hard futon; a futon as flat as a pancake.

せんべつ【餞別】a「parting [farewell, going-away] gift [present].　◐ ご餞別の印までに差し上げます.《文》Kindly accept this as a token of my best wishes for your journey. / 餞別を贈る give a parting gift.

せんまいづけ【千枚漬け】thin slices of turnip pickled in vinegar and other ingredients.

せんめんき【洗面器】a washbowl; a (wash)basin;〔据えつけの〕a lavatory.

せんめんじょ【洗面所】a lavatory; a toilet; a toilet room;(レストランや公共建築物の) a washroom.　◐ 浴室兼(ヶ)洗面所 a combined bathroom and lavatory; a room containing both a bath and a toilet.

せんりゅう【川柳】a *senryū*; a humorous or ironical haiku.　◐ 川柳を一句ひねる compose a *senryū*.

そ

ぞう【象】 an elephant; a jumbo. ◐ 雄[雌]の象 a「bull [cow] elephant / 象に乗る ride an elephant / 象の鼻 an elephant's trunk; the「trunk [proboscis] of an elephant / 象の墓場 the elephants' graveyard.
 ■ アフリカ象 an African [a bush] elephant.　インド象 an Indian elephant.　白象 a white [an albino] elephant.

そうがんきょう【双眼鏡】 a binocular (telescope); 《a pair of》 binoculars.

そうきょく【箏曲】 《a piece of》 koto music. ◐ 箏曲教授.〔看板の文句〕Koto Lessons.　■ 箏曲家 a koto player.

ぞうげ【象牙】 ivory. ◐ 象牙狩りをする hunt ivory / 象牙の箸 ivory chopsticks.

そうこうかい【壮行会】 a「send-off [farewell] party; a rousing send-off. ◐ 壮行会を開く give a send-off party 《in honor of *somebody*》; give *somebody* a fine send-off.

そうしき【葬式】 a funeral (ceremony); a「funeral [burial] service; funeral [burial] rites; obsequies. ◐ 葬式に参列する attend [be present at] a funeral.

そうじき【掃除機】 a (vacuum) cleaner. ◐ 掃除機で掃除する vacuum 《the floor》/ 部屋に掃除機をかける vacuum a room.
 ■ 真空[電気]掃除機 a vacuum「cleaner [sweeper]; 《口》 a vacuum.

ぞうに【雑煮】 soup containing *mochi* (rice cakes), vegetables and other ingredients, a standard New Year's dish.

そうべつかい【送別会】 a「farewell [going-away] party; a send-off dinner. ◐ 水野所長の送別会を開く hold [give] a farewell「dinner [party] for [in honor of] Director Mizuno.

そうまとう【走馬灯】 a revolving lantern. [＝まわりどうろう] ◐ 走馬灯のような kaleidoscopic; ever-changing[-shifting] / 走馬灯のように変

転する make a kaleidoscopic change / いろいろな思い出が走馬灯のように去来した. Ever-changing scenes from the past rose before my eyes and vanished. | A kaleidoscope of memories passed before my mind's eye.

そうめん【素麺】thin [fine] noodles (for eating cold in summer); Japanese vermicelli.

ぞうり【草履】zori; (Japanese) sandals

ソープランド a massage parlor; a bathhouse (where customers pay for sex); a "soapland"; a brothel;《口》a whorehouse.

そくせきめん【即席麺】instant (Chinese) noodles.

そしな【粗品】a「small [little] present [gift]; an [a marketing] incentive. ◐ ご来店のお客様にもれなく粗品を進呈いたします.〔掲示〕A free gift for every customer.

そせん【祖先】an ancestor; a forefather; a progenitor; *one*'s forebears.

そとば【卒塔婆】〖仏教〗**1**〔仏舎利塔〕a stupa; a dagoba; a Buddhist monument. **2**〔板塔婆・板石塔婆〕a grave tablet; a narrow wooden plank with Sanskrit characters written on it.

そとぶところ【外懐】〔着物の上前と下前の間のふところ〕the bosom (of a kimono); the space between the two overlapping folds of the front of a kimono.

そとぼり【外堀】an outer moat. ◐ 外堀を埋める fill in an outer moat;〔比喩的に〕get rid of obstacles to what *one* wants to do.

そなえもち【供え餅】rice cakes offered (in front of a household Shinto altar); an offering of rice cakes.

そば【蕎麦】**1**【植】〔タデ科の１年草; 東アジア原産〕buckwheat. **2**〔食品〕soba; buckwheat「noodles [vermicelli]. ■そば焼酎 a spirit distilled from buckwheat. そばずし a sushi roll made with soba (instead of rice). そばつゆ *soba* dipping「sauce [broth]. そば屋〔店〕a *soba*「restaurant [shop, stall];〔人〕a *soba*「seller [vendor]. そば湯〔そばをゆでた湯〕*soba* water; the water in which noodles have been boiled;〔そば粉を湯でといたもの〕buckwheat flour mixed with water.

そぼろ sweetened ground「meat [fish]; ground [minced] fish [meat] flavored and preserved with soy sauce and sugar. ◐ 鳥そぼろ弁当 a box lunch with minced chicken *soboro* on top of rice.

そらなみだ【空涙】crocodile [sham, false, forced] tears. ◐ 空涙を流す

shed [weep] crocodile [sham] tears.

そらに【空似】 an accidental resemblance; a chance likeness. ◐ 他人の空似ということがある. There is such a thing as resemblance between strangers.

そらべん【空弁】〔空港で売っている弁当〕a「packed meal [box lunch, packed lunch] sold at airports.

そらまめ【空豆】〔マメ科の1・2年草; 北アフリカから中央アジア原産の食用作物〕(大粒種) a broad bean;(中粒種) a horse bean;(小粒種) a pigeon bean.

そらみみ【空耳】 mishearing. ◐ それは君の空耳だ. You only「fancy [imagine] you heard that.

そろばん【算盤】1〔計算器〕an abacus 《*pl.* ～es, -ci》; a calculating device with parallel rows of sliding beads strung on wires. ◐ そろばんが上手だ be good at the abacus / そろばんで計算する count [reckon] on the abacus / そろばんをはじく[使う, 置く] use [work] an abacus. **2** 〔損得の計算〕◐ そろばんが合う[合わない] pay [do not pay]. ■**そろばん勘定** counting [reckoning] on the abacus. **そろばん塾** an abacus school; 《take》abacus classes. **そろばんずくの** mercenary; calculative; commercial-minded; commercially minded.

た

たい【鯛】〔スズキ目タイ科の魚〕a sea bream; a porgy (its name rhymes with *medetai*, "auspicious," and the fish is used as an emblem of happy occasions).

たいあん【大安】〔六曜の〕a day, in a recurring six-day calendrical cycle, when all is auspicious; a lucky day (sought for weddings).

たいいくのひ【体育の日】〔10月の第2月曜日〕Health-Sports Day.

たいおんけい【体温計】 a (clinical) thermometer. ◐体温計を当てる place a thermometer 《under *one*'s tongue》/ 体温計を当ててみると熱が38度もあった. When I took my temperature, the thermometer showed I had a fever of「38 (degrees) [over 100 (degrees) Fahrenheit]. / 脇の下に体温計をはさむ place a thermometer in *one*'s armpit / 体温計をくわえる put [keep] a thermometer「under *one*'s tongue [in *one*'s mouth] ▶ 欧米での普通のやり方. ■水銀体温計 a mercury thermometer. **電子体温計** a digital thermometer; an electronic thermometer. **婦人体温計**〔基礎体温測定用〕a basal thermometer; a basal body thermometer.

だいがく【大学】〔総合〕a university;〔単科または分科〕a college. ◐大学1 [2, 3, 4] 年生 *a freshman [sophomore, junior, senior]; "a first-year [second-year, third-year, fourth-year] student / 大学で考古学を専攻する *major ["specialize] in archaeology at「college [university] / 大学に入る enter [enrol in] a university; matriculate / 大学に進む[進学する] go「on to college ["up to university] / 大学に行く go to「college [university] / 大学を受験する take ["sit] a university entrance examination / 大学を出る[卒業する] leave [graduate from] college [university].
■**一流 [二流, 三流] 大学** a「top-notch [second-rate, third-rate] university. **県立[市立]大学** a「prefectural [city] university. **公立大学** a public university. **国立大学** a national university. **私立大学** an in-

dependent [a private] university.　**マンモス大学**〔学部が各地に散在する〕a multiversity.　**名門大学** a「prestigious [famous] university.　**大学芋** candied sweet potatoes.　**大学教授** a「university [college] professor.　**大学入試[入学試験]**《take》a university entrance examination.　**大学ノート** a close-ruled notebook; a large (B5-sized) notebook (for taking lectures).　**大学病院** a university hospital; a teaching hospital.

だいかぐら【大神楽・太神楽】〔大道で行う曲芸〕street performances including a lion dance and juggling;〔伊勢神宮で行う太々神楽〕a grand performance of「*kagura* [sacred music and dancing] (at Ise Shrine).

たいきょく【対局】a game of「go [*shōgi*].

だいぎんじょう(しゅ)【大吟醸(酒)】〔精米歩合 50％以下のもの〕*daiginjō* (sake); top-quality sake brewed at low temperatures from rice grains milled to 50 percent of their weight or less.

だいきんひきかえ【代金引き換え】cash on delivery (略: COD).　◐ 代金引き換えで宅配便を送る send a parcel COD / お支払いは代金引き換えでお願いいたします. We request payment by cash on delivery. / 代金引き換えの宅配便 a COD parcel delivery.

だいぐうじ【大宮司】the chief priest of a major (Shinto) shrine.

たいこうぼう【太公望】1〔人名〕Tai Kung Wang.　2〔魚を釣る人〕an ["compleat"] angler; a Waltonian.　▶ 後者は『釣魚大全』の著者 I・ウォールトンの名から.　◐ 太公望を決め込む give *one*self up to the pleasure of angling.　■ **太公望連** a group of anglers; disciples of Sir Izaak Walton.

だいこくてん【大黒天】〔七福神の一〕Daikoku(ten);〚Skt〛Mahākāla; the God of Wealth (one of the seven gods of good fortune, he is usually depicted carrying a magic mallet and standing atop two bags of rice).

だいこくばしら【大黒柱】1〔柱〕the principal post; the central pillar《of a house》.　2〔支える人〕a「pillar [tower] (of strength); a mainstay; a chief support; a breadwinner.　◐ 一家の大黒柱 the「breadwinner [chief support] of a family.

たいこばら【太鼓腹】a potbelly; a (prominent) paunch;《口》a bay window; a pot.　◐ 太鼓腹をした男 a「potbellied [paunchy] man / 太鼓腹を抱える《口》have [carry] a spare tire.

たいこむすび【太鼓結び】a puffed-out bow (of an obi).

たいこもち【太鼓持ち】〔幇間(ほうかん)〕a professional jester; a buffoon; a funnyman; a comedian (hired to entertain at parties).

だいこん【大根】1 〔アブラナ科の 1, 2 年草; 中央アジア原産の栽培野菜〕 a daikon; a mooli; a「Japanese [Chinese, giant white] radish. **2** 〔下手な役者〕 a bad [poor] actor; a ham. ■**大根おろし**〔食物〕grated daikon.

たいしぼう【体脂肪】 body fat. ◖体脂肪の指標 a body mass index (略: BMI). 体格指数・肥満指数・ボディマス指数などと呼ばれている / 体脂肪を燃やす burn (off) *one*'s body fat. ■**体脂肪計** a body(-)fat「scale [meter, gauge, analyzer]. **体脂肪率** body fat ratio.

たいしゅう【体臭】〔体のにおい〕the「odor [smell] of a (person's) body; *one*'s body odor; the distinctive smell 《of a person》;〔主にわきがのにおい〕body odor (略: BO). ◖(人が)体臭がきつい have (a) strong body odor; have BO

たいじゅうけい【体重計】 a scale; scales; a weighing「device [machine].

だいじょ【大序】〔歌舞伎や浄瑠璃の〕a prologue; an opening act.

たいしょうごと【大正琴】 a Taishō lyre.

たいしょうじだい【大正時代】 the Taishō period (1912–1926).

だいじんぐう【大神宮】 a「major [Grand] Shinto shrine. ◖伊勢大神宮 the Grand Shrine at Ise.

だいす【台子】〔茶道具〕a display stand for tea ceremony utensils.

だいず【大豆】〔マメ科の 1 年草; 食用栽培種〕(a) soybean; (a) soya [soja] (bean);〔その豆〕soybean(s); soya bean(s); soya; soja; soy. ■**遺伝子組み換え大豆** genetically「modified [engineered, altered] soybeans; GM soybeans. **大豆油** soybean oil; soy [soya-bean] oil; Chinese bean oil. **大豆加工食品** a processed-soybean product.

だいだいり【大内裏】〔内裏を中心とする一郭〕the Outer Palace Precincts.

たいちょう【体調】体調管理 control [management] of *one*'s physical condition. ◖体調管理に気をつかう monitor *one*'s physical condition closely; keep a close eye on *one*'s「physical condition [health] / 体調不良 a health problem; poor [bad] health / 体調不良のため欠席いたします. I will be absent due to poor health. | I'm not well, so I won't be able to come today.

だいどうげい【大道芸】 a street performance. ◖大道芸をする perform 《tricks》 on the street.

だいびき【代引き】＝だいきんひきかえ.

たいびょう【大廟】1〔天皇家の〕an Imperial Mausoleum. 2〔伊勢の〕the Great Shrine of Ise.

たいふう【台風・颱風】a typhoon. ▶「風力12の風」の意では a hurricane. ◯伊勢湾台風 the Ise Bay Typhoon / 超大型の[大型の, 中型の, 小型の, ごく小さい]台風〔強風域の半径による区分〕a super [major, medium, minor, small] typhoon / 台風18号 typhoon (no.) 18; the season's 18th typhoon. ■台風一過 ◯台風一過の青空 a (clear) blue sky after a typhoon (has passed, has blown over). 台風銀座 the typhoon Ginza; the area (of Japan) where typhoons frequently pass.

たいふうのめ【台風の目】the eye of a typhoon; a typhoon eye;〔(比喩的に)激動の中心〕the eye of a storm; the「center [focus] of a「commotion [disturbance].

だいふくちょう【大福帳】an (old-fashioned) account book (literally, "Great Happiness Book"); a daybook.

だいふくもち【大福餅】a soft rice cake filled with sweet bean jam.

だいぶつ【大仏】a great [giant, huge] statue [image] of Buddha. ■奈良の大仏 the Great Buddha of Nara. 大仏殿 the Temple of the Great Buddha; the「Great [Grand] Buddha Hall.

たいへいらく【太平楽】〔雅楽の一曲目〕(the tune of) "Blessed Peace".

たいみそ【鯛味噌】miso paste with bream.

だいみょう【大名】a daimyo; a feudal「lord [chief]; a (great) feudatory. ■大名行列〔大名の〕a daimyo's procession;〔供の多い行列〕a long procession. 大名屋敷 a daimyo's mansion. 大名旅行 ◯大名旅行をする travel like a「lord [prince]; travel in「an extravagant way [grand style];〔公金を使って〕go on a「junket; junket《around the country》.

たいめし【鯛飯】boiled rice with (minced) sea bream.

だいもく【題目】〔日蓮宗の〕the prayer of the Nichiren sect. ■題目講 a fraternity of Nichiren Buddhist adherents. 題目堂 the Prayer Hall.

だいもん【大門】the great outer gate (of the grounds of a Buddhist temple).

たいやき【鯛焼き】a pancake in the shape of a sea bream filled with bean jam.

だいり【内裏】the Imperial Palace. ■内裏雛(びな) Emperor and Empress dolls; a pair of dolls representing the Emperor and Empress in ancient costume (displayed on 3 March, the day of the Doll Festival).

だいりせき【大理石】 marble. ◐大理石の浴槽 a marble bath(tub).

たうえ【田植え】 rice planting; planting out rice seedlings; rice transplantation. ◐田植えをする transplant [plant out, bed out] rice seedlings; plant rice. ■田植え歌 a rice planters' song. 田植え機 a rice-planting machine. 田植え時 the rice-planting season. (お)田植え祭り a rice-planting festival.

たかげた【高下駄】 high clogs; clogs with high supports.

たかさご【高砂】 ◐〔謡曲〕高砂を歌う sing the Noh song of Takasago 《at a wedding》(a song celebrating people upon the land).

たかしまだ【高島田】 a hairstyle favored by women during the Meiji period and, subsequently, by brides wearing kimono.

たかはり(ぢょうちん)【高張(提灯)】 a (large paper) lantern on a pole.

たかびしゃ【高飛車】 〜な haughty; high-handed; overbearing; domineering; peremptory. ◐高飛車な物言い a high-handed [an overbearing] way of speaking / そんな高飛車な言い方はやめてくれ. Enough of that high and mighty「tone attitude of yours!

たかまがはら【高天原】 "the High Plain of Heaven"; the「abode [seat] of the (Japanese) gods; the Japanese Olympus.

たかまきえ【高蒔絵】 embossed gilt lacquer; raised lacquer work.

たかまくら【高枕】 a high pillow. ◐高枕で寝る sleep「in peace [free from care]; slumber peacefully.

たからくじ【宝籤】 a (public) lottery. ◐宝くじを買う buy a lottery ticket / サマージャンボ宝くじ the Summer Jumbo Lottery.

たからぶね【宝船】 a treasure ship; a ship loaded with treasure; 〔七福神のいる絵〕a picture of a treasure ship (bearing the Seven Gods of Good Fortune).

たきぎのう【薪能】 torchlight [firelight] Noh; a Noh drama presented on a torch-lit outdoor stage; a Noh performance formerly given at the offering of firewood to Kōfukuji, a temple in Nara.

たきこみごはん【炊き込み御飯】 rice seasoned with soy sauce and boiled with meat or seafood, and savory vegetables.

たきだし【炊き出し・焚き出し】 distribution of (boiled) rice. 〜する distribute [provide] rice 《to disaster victims》/ 災害地ではただちに炊き出しが行われた. Food was distributed without delay in the devastated area.

たくあん【沢庵】yellow pickled radish.

たくはい【宅配】home (parcel) delivery; doorstep delivery. ～する deliver 《*something* to *somebody*'s「house [home]」》/ ピザを宅配する deliver a pizza / 荷物を前もって宅配で[にして]送る send *one*'s luggage ahead by delivery service / 宅配もできます.〔掲示〕Delivery Service Available. | We Deliver. / 即日宅配いたします. We provide same-day delivery service. ■宅配業 a (parcel) delivery service. 宅配業者[会社] a home-delivery company; a delivery agent [agency]. 宅配ピザ〔業種〕pizza delivery;〔ピザ〕a home-delivered pizza. 宅配便 a「home (parcel) delivery service; a courier service;〔その荷物〕a (home-delivered)「parcel [package]. 宅配ボックス〔宅配便受け取り用の〕a delivery box.

たけ【竹】〔イネ科タケ類の総称〕bamboo. ▶竹の葉[桿] a bamboo stem; a「culm [stem] of bamboo. ■竹を割る split bamboo. 竹かご a bamboo basket. 竹釘 a bamboo「peg [nail]. 竹細工 bamboo「work [ware]. 竹細工職人 a bamboo-ware craftsman. 竹竿 a bamboo pole. 竹ぼうき a bamboo broom. 竹楊子 a bamboo toothpick.

たけうま【竹馬】(a pair of) bamboo stilts. ▶竹馬に乗る walk [play] on stilts.

たげた【田下駄】large geta worn in the paddy fields.

たけとんぼ【竹蜻蛉】a bamboo dragonfly; a T-shaped bamboo flying toy; a simple helicopter-like bamboo toy.

たけのこ【筍・竹の子】a bamboo「shoot [sprout]. ▶たけのこの皮をむく peel a bamboo shoot.

たけや【竹屋】a bamboo dealer; a washing-pole seller. ▶竹屋, 竿竹 (さおだけ).〔売り声〕Washing poles, washing poles for sale!

たこ¹【凧】a kite. ▶凧の糸 kite string; string [twine] for a kite. ■絵凧 a「picture [decorated] kite. 字凧 a kite with a Chinese character written on it. 奴(やっこ)凧 a kite with a picture of a samurai's valet (on it). 凧揚げ kite-flying.

たこ²【蛸・章魚】an octopus 《*pl.* ～es, -pi, -podes》; a poulp(e).

たこあしはいせん【蛸足配線】octopus wiring; plugging many leads into one (electrical) outlet; a spaghetti junction (of leads from one outlet). ▶たこ足配線にする have many electrical cords connected to a single outlet.

たこやき【蛸焼き】*takoyaki*; an octopus「ball [cake]; a ball of cooked batter containing small pieces of octopus.

たしざん【足し算】addition; adding up. ◐四桁の足し算 four-digit [four-figure] addition / 足し算をする do a sum; add 《figures》 up; total (up).

だじょうだいじん【太政大臣】〖日本史〗〔太政官の長〕the chancellor of the realm; the grand minister (an office created in 702 under the Taihō Code).

たすき【襷】〔袖をまとめる〕a band of cloth used for holding 《kimono, *yukata*》 sleeves out of the way;〔肩から斜めにかける〕a white sash crossing from one shoulder to the opposite hip, worn by an election candidate;(駅伝などの) a sash of cloth worn by relay marathon runners.

たたき【叩き・敲き】〖料理〗◐カツオのたたき ⇒かつお / アジのたたき minced raw horse mackerel / 牛肉のたたき〔表面をあぶった〕raw beef, lightly grilled on the outside;〔細かく刻んだ〕minced raw beef (similar to steak tartare).

たたみ【畳】a tatami 《*pl.* ~, ~s》; a tatami mat; a straw(-and-rush) mat used for flooring;〔総称〕straw matting.

たたみいわし【畳鰯】〔食品〕baby sardines dried in sheets.

たたみや【畳屋】〔人〕a tatami「maker [dealer];〔店〕a tatami store.

たちおうじょう【立ち往生】〔立ったままで死ぬこと〕dying on *one*'s feet. ◐弁慶の立ち往生 "the last stand" of Benkei, who died on his feet.

たちぐいずし【立ち食い寿司】a stand-up sushi「bar [counter].

たちぐいそばや【立ち食いそば屋】a stand-up *soba*「shop [stall, counter].

たちとり【太刀取り】〔切腹の介錯をする人〕an assistant [a second] at *hara-kiri*;〔罪人の首を切る人〕an executioner.

たちのみ【立ち飲み】stand-up drinking 《at a stall》.

たつ【辰・竜】〔十二支の〕the Dragon, one of the twelve animals of the oriental zodiac. ◐辰の日 the day of the Dragon / 辰の刻(ᴈ) the hour of the Dragon(; 7-9 a.m.) / 辰の方(ホラ)〔東南東〕the direction of the Dragon(; east-southeast). ■辰年 the year of the Dragon. ◐辰年生まれの born in the year of the Dragon.

たづくり【田作り】**1**〔田を耕すこと〕tilling a「rice [paddy] field;〔人〕a

rice-field tiller; a person who tills a paddy field.　**2**〘料理〙〔ごまめ〕small sardines, dried and then simmered in sugar and soy sauce.

たつたあげ【竜田揚げ】〔薄い衣で揚げること〕deep-frying fish or pieces of chicken coated in seasoned flour or potato starch;〔その食品〕deep-fried 《flatfish》.

たづな【手綱】 1〔馬を操る綱〕reins;（頭絡）a bridle.　◐手綱をさばく use [handle] the reins 《well》／手綱を引き締める tighten [shorten, gather up] the reins／手綱を引く pull [tighten, draw in] the reins; rein in 《a horse》; check 《a horse》(with the reins).　**2**〔人を管理する力〕control; the reins; the bit.

だっぱん【脱藩】leaving [deserting] *one*'s *han* [domain]; secession from *one*'s domain [*han*].

たてえぼし【立て烏帽子】a tall, usually lacquered, hat worn by noblemen.

たてぎょうじ【立て行司】one of the two top-ranking referees at a sumo tournament.

たてさくしゃ【立て作者】the chief Kyōgen playwright (attached to a Noh theater).

たてじとみ【立蔀・竪蔀】〔古建築の〕a screen consisting of a wooden lattice covered with a board.

たてじゃみせん【立て三味線】〔脇三味線に対し〕the chief samisen player.

だてまき【伊達巻き】〔料理〕a fish omelette (tightly rolled and traditionally served at New Year's).

たなばたまつり【七夕祭り】the Tanabata Festival; the Star Festival; a festival celebrating the legend of the weaver girl and the cowherd who are allowed to meet only once a year on the night of the 7th of July, when slips of colored paper with poems and wishes written on them are attached to branches of bamboo and displayed in doorways.

たにし【田螺】〘貝〙a mud snail; a pond snail; a river snail.

たにまち【谷町】〘相撲〙a sumo wrestler's「patron [backer, financial supporter].

たぬき【狸】〔イヌ科の動物〕a raccoon dog; a tanuki.　◐たぬきが化ける a raccoon dog「disguises itself [assumes another form]／たぬきの置物 an earthenware figurine of a male raccoon dog standing erect on its hind legs, with exaggerated belly and testicles. ■ **たぬきうどん** an *udon* noodle dish with bits of deep-fried batter added. ⇨ たぬきそば **たぬきおやじ** a「crafty [sly, cunning] old man. **たぬき汁** raccoon dog's meat soup. **たぬきそば** a *soba* noodle dish with bits of deep-fried「batter [bean curd] added. ▶ 関東では揚げかす (deep-fried batter), 関西では油揚げ (deep-fried bean curd) を入れる.

たぬきねいり【狸寝入り】pretending to be asleep; playing possum; sham [feigned, pretended] sleep. ◐ たぬき寝入りをする[決め込む] pretend to be asleep; feign sleep.

たび【足袋】thick-soled socks made with a cleft between the big toe and second toe; (Japanese) split-toe socks. ■ **白[紺]足袋** white [dark blue] split-toe socks. [⇨ じかたび]

たまぐし【玉串】a sprig of cleyera [*sakaki*] with white paper-strips attached(, used by Shinto priests in ceremonies). ◐ **玉串を捧げる** offer a「sprig [branch] of the sacred *sakaki* tree to a god. ■ **玉串奉納[奉奠]** offering a sprig of the sacred *sakaki* tree in front of a shrine altar. **玉串料**〔初穂料〕a cash offering made on the occasion of *one*'s visit to a shrine.

たまご【卵】**1** an egg;〔魚・エビ・カニ・カエルなどの〕eggs;（塊）spawn;（粒）a berry;（はらご）roe;〔貝, 主にカキの〕spat;〔ロブスター・蚕などの〕seed;〔シラミなどの〕a nit;【玉子】〔寿司の〕sweet egg「custard [omelette]. ◐ **アヒル[ウズラ]の卵** a duck('s) [quail('s)] egg /（カエルなどの）**無数の卵** countless eggs 《of a frog》/ **黄身が 2 つある卵** a double-yolked egg / **産みたての卵** a「freshly laid [new-laid] egg / **腐った卵** an addled [a rotten] egg / **卵の殻** an eggshell / **卵の殻をむく** peel a (hard-)boiled egg / **卵の白身[黄身]** the「white [yolk] of an egg / **卵のカラザ**〔白いひも状の〕a chalaza 《*pl.* ~s, chalazae》/ **卵を産む**〔鳥・は虫類・昆虫などが〕lay an egg;〔魚が〕spawn / **卵をかえす** hatch an egg / **卵を焼く** fry an egg / **卵を吸う** suck an egg / **卵を割る** break [crack] an egg **2**〔一人前ではない者〕**記者の卵** a「journalist [reporter] in the making; a budding「journalist [reporter]. ◐ **医者の卵** a doctor in the making; a student doctor. ■ **いり卵** scrambled eggs. **落とし卵** a poached egg. **地卵** locally produced eggs. **溶き卵** (a) beaten egg. **生卵** a raw egg. **半熟(の)卵** a soft-boiled egg. **ゆで卵** a (hard-)boiled egg.

たまござけ【卵酒】hot sake with beaten egg in it; a sake「eggnog [flip].

たまごとじ【卵綴じ】 egg soup; a hot dish over which a lightly beaten egg is poured just before serving.

たまごどんぶり【玉子丼】 a bowl of rice topped with eggs lightly beaten and simmered in soy sauce with vegetables.

たまごやき【卵焼き】 a (sweetened and) soy-flavored omelet(te).

たまてばこ【玉手箱】 1 〔伝説の〕Urashima's casket received from the princess of the Dragon Palace. ◐開けて悔しい玉手箱だった. It was a「Pandora's box [can of worms]. **2** 〔容易に他人に明かさない大切なこと〕*one*'s carefully guarded treasure.

たまねぎ【玉葱】 〔ユリ科の 2 年草; 中央アジア原産の食用野菜〕an onion; a common onion. ◐たまねぎの皮 the「coats [peels] of an onion; (an) onionskin / たまねぎの皮をむく peel an onion.

たまのこし【玉の輿】 a palanquin for the nobility. ◐玉の輿に乗る marry into wealth; get married to a man of「wealth [high status].

たまむしいろ【玉虫色】 1 iridescent coloring. ◐玉虫色の iridescent / 玉虫色の絹布 shot silk. **2** 〔異なった解釈のできるあいまいさ; 見る角度で異なる色合い〕◐玉虫色である *its* appearance changes depending on the angle of light; *its*「meaning [interpretation] changes depending on *one*'s standpoint / 玉虫色の合意 an ambiguous [an equivocal, a chameleonic, a weasel-word] agreement / 玉虫色の発言 a statement whose meaning is hard to pin down; an ambiguous [a vague, an equivocal] statement; weasel words / 玉虫色の人事 an ambiguous personnel change.

ためぐち【ため口】 peer language. ◐ため口をきく speak in *one*'s peer language (to *somebody* who is not a peer).

だめもと【駄目元】 〔「だめでもともと」の略〕◐だめもとである it can't be worse (so give it a try); 〈人が主語〉will be no worse off (if *one* fails); 〈事物が主語〉will not do any harm (even in the event of failure) / だめもとでやってみる try on the assumption that「it won't do any harm [it can't get any worse].

たゆう【太夫・大夫】 1 〔能〕〔仕手を勤める有資格者〕an actor qualified to play the protagonist in a Noh play; 〔家元〕the headmaster of a school of Noh performance. **2** 〔浄瑠璃の〕the narrator in a *Jōruri* performance. **3** 〔歌舞伎の〕a female-role actor in a Kabuki play. **4** 〔おいらん〕a courtesan of the highest rank.

たらこ【鱈子】cod roe.

だるま【達磨】〔達磨大師〕Bodhidharma; 〔張り子細工の縁起物〕a *daruma* (doll); a round, red-painted good-luck doll in the shape of Bodhidharma (with an unfilled eye to be painted in when a person's wish is granted). ■ **だるまさんが転んだ**〔遊戯〕the Bodhidharma fell down; a children's game similar to statues. **だるまストーブ** a pot-belly (stove).

だるまいち【達磨市】a *daruma* fair; a fair at which round red Bodhidharma dolls and other good-luck decorations are sold.

たろうかじゃ【太郎冠者】Tarokaja; a common name for a manservant in「*kyōgen* [Noh farce].

たん【反】〔尺貫法における土地の面積の単位〕a *tan*《pl. ~》(=約 991.7 m²).

たんか【短歌】a tanka; a short Japanese poem of 31 syllables, arranged in lines of five, seven, five, seven and seven syllables

だんか【檀家】a「supporter [patron] of a Buddhist temple. ◯ 檀家の多い[少ない]寺 a temple with「many [few] patrons.

たんご【端午】the festival on the fifth day of the fifth month《of the lunar calendar》. ■ 端午の節句 the Boys' Festival (on May 5); the Iris Festival; the Feast of Irises.

だんご【団子】**1**〔米の粉で作る菓子〕a dumpling; a doughboy; a boiled or steamed ball of (rice) flour. ◯ 串刺し(の)団子 *dango* on a stick / 団子を串に刺す put *dango* on a stick / 十五夜に[仏壇に]団子を供える make an offering of *dango*「on the night of the harvest moon [at a Buddhist altar]. **2**〔だんごの形に似たもの〕a (small) round object; a ball-shaped object. ◯ 団子に目鼻 a round [plump, bulbous] face. **3**〔並んで続く様子; 一つにかたまった様子〕a lump; a clump; a knot (of people); a tight crowd. ◯ 団子(状態)になる become「crowded [clumped] together; lump together. ■ 甘辛[みたらし]だんご a (sweet) soy-glazed *dango* (on a stick). **ごまだんご** a sesame(-seed) *dango*. **泥だんご** a mud pie. **肉だんご** a meatball. **だんご状態** ◯ (競争者が)団子状態である be (all) crowded together; be strung out in knots. **だんご鼻** ⇨ だんごばな. **だんごレース** a crowded race; a race where the runners stay close together. ◯ 団子レースの様相を呈しはじめた. It's turning into a crowded race, with all the runners

だんごう【談合】collusion; collusive「bidding [tendering]; bid-rigging. ~する rig a bid; collude; agree (illegally) in advance. ■**官製談合** government-led bid-rigging.

だんごばな【団子鼻】a button(-shaped) nose; a「flat [squat, snub] nose; a「bulbous [potato, cauliflower] nose.

たんざく【短冊】a strip of (fancy) paper (for writing a tanka or a haiku on). ■**短冊掛け** a frame for (displaying) *tanzaku*. **短冊切り**〔ニンジンなどの〕cutting [slicing] into thin rectangles [rectangular slabs].

たんさんでんち【単三電池】an *AA size [a size AA] battery; an ⅡR6 battery.

たんぜん【丹前】a padded large-size kimono.

たんだい【探題】〖日本史〗a (feudal, military) commissioner.

だんちょうのおもい【断腸の思い】heartbreaking [heart-rending, gut-wrenching, stomach-sickening] grief. ◐断腸の思いがする feel「*one*'s heart rent [torn to pieces]; feel as if *one*'s heart were breaking; be brokenhearted; be sick to the stomach.

たんにでんち【単二電池】a *C size [size C] battery; an ⅡR14 battery.

たんぽぽ【蒲公英】〔キク科タンポポ属植物の総称〕a dandelion;〔セイヨウタンポポ〕a common dandelion ◐タンポポの綿毛 a dandelion tuft; dandelion fluff.

たんめん【湯麺】Chinese noodles served in a salty soup and topped with stir-fried vegetables and meat.

たんよんでんち【単四電池】an *AAA size [a size AAA] battery; an ⅡR03 battery.

ち

ちかてつ【地下鉄】*a subway; ǁan underground (railway); 〔ロンドンの〕the tube; the underground; 〔パリの〕the Metro.　◐ 地下鉄で行く *go by subway; ǁgo by「tube [underground] / 地下鉄で30分のところにある be half an hour (away) by subway / 地下鉄に乗る board [get on] a subway (train); board [get on] the underground / 地下鉄の駅 *a subway「station [stop]; an underground [a tube] station / 地下鉄を降りる get off a subway train.

ちかみち【近道】a「shorter [faster] route;〔手っ取り早い方法〕a shortcut.　◐ 上野へ行く近道 a shorter route to Ueno / 野原を抜ける近道 a shortcut across the fields / 一番の近道 the「shortest [fastest] route [way] / 知識を得る近道 a shortcut to acquiring knowledge / 英語をマスターする近道 the quickest way to master English / 近道をする take a「shorter route [shortcut]; cut across《a field》;〔角を曲がらずに〕cut a corner / 学問に近道はない. There is no royal road to「knowledge [learning].

ちからうどん【力饂飩】a bowl of thick white noodles with a rice cake in it.

ちからみず【力水】〖相撲〗*chikara mizu*; purifying water with which a sumo wrestler rinses his mouth before a bout.

ちくわ【竹輪】a kind of fish paste, shaped into a tubular form and grilled.

ちくわぶ【竹輪麩】a tube-shaped cake of flour paste.

ちご【稚児】〔小児〕an infant; a boy;〔小姓〕a page;〔祭事の〕a child in a traditional festival procession;〔陰間(かげま), 男娼〕a catamite.　■ 稚児行列 a kimono-clad children's procession in a traditional festival.　稚児髷(まげ)[輪] a hairstyle formerly worn by children, now worn by children in traditional festival processions.

ちとせあめ【千歳飴】a long rope of pink and white candy given to

children celebrating their seventh, fifth, or third birthday.

ちまき【粽】a steamed rice-dumpling wrapped in bamboo leaves; eaten on Children's Day (5 May).

チャーハン【炒飯】Chinese-style fried rice.

ちゃかいせき【茶懐石】a simple Japanese meal served before a tea ceremony.

ちゃがけ【茶掛け】〔掛け物〕a 「kakemono [hanging scroll] in a tea ceremony room.

ちゃきん【茶巾】a tea 「cloth [napkin]. ■茶巾しぼり 『料理』the technique of squeezing 《bean paste》 into shape in a cloth;《chestnut paste》squeezed into shape in a cloth. 茶巾寿司 sushi wrapped in a layer of egg.

ちゃくうた【着歌】〔歌が流れる着メロ〕a ring song.

ちゃしつ【茶室】a 「tea house [tea room, tea hut].

ちゃしゃく【茶杓】〔茶をすくう匙〕a tea scoop;〔茶柄杓〕a tea 「ladle [dipper].

ちゃせん【茶筅】a tea whisk.

ちゃそば【茶蕎麦】buckwheat noodles containing tea.

ちゃたく【茶托】a teacup holder; a saucer 《for a teacup》.

ちゃづけ【茶漬け】boiled rice soaked with 「tea [hot water];〔簡単な食事〕a simple meal. ■鯛(たい)[鮭, 海苔]茶漬け boiled rice with 「raw sea bream [salmon, seaweed], soaked in tea.

ちゃつみ【茶摘み】〔事〕tea-picking;〔人〕a tea picker. ◐一[二]番茶の茶摘み a 「first [second] tea-picking. ■茶摘み歌 a tea pickers' song.

ちゃのま【茶の間】a living room; a sitting room; a parlor;〔茶室〕⇨ちゃしつ.

ちゃのみともだち【茶飲み友達】a tea-drinking companion; a crony;〔年をとってから結婚した配偶者〕a person married late in life for the purpose of companionship; a late-life marriage partner.

ちゃばしら【茶柱】茶柱が立つ a (lucky) tea stalk floats vertically in *one*'s tea.

ちゃぱつ【茶髪】hair dyed brown.

ちゃわんむし【茶碗蒸し】egg custard hotchpotch steamed in a cup.

ちゃんこりょうり[なべ]【ちゃんこ料理[鍋]】a stew made from fish, meat, and vegetables for sumo wrestlers.

ちゃんちゃんこ a padded sleeveless kimono jacket.

ちゃんばら a sword battle;〔乱闘〕fighting; a fight. ■ちゃんばら劇[映画, 物] plays [pictures] featuring swordplay; samurai films. ちゃんばらごっこ playing at「sword-fighting [a samurai duel]; a pretend swordfight.

ちゃんぽん 1 〔まぜ合わせ〕a mixture; a medley;〔交互〕alternation. ◐ ちゃんぽんに〔いっしょに〕together;〔交互に〕alternately; by turns; one after「the other [another] / 酒とビールをちゃんぽんに飲む drink sake and beer「alternately [on the same occasion]. 2 〔長崎の郷土料理〕a Chinese-style hotchpotch originating in Nagasaki which consists of meat and vegetables in a thick sauce on top of Chinese noodles.

ちゅうかそば【中華そば】 Chinese「noodles [vermicelli].

ちゅうかりょうり【中華料理】 Chinese「food [cooking, cuisine]; a Chinese「dish [meal]. ◐ 中華料理店 a Chinese restaurant; *a chop suey「house [restaurant].

ちゅうげん【中元】 the fifteenth day of the seventh month (according to the lunar calendar); the summer gift period (about July 1–15);〔贈物〕a「summer [midyear] present [gift].

ちゅうしんぐら ⇨ かなでほんちゅうしんぐら「仮名手本忠臣蔵」.

ちゅうとろ【中とろ】 medium-fatty tuna「meat [flesh].

ちゅうのり【宙乗り】 a midair「stunt [feat, performance] in Kabuki.

ちゅうハイ【酎ハイ】 an alcoholic drink of「*shōchū* [clear distilled liquor] mixed with soda water or soda pop.

ちょう¹【蝶】 a butterfly. ◐ 蝶のように飛ぶ flit around [fly] like a butterfly

ちょう²【町】〔尺貫法における面積の単位〕a *chō*《*pl.* ~》(=約 99.2 ares);〔尺貫法における長さの単位〕a *chō*《*pl.* ~》(=約 109 m).

ちょうし【銚子】〔徳利〕an earthenware [a ceramic] serving vessel; a sake bottle;〔ひしゃく〕a sake holder. ◐ 酒を銚子に移す pour sake into a serving vessel / 銚子のお代わり《asking for》another bottle of sake.

ちょうじ【弔辞】 a message [letter] of condolence [sympathy]; words of condolence;〔葬儀場での〕a「memorial [funeral] address; a eulogy. ◐ 弔辞を述べる express *one*'s condolence(s);〔演説をする〕give a memorial address / 弔辞を読む read *one*'s message of condolence.

ちょうしゅうぶろ【長州風呂】 a bath consisting of a cast-iron tub

heated directly by a fire.

ちょうせんにんじん【朝鮮人参】〔ウコギ科の多年草; 中国東北部・朝鮮原産の薬用植物〕an Asiatic ginseng.

ちょうだ【長蛇】◐ 長蛇の列 a long「line [file, row];〔順番を待つ〕a long queue《snaking along the street》/ 長蛇の列を作って in a long「line [queue].

ちょうちん【提灯】a (paper) lantern. ◐ 祭りのちょうちん a festival lantern / ちょうちんで足元を照らす light *one*'s way with a lantern / ちょうちんを持つ carry [hold] a lantern;〔ほめそやす〕sing *somebody*'s praises; puff; give *somebody* a boost; boost [favor] *somebody*.
  ■ 小田原提灯 ⇨ おだわらちょうちん. 岐阜提灯 a「Japanese [Chinese] lantern. 高張提灯 a paper lantern on pole. 提灯行列 ◐ ちょうちん行列を催す hold a lantern「procession [parade, march].

ちょうちんもち【提灯持ち】〔提灯を持つ人〕a lantern bearer; a lantern-man;〔ほめそやし〕puffery;《俗》boosting;《口》〔新聞紙上などでの〕a write-up;〔人の手先となってほめそやす者〕a puffer; a booster.

ちょうないかんきょう【腸内環境】the intestinal environment. ◐ 腸内環境を整えるビフィズス菌 bifidobacteria that「improve [have a beneficial effect on] the intestinal environment.

ちょうないバランス【腸内バランス】intestinal balance. ◐ 強いストレスは腸内バランスを崩すことがある. Severe stress may disturb intestinal balance.

ちょく【猪口】a sake cup. ◐ 猪口で3杯飲む drink three cups of sake / 酒を猪口に注ぐ fill a cup with sake / 猪口を干す[空ける] empty [drain] *one*'s sake cup.

ちょんまげ【丁髷】a Japanese topknot; a men's hairstyle of the Edo period, with the forehead shaved and the remaining hair tied back in a knot, a variant of which is now worn by high-ranking sumo wrestlers. ◐ ちょんまげに結う wear a topknot; wear *one*'s hair in a knot.

ちらしずし【散らし鮨】rice dressed with vinegar and topped with egg and seafood (served in a box or bowl).

ちりめん【縮緬】(silk)「crepe [crape]. ◐ ちりめんのような crepe-[crape-]like; resembling crepe.

ちりめんじゃこ【縮緬じゃこ】dried and seasoned baby sardines or other fish.

ちんとんしゃん〔三味線の擬音〕(an onomatopoeic word for) the (sound of a) samisen.

ちんどんや【ちんどん屋】a group of eccentrically dressed musicians who parade through the streets advertising and announcing events.

つ

つかいきり【使い切り】～の single-use;〔使い捨ての〕. [⇒ つかいすて]　■使い切りカメラ[万年筆] a「single-use [disposable, throwaway] camera [fountain pen].

つかいすて【使い捨て】◐使い捨てにする〔一度だけ使って〕use *something* only once and then throw it away;〔使えるだけ使って〕get all the use out of *something* and then discard it / 使い捨ての disposable; throwaway; single-use; one-time-use; use-once, throw-away / 使い捨ての紙おむつ a「disposable [throwaway] *diaper [''nappy].

つぎ【次】〔宿場〕a post town; a station; a stage.　◐東海道五十三次 the 53 stages on the Tōkaidō.

つきだし【突き出し】1〘相撲〙a frontal thrust out.　2〘料理〙an appetizer; an *hors d'oeuvre*.

つきみ【月見】1〔月の鑑賞〕viewing [enjoying] the moon;〔月見の宴〕a「moon-viewing [moonlight] party.　◐お月見〔十五夜・十三夜の〕a moon-viewing party (on August 15 [on September 13] on the lunar calendar).　2〔そば・うどん〕*soba* [*udon*] with an egg on top.　■月見酒 moon-viewing sake.　月見団子 dumplings offered to the moon.

つくし【土筆】〘植〙〔スギナの胞子茎〕a fertile「shoot [stalk] of field-horsetail.

つくしごと【筑紫琴】a koto; a Japanese zither with 13 strings.

つくだに【佃煮】food boiled down in soy; *tsukudani*.　◐アサリの佃煮 simmered *asari* / のりの佃煮 nori boiled down in soy.

つくね【捏ね】〘料理〙鳥のつくね minced chicken (formed into bite-sized balls); a chicken meatball.　■つくね揚げ a deep-fried meatball.　つくね焼き a「fried [baked] meatball.

つくばい【蹲い】〔茶庭の手水(ちょうず)鉢〕a stone washbasin.

つげ【柘植・黄楊】〔ツゲ科の常緑低木〕Japanese (little-leaf) boxa.　◐つ

げの櫛(˳) a boxwood comb.

つけしょいん【付け書院】a writing alcove.

つけめん【付け麺】Chinese noodles served with a sauce to dip them in.

つけもの【漬け物】pickles; pickled [salted] vegetables; *tsukemono*. ■漬け物石 a stone weight. 漬け物おけ a pickle「tub [barrel]. 漬け物屋〔店〕a pickle shop;〔人〕a pickle「seller [dealer].

つた【蔦】〔ブドウ科の落葉つる性木本; ナツヅタ〕Boston [Japanese] ivy. ◐壁につたをはわせた建物 an ivy-walled building.

つつじ【躑躅】〔ツツジ科ツツジ属植物の総称〕(an) azalea; (a) rhododendron; (a) rosebay.

つづみ【鼓】a hand drum; a long hourglass drum beaten with the hand;〔小鼓〕a tabor.

つつもたせ【美人局】《俗》a badger game; a scheme in which a man and a woman trick a mark into a compromising position and then blackmail him. ◐美人局をやる play a badger game; carry out a blackmail scheme.

つなひき【綱引き】**1**〔競技〕a tug of war; a rope pulling contest. ◐綱引きのチーム a tug-of-war team / 綱引きをする have a tug of war. **2**〔取り合い〕a dispute over possession of *something*. ◐政権をめぐる両党間の激しい綱引き a fierce「dispute [tug-of-war] over political ascendancy between the two parties.

つなみ【津波】a tsunami 《*pl.* ~(s)》; a tidal wave. ■津波警報 a tsunami warning. ■津波地震〔ゆれのわりに大きな津波を生じる〕a tsunami earthquake.

つのかくし【角隠し】a bride's white head covering 《at a traditional Japanese wedding》.

つばき【椿】〔ツバキ科ツバキ属植物の総称〕a (common) camellia. ◐椿油 tsubaki [camellia] oil.

つぶししまだ【潰し島田】〔髪型〕a low shimada coiffure.

つぼ【坪】〔尺貫法における土地の面積の単位〕a *tsubo* 《*pl.* ~》(=約 3.3 m^2).

つぼね【局】**1**〔部屋〕an apartment [a chamber] 《for a court lady》. **2**〔女官〕a court lady; a lady-in-waiting.

つまみざいく【摘み細工】〔江戸手芸〕(a) folded-cloth collage.

つまようじ【爪楊枝】a toothpick. ◐爪楊枝で歯をせせる pick *one*'s

teeth / 爪楊枝をくわえたまましゃべる talk with a toothpick in *one*'s mouth.

つみれ〚料理〛(fish) dumplings (for [in] soup). ◐ イワシのつみれ汁 sardine dumpling soup. ■ **つみれはんぺん** fish balls.

つやもの【艶物】〔義太夫の〕a chanted narration of a love story in the *gidayū* school of *Jōruri* puppet drama.

つゆ【梅雨】the long spell of rainy weather in early summer; the「rainy [wet] season. ◐ 梅雨が明けた. The rainy season is over. / 梅雨に入った. The rainy season has「begun [set in]. ■ **梅雨明け** the end of the rainy season. **梅雨入り** the「beginning [start] of the rainy season. **梅雨寒** cool weather during the rainy season. **梅雨空** an overcast [a cloudy] sky during the rainy season. **梅雨時** the「rainy [wet] season. ◐ 梅雨時の小糠雨 a drizzle in the rainy season. **梅雨晴れ**〔梅雨以降の〕clear weather after the rainy season;〔梅雨の最中の〕a sunny spell during the rainy season. **梅雨冷え** a cold spell during the rainy season.

つゆだく【汁だく】◐ つゆだくでお願いします.〔牛丼屋で〕Plenty of broth, please.

つれじゃみせん【連れ三味線】playing the samisen together.

て

ていきけん【定期券】 a ⌈rail [bus, train, subway] pass; a ⌈commuting [commuter, commuter's] pass; *a ⌈commutation [commuting, commuter's] ticket; ⁽a season ⌈ticket [pass]; 《口》a season.　■**通学[通勤]定期券** a ⌈commuting [commuter] pass for travel to ⌈school [work].　**定期券入れ** a commuter pass holder.

ティッシュペーパー (a) tissue;〔化粧用〕a facial tissue.

てうちそば[うどん]【手打ちそば[うどん]】 handmade ⌈*soba* [*udon*].

ておどり【手踊り】〔小道具を使わない踊り〕a Kabuki dance performed without props independently of the main plot.

でがたり【出語り】 the two groups of on-stage musicians who provide the main accompaniment in Kabuki.

できちゃったこん【出来ちゃった婚】 a wedding prompted by the bride's pregnancy.

てづかいにんぎょう【手遣い人形】 a puppet manipulated not by strings but directly by hand.

てっかどん【鉄火丼】 a bowl of vinegared boiled rice with slices of raw tuna on top.

てっかまき【鉄火巻き】 raw tuna slices rolled in vinegared boiled rice and covered with dried laver.

てっちり【鉄ちり】〔フグのちり鍋〕a fugu and vegetable hotpot.

てぬぐい【手拭い】 a (hand) towel; a cotton towel.　◐ 手ぬぐいでふく wipe [rub] with a towel; dry 《*one*'s hands》on a towel / 手ぬぐいを絞る wring a towel (out).

てば【手羽】〔鶏肉の羽のつけ根の部分〕a chicken wing.　■**手羽先** a chicken wing tip.

でばかめ【出歯亀】 a Peeping Tom; a voyeur (derives from the name of a man committed of sexual crimes in the Meiji period).

デパちか【デパ地下】〔デパートの地下の食料品・惣菜売場〕the food department in a department store basement.

てまえ【点前】〔茶の湯の作法〕tea ceremony「etiquette [procedure]. [＝おてまえ] ◐けっこうなお点前でございます. That was a beautifully performed ceremony. ■薄茶点前 the tea ceremony procedure for serving weak tea. 濃茶(ごいちゃ)点前 the tea ceremony procedure for serving strong tea.

でまえ【出前】a restaurant meal delivery service; outside catering. ■出前持ち a delivery person.

てまえみそ【手前味噌】〔自慢〕 self-glorification[-praise, -admiration, -flattery]. ◐いささか手前味噌だが… I may be flattering myself, but …; …though I say it myself; at the risk of blowing my own horn… / 手前味噌を言う[並べる] sing *one*'s own praises; blow *one*'s own horn; flatter [praise] *one*self; call *one*'s geese swans.

てまきずし【手巻きずし】hand-rolled sushi; sushi rolled in a crispy seaweed cone.

てまり【手鞠】a traditional ball with a cloth core around which multicolored threads are wound. ■手鞠唄 a handball song.

てらこや【寺子屋】a commercially operated elementary school in the Edo period.

てりかえし【照り返し】reflection; reflected「light [heat]; glare. ◐(道路の)アスファルトの照り返し reflected heat from asphalt / 強い照り返し (a) strong「reflection [glare].

てりやき【照り焼き】teriyaki; grilled meat or fish marinated in sweetened soy sauce. ◐ブリの照り焼き yellowtail broiled with sweet soy sauce / 照り焼きにする broil [grill]《fish》with sweet soy sauce.

てるてるぼうず【照る照る坊主】a paper doll which children hang by the window in hopes of it bringing fine weather.

てんがい【天蓋】1〔仏像・棺などの上にかざす絹がさ〕 a canopy; a baldachin(o) [baldaquin]; a ciborium《*pl.* -ria》. 2〔虚無(こむ)僧の深編みがさ〕a basket of woven rush worn by mendicant Zen monks so as to cover the head and face completely.

でんがく【田楽】1〔舞楽の一種〕ritual music and dancing performed in association with rice planting. 2〔田楽豆腐の略〕bean curd skewered, roasted over coals, and coated with miso. ■田楽焼き a kabob glazed with miso.

でんきかとりき【電気蚊取り器】an electric mosquito zapper.

でんきがま【電気釜】an electric rice cooker.

でんきくらげ【電気水母】a Portuguese man-of-war.

でんきごたつ【電気ごたつ】a kotatsu whose source of heat is electricity.

てんぐ【天狗】〔山の神または妖怪〕a mountain spirit (portrayed as winged and having a long nose); a long-nosed goblin.

てんじゃ【点者】a critic of renga or haikai.

てんじん【天神】**1**〔天の神々〕the gods of heaven. **2**〔天神様〕the deified spirit of Sugawara no Michizane. ■天神講[祭り] the Tenjin Festival.

てんとうむし【天道虫】a ladybug; ⁿa ladybird (beetle); a lady beetle.

てんにょ【天女】〔女性の天人〕a celestial nymph; a heavenly maiden.

てんのう【天皇】a *tennō*; an emperor. ■明治天皇 the Emperor Meiji; the Meiji Emperor. 天皇杯 the Emperor's「Trophy [Cup].

てんのうざん【天王山】**1**〔山名〕Tennōzan Hill. **2**〔勝敗の分かれ目〕a「strategic [make-or-break] point (in a contest); a crisis. ◐天王山の戦い (from the role the taking of this mountain played in the defeat in 1582 of Akechi Mitsuhide by Toyotomi Hideyoshi) a decisive battle.

てんのうたんじょうび【天皇誕生日】(the) Emperor's Birthday.

でんぱソーラーどけい【電波ソーラー時計】a radio-solar clock;〔腕時計〕a radio-solar watch.

てんびんざ【天秤座】〖天・占星〗the Balance; the Scales; Libra (略: Lib). ◐天秤座生まれの人 a Libra; a Libran.

てんぷら【天麩羅】tempura; vegetables or fish dipped in batter and deep-fried. ◐エビのてんぷら prawn tempura; deep-fried prawns in batter. ■てんぷら油 tempura (deep-frying) oil. てんぷらうどん[そば] (a bowl of) *udon* [*soba*] noodles in a hot broth with (prawn) tempura on top.

てんまんぐう【天満宮】a shrine dedicated to Sugawara no Michizane, the patron saint of scholarship.

てんむす(び)【天むす(び)】〔小エビの天ぷらが上に載っているおにぎり〕a rice ball topped with deep-fried shrimp.

と

と【斗】〔尺貫法における容積の単位〕a *to* 《*pl.* ~》(＝約 18.04 l).

といたがえし【戸板返し】〔歌舞伎の〕a revolving panel (with a life-size doll on either side).

とう【籐】〔熱帯産つる性ヤシ類の総称〕rattan (palm). ◖籐で編む weave with rattan. ■籐椅子 a「rattan [cane] chair; a chair with a cane seat; a cane-bottomed chair.

どう【胴】〔よろいなどの〕the plastron; the body armor;〘剣道〙(防具) a breastplate; (決まり手) a「blow [stroke] to the torso.

とうがらし【唐辛子】〔ナス科の 1-多年草; 南アメリカ原産の食用作物〕red [sweet] pepper;〘生薬〙(果実) capsicum;〔香辛料〕(実) a (red, chili) pepper; a chili; (粉) cayenne [red] pepper; chili [chilli] (powder). ■一味唐辛子 (hot) red pepper powder (unmixed with other spices).

とうじ【冬至】〔二十四節気の一にも数えられる〕the winter solstice. ◖今日は冬至だ. Today is the winter solstice.

とうじき【陶磁器】ceramics; ceramic ware; pottery (and「porcelain [china]).

どうそじん【道祖神】the travelers' guardian deity.

とうどり【頭取】〔銀行などの〕a president. ◖N 銀行の頭取 the President of the N. Bank.

とうにゅう【豆乳】soya [soybean] milk.

とうば【塔婆】〔卒塔婆〕a wooden symbol of a fivefold tomb. [＝そとば]

とうふ【豆腐】bean [soybean] curd; tofu. ◖豆腐 1 丁 a「piece [cake] of bean curd. ■焼き豆腐 toasted bean curd. 豆腐がら ＝おから. 豆腐屋 a「tofu [bean curd] dealer [store, seller, maker].

とうもろこし【玉蜀黍】〔イネ科の 1 年草; ペルー原産の穀物〕Indian corn; maize; *corn; Zea mays. ■とうもろこし色 maize; pale yellow. とうもろこし畑 *a cornfield; a field of「*corn [maize]. とうも

[189]

とおし

ろこしパン *corn bread; *《南部》(corn) pone.

とおし【通し】〖料理〗〔つき出し・前菜〕〚F〛 *hors d'oeuvre*; a relish.

とき【鴇・桃花鳥・朱鷺】〖鳥〗a Japanese crested ibis 《*pl.* -ses, 〈集合的に〉～》.

ときいろ【鴇色】pink; pale rose; damask. ◖鴇色のドレス a (pale) pink dress.

ときわず【常磐津】〔浄瑠璃の〕a *tokiwazu* ballad.

どくみやく【毒味役】a taster.

どげざ【土下座】getting down on *one*'s hands and knees (in obeisance); kowtowing. ～する kneel [squat, sit down, prostrate *one*self] on the ground; strike the ground with the forehead; kneel 《to [before]…》.

とこのま【床の間】a tokonoma; an alcove; the recess in a Japanese room in which a scroll may be hung.

ところてん【心太】gelidium jelly.

とさいぬ【土佐犬】a Tosa dog.

とさじょうゆ【土佐醤油】a sweet soy-based dip for sashimi.

とさは【土佐派】the Tosa school of painting.

とさぶし【土佐節】1〔浄瑠璃の一派〕the Tosa style of singing. 2〔かつお節〕fine-quality dried bonito.

としごい(の)まつり【祈年祭】a Shinto service to pray for a good crop.

としこしそば【年越しそば】buckwheat noodles eaten on New Year's Eve.

としのまめ【年の豆】lucky beans scattered at the ritual *setsubun* welcoming of spring.

どじょう【泥鰌・鰌】a dojo; a loach. ■ どじょうすくい scooping loaches; catching loach with a basket;〔踊り〕a loach-scooping[-catching] dance.

とそ【屠蘇】spiced sake (drunk in celebration of the New Year).

とそきげん【屠蘇機嫌】《be》under the influence of [drunk with] the New Year's sake.

とそきぶん【屠蘇気分】《in》a festive New Year's mood.

とそさん【屠蘇散】spices for flavoring New Year's sake.

とっくり【徳利】a sake bottle.

どてら【褞袍】a padded kimono.

どどいつ【都々逸】a Japanese popular love song of the Edo period in the 7-7-7-5 syllable pattern.

とび【鳶】 **1** 〘鳥〙〔一般に〕a kite; 〔日本の〕a black kite; a black-eared kite. ◐ 鳶が空を舞う a kite wheels in the air / 鳶が鷹(たか)を生んだとはこのことだ. It is a case「of a black hen laying white eggs [of the child excelling the parents]. / 鳶に油揚げをさらわれたように with a look of surprise; with a look of astonishment. **2** 〔鳶職〕a fireman; 〘建〙a scaffolding man.

とびいろ【鳶色】 brown; auburn.

とびうお【飛び魚】 a flying fish.

どひょう【土俵】 **1** 〔土を詰めた俵〕a sandbag; a gabion. **2** 〔土俵場〕the sumo (wrestling) ring. ◐ 土俵で in the ring / 土俵に上がる〔力士が〕step up into the ring / 土俵につまる be pushed to the edge of the ring / 土俵を割る be pushed out of the ring / 土俵を退く retire from the ring. **3** 〔対決や話し合いの場〕a forum for「deciding [discussing] an issue. ◐ 相手の土俵で相撲を取る contest an issue on *one*'s opponent's terms / 同じ土俵で勝負する negotiate an issue on the basis of a common understanding. ■ **土俵入り** a parade around the ring of sumo wrestlers wearing their brocaded aprons. **土俵ぎわで** on the「edge [brink] of the ring; at the ring's edge;〔きわどい時〕at the「last [critical] moment; at the eleventh hour. ◐ 土俵ぎわに追いつめられる be driven to the edge of the ring 《by...》.

とめそで【留め袖】 a married woman's formal kimono decorated with five crests and a pattern around the skirt. ■ **色留め袖** a married woman's formal kimono with a colored ground, decorated with five crests and a pattern around the skirt. **黒留め袖** a married woman's formal kimono with a black ground, decorated with five crests and a pattern around the skirt.

ともびき【友引】〔六曜の〕a day, in a recurring six-day calendrical cycle, when *one*'s luck affects other people; hence, a good day for weddings and a bad day for funerals.

どよう【土用】 the hottest part of summer; midsummer; the dog days; the *doyō* season. ◐ 土用の暑さ the heat of the dog days; the canicular heat / 土用の入り[明け] the「beginning [end] of the *doyō* season / 土用の丑の日 ⇒ うし[1]. ■ **土用波** high waves in the dog days.

とら[1]【虎】 **1** 〔ネコ科の動物〕a tiger;（雌）a tigress. ◐ 虎がほえた. A

tiger roared. / 虎の威を借る狐 a fox borrowing a tiger's authority; a small man acting arrogantly by hanging onto the shirttails of a powerful figure.　**2**〔酔っ払い〕a drunkard; a sot;《口》a boozer.　◐虎になる get「beastly [riotously, dead] drunk; get「boozed up [boozy].

とら²【寅】〔十二支の〕the Tiger, one of the twelve animals of the Oriental zodiac.　◐寅の日 the Day of the Tiger / 寅の刻(ᶜ) the Hour of the Tiger(; 3-5 a.m.) / 寅の方(ᵏᵃ)〔東北東〕the Direction of the Tiger(; east-northeast).　■**寅年** the year of the Tiger.　◐寅年生まれの born in the year of the Tiger.

どらやき【どら焼】a confection of bean jam sandwiched between gong-shaped pancakes.

とり¹【酉】〔十二支の〕the「Cock [Rooster], one of the twelve animals of the Oriental zodiac.　◐酉の日 the Day of the「Cock [Rooster] / 酉の刻(ᶜ) the Hour of the「Cock [Rooster](; 5-7 p.m.) / 酉の方(ᵏᵃ)〔西〕the Direction of the「Cock [Rooster](; west).　■**酉年** the year of the「Cock [Rooster].　◐酉年生まれの born in the year of the「Cock [Rooster].

とり²【鳥】　1〔鳥類〕a bird; a fowl; a「feathered [winged] creature.　◐かごの鳥 a caged bird;〔自由のない人〕a bird in a cage.　**2**〔食用の〕a fowl;〈集合的に〉poultry;〔鶏〕(雌) a hen; (雄) a cock; a chicken;〔鳥肉〕chicken; fowl.

とりい【鳥居】a torii《*pl.* ~》; an archway to a Shinto shrine.

とりいは【鳥居派】〔浮世絵の〕the Torii school of ukiyo-e.

とりがい【鳥貝】an edible cockle; an egg cockle.

とりのいち【酉の市】a "Tori-no-ichi" Fair; a Cock Fair; a fair held at Ōtori Shrine on each Day of the Cock in November.

とりふだ【取り札】〔百人一首で, 読み札に対し〕(in the game of hyakunin isshu) cards spread face up from which players capture the one that completes a poem read to them.

とろ〔マグロなどの〕oily bluefin tuna meat; fatty flesh of「tuna [tunny].

とろろこんぶ【とろろ昆布】tangle shaved into stringy, paper-thin shavings.

とんカツ【豚カツ】a breaded pork cutlet.

どんぐり【団栗】an acorn.　◐彼らはどんぐりの背比べだ. They are all much of a muchness. | There is little to choose between them.

とんこつ【豚骨】pig bones.　◐豚骨スープ pig bone soup.

とんじる【豚汁】miso soup with pork and (several) vegetables; pork miso soup.

どんたく〚<Du. *Zondag*〛Sunday; a holiday.　■博多どんたく a festival held at Kushida Shrine in Hakata on May 3–4.

どんど(やき)【どんど(焼き)】making a bonfire of the New Year's decorations (such as pine branches, bamboos, and straw festoons), at a shrine on the 15th of January.

とんぼ【蜻蛉】**1** a dragonfly; a devil's darning needle.　**2**〔グラウンド整備用のレーキ〕a (ground) rake.

とんぼがえり【蜻蛉返り】〔行ってすぐ帰ること〕go and come back without resting.　～する make a round-trip without stopping for a rest / 大阪へ行ってとんぼ返りで戻ってくる go to Osaka and come back without stopping over.

な

なえ【萎え】1〔気力・体力が抜けること〕weakening; (a) loss of strength. ●気持ちの萎え a feeling of depression;《口》the blues / 仕事で失敗が続き, 最近気分が萎え気味だ. Recently I've been feeling a bit down because of a series of missteps [mistakes] at work. **2**〔アニメ・漫画ファンの間で, キャラクターへの興味が冷めること〕a loss of interest; a letdown feeling;〔嫌悪感を抱くこと〕disgust; dislike. **3**〔がっかりすること〕disappointment. ●明日は休日出勤しなきゃならなくなっちゃった. 激萎えだあ. Tomorrow I have to go to work on what was supposed to be my day off.「What a「letdown [drag]! ■萎え要素 a disappointing「feature [aspect]. ●あのゲームの下手な効果音は萎え要素だ. That game's clumsy sound effects are a real turnoff.

なかいり【中入り】〔寄席・相撲などの〕an intermission; a break; an interval;〔能で〕a temporary exit from the stage by the principal actor.

ながうた【長唄】*nagauta*; ballads usually sung to samisen accompaniment; originally developed for use in Kabuki in eighteenth-century Edo out of elements of folk music and Noh.

ながしびな【流し雛】dolls floated「down a river [out to sea] as part of the Girl's Festival held on March 3.

ながばおり【長羽織】a long *haori* coat.

ながばかま【長袴】a trailing *hakama* trousers.

なかまく【中幕】a short play enacted between the feature performances of a Kabuki program; the middle piece of a three-item Kabuki program.

ながもち【長持】a large oblong chest《for clothing》.

ながや【長屋】*a row house; a terrace(d) house. ●長屋住まいをする, 長屋に住む live in a row house / 長屋の住人 a row house tenant. ■裏長屋 a row house along a back alley. **2軒長屋** a two-family house; *a duplex (house); "a semidetached house. **3軒長屋** a row house divided into three units. **長屋造りの** built in「row-house ["terrace-house] style;〔安普請の〕jerry-built.

なぎなた【薙刀】a Japanese halberd; a partisan.

なげいれ【投げ入れ】〔華道〕a style of creating a simple arrangement of flowers and other plants in a vase without a pin frog; freestyle flower arrangement; the *nageire* style (of flower arrangement).

なげこみでら【投げ込み寺】〔江戸時代の〕a temple where unidentified or unclaimed bodies《of travelers or prostitutes》were buried.

なこうど【仲人】〔人〕a go-between; a matchmaker;〔役割〕matchmaking. ◐ 仲人をする act as「a go-between [go-betweens]; arrange a「marriage [match]《between A and B》.

なし【梨】〔実〕a pear;〔特に洋梨と区別して〕an Asian [a Japanese] pear;〔木〕a pear tree.

なす【茄子】〔ナス科の1年草; インド原産の野菜〕an [a garden] *eggplant; an "aubergine.

なすこん【茄子紺】dark purple; aubergine [eggplant, bishop's] purple.

なたね【菜種】rapeseed; coleseed; colza. ■ **菜種油**〚薬〛rapeseed oil.

なっとう【納豆】fermented soybeans; *nattō*. ■ **納豆売り** a vendor of fermented soybeans. **納豆菌** *Bacillus nattō*. **納豆汁** miso soup with (minced) fermented soybeans. **納豆巻き** a sushi containing *nattō* and rolled in nori.

なつみかん【夏蜜柑】〔木・実〕a Chinese citron; a Watson pomelo; a summer orange.

なつメロ【懐メロ】a favorite old tune; an old favorite; a golden oldie. ■ **懐メロ歌手** a singer of「old-time favorite songs [golden oldies].

なとり【名取り】an accredited master《of Japanese dance》.

ななくさ【七草】〔春の〕the seven spring herbs;〔秋の〕the seven autumn flowers;〔正月の七日〕the seventh of January. ▶「春の七草」は、セリ (dropwort), ナズナ (shepherd's purse), ゴギョウ ((a) cudweed), ハコベラ (chickweed), ホトケノザ (henbit), スズナ ((a) turnip), スズシロ ((a) garden radish),「秋の七草」は、ハギ (bush clover), ススキ (miscanthus), クズ (a *kudzu*), ナデシコ ((a) fringed pink), オミナエシ ((a) patrinia), フジバカマ ((a) thoroughwort), キキョウ ((a) Chinese bellflower) を言う. ◐ 七草の節句 the Festival of Seven Herbs (7 January). ■ **七草がゆ**

rice porridge with seven spring herbs, traditionally taken on the 7th of January to invoke health in the new year.

なにわぶし【浪花節】a narrative ballad chanted solo to samisen accompaniment.

なのはな【菜の花】rape. ◐一面の菜の花 a broad expanse of rape blossoms. ■菜の花畑 a rape field; a field of rape.

なべぶぎょう【鍋奉行】a person who delights in directing the cooking of food in a pot at the table; a pot boss.

なべやきうどん【鍋焼きうどん】an individual meal of vegetables, fish, and meat morsels in clear broth served, with wheat-flour noodles, in the pot in which it is cooked.

なまこ【海鼠】a sea「slug [cucumber]; [西洋の] a trepang.

なます【膾】a dish of raw fish and vegetables seasoned in vinegar; Japanese fish salad; a pickled salad of daikon and carrots.

なまず【鯰】a catfish. ◐鯰は地震を予知するというのは本当かしら? I wonder if it's true that catfish can predict an earthquake?

なまたまご【生卵】a raw egg.

なまはげ【生剥】*namahage*; a custom still current on the Oga Peninsula in Akita of young men, on the night of the fifteenth of January, wearing large troll masks and straw capes and, brandishing swords, going from house to house, where they offer new year felicitations and are fêted.

なまり【訛り】an [a provincial] accent;〔方言〕a dialect; a patois; a provincialism;〔転訛〕a corrupted form; a corruption. ◐鹿児島なまり丸出しで話す speak in a「heavy [broad] Kagoshima accent.

なまりぶし【生り節】half-dried bonito.

なめし【菜飯】rice boiled with vegetable greens.

ならじだい【奈良時代】the Nara period (710–794).

ならづけ【奈良漬】pickles seasoned in sake lees (a practice originating in Nara).

なんが【南画】the「Nan-ga [Bunjin-ga] school of Japanese painting; Southern [Literati] painting (a style of painting that originated in China).

なんきんたますだれ【南京玉簾】a style of street performance using bamboo screens.

ナンバはしり[あるき]【ナンバ走り[歩き]】◐〔同側の手と足が同時に前に出る走り方[歩き方]〕running [walking] with the arm and leg on the same side of the body swinging synchronized.

なんばん【南蛮】〔南方の蛮人〕southern barbarians; 〔唐辛子〕cayenne [red] pepper. ■ 南蛮人[船] an early European「visitor [ship] (principally from Spain and Portugal and arriving from the south). ■ 南蛮漬 roasted or deep-fried fish or meat marinated in a spicy sauce. 南蛮寺 a Christian church (*nanban dera* as it was called in pre-Meiji times). 南蛮煮 a dish of boiled vegetables and meat or fish, with peppers and leeks. 南蛮屏風 a painted screen depicting scenes of sixteenth- and seventeenth-century European visitors. 南蛮文化 European and Christian culture brought in by Portuguese visitors in the sixteenth century. 南蛮貿易 Japan's trade with Spain and Portugal in the sixteenth and seventeenth centuries.

なんぶてつびん【南部鉄瓶】a Nanbu iron kettle cast in Iwate and Morioka prefectures.

なんほくちょうじだい【南北朝時代】the Period of the Northern and Southern Courts (1334–1392).

に

におう【仁王】the two Deva kings; the guardian gods (at either side temple gate). ■仁王門 a「Deva [temple] gate.

にがり【苦汁】bittern《used to firm tofu》.

にぎりずし【握り鮨】sushi shaped by hand.

にくじゃが【肉じゃが】boiled [simmered] meat and potatoes (with soy sauce and sugar).

にくだんご【肉団子】a meat「ball [dumpling]; a quenelle.

にくまん【肉饅】a meat bun; a soft, steamed bun with a filling of meat.

にしき【錦】〔織物〕Japanese brocade;〔美しい衣装〕fine dress. ◐錦の御旗 the Imperial standard (made of gold brocade); the banner of《democracy》.

にしきえ【錦絵】a color print; a colored woodblock print.

にしきごい【錦鯉】a「dappled [multi-colored, brocade, *nishiki*] carp; a *nishikigoi*.

にしじんおり【西陣織】*Nishijin* brocade (woven at Nishijin in Kyoto).

にじます【虹鱒】〔サケ科の魚〕a rainbow trout.

にじゅうしせっき【二十四節気】the 24 seasonal divisions of a year in the old lunisolar calendar. ▶順に, 立春・雨水・啓蟄・春分・清明・穀雨・立夏・小満・芒種・夏至・小暑・大暑・立秋・処暑・白露・秋分・寒路・霜降・立冬・小雪・大雪・冬至・小寒・大寒.

にじりぐち【躙り口】a low entrance to a teahouse that requires a participant in a tea ceremony to bend his head to enter.

にしん【鰊・鯡】a herring. ◐ニシンの燻製 a「red [smoked] herring;〔開きにした〕a kippered herring; a kipper;〔丸干しの〕a bloater. ■身欠き鰊 a dried (gutted) herring.

にせたいじゅうたく【二世帯住宅】a two-family house; a house for a two-generation family.

に(っ)ころがし【煮(っ)ころがし】〔いもの〕taro corms, stirred constantly to prevent scorching, that have been cooked until all the natural juices evaporate.

にはいず【二杯酢】『料理』two-flavor vinegar; vinegar with soy sauce added; a「combination [mixture] of vinegar and soy sauce (with a little *dashi*).

にぼし【煮干し】dried small sardines.

にほんさんけい【日本三景】the Three (Great) Sights of Japan; the「three noted views of [scenic trio of, three most famous scenic places in] Japan (Matsushima, Miyajima and Ama-no-Hashidate).

にほんしゅ【日本酒】sake; rice wine.

にほんていえん【日本庭園】a Japanese (-style) garden; a traditional Japanese landscape garden.

にほんとう【日本刀】a Japanese sword; a *katana* 《*pl.* ~s》.

にほんぶよう【日本舞踊】(classical) Japanese dance [dancing].

にゅうばい【入梅】the beginning of the「rainy [wet] season. ◐入梅になった. The rainy season has「begun [set in].

にゅうよく【入浴】a bath; bathing. ～する have [take] a (hot) bath; go in the bath; bathe. ◐たびたび入浴する enjoy frequent baths. ■入浴介助 bathing assistance. 訪問入浴サービス a home [an in-home, a visiting] bath(ing) service. 入浴剤 bath「salts [oil]; bubble bath; a bath「additive [agent]; spa powder.

にわかあめ【俄雨】a (sudden, rain) shower. ◐にわか雨にあう be「caught in [overtaken by] a shower.

にわかきょうげん【俄[仁輪加]狂言】a mime; a farce.

にんぎょうじょうるり【人形浄瑠璃】a Japanese puppet drama [the *Jōruri* puppet theater] (in which dialogue and narrative are recited to samisen accompaniment).

にんぎょうやき【人形焼き】〔人形の形をした和菓子〕a small cake with sweet beanjam filling shaped like a doll.

にんげんドック【人間ドック】a thorough physical「examination [checkup]. ◐日帰りの人間ドック a thorough physical「examination [checkup] without an overnight stay in a hospital / 1泊2日の人間ドック a thorough physical「examination [checkup] with an overnight stay in a hospital / 人間ドックに入る have [undergo] a thorough physical examination.

にんじゃ【忍者】a ninja; a secret agent (in feudal Japan) highly skilled in stealth and secrecy.

にんじゅつ【忍術】the art of spycraft [stealth, a ninja]. ◐忍術を使う use one's skills as a secret agent.

にんじん【人参】〔セリ科の1-2年草; 野菜〕a carrot. ◐にんじん色の carroty; carrot-colored.

にんにく【大蒜】〔ユリ科の多年草; 中央アジア原産の香辛料植物〕a garlic;〔香辛料〕《a clove of》garlic. ◐にんにく臭い garlicky; smelling of garlic / にんにくのみじん切り minced garlic.

ぬ

ぬか【糠】rice「bran [polish]. ◐ ぬか臭い smell of bran; be redolent of bran / キュウリをぬかに漬ける pickle cucumbers in bran / ぬかを取る〔米をといで〕polish 《a bag of rice》 remove the bran (coating)《from the rice》/ 糠に釘(を打つ) plow the sand(s); sow (*one*'s seeds in) the sand; have no effect 《on…》; be lost upon *somebody*.

ぬかづけ【糠漬け】vegetables pickled in a fermented medium of rice bran and brine.

ぬかどこ【糠床】a fermented mixture of rice bran and brine used as a pickling medium.

ぬかみそ【糠味噌】a fermented mixture of rice bran and brine used as a pickling medium.

ぬた〘料理〙finely chopped fish or vegetables in a sauce of vinegar and miso.

ぬりげた【塗り下駄】lacquered「getas [clogs].

ぬれえん【濡れ縁】an open veranda(h).

ぬれぎぬ【濡れ衣】a false [an unjust, a trumped-up] charge [accusation, imputation]; groundless [unfounded] suspicion. ◐ ぬれぎぬを着せる unjustly accuse 《*somebody* of theft》; make [bring] a false charge 《of espionage》 against *somebody*; charge *somebody* unjustly 《with bribery》/ ぬれぎぬを着せられる[着る] be「falsely [unjustly, wrongly] accused 《of stealing》; be falsely charged 《with murder》; be unjustly suspected of a guilt.

ぬれティッシュ【濡れティッシュ】a pre-moistened [moist] tissue; a (pre-moistened) wipe.

ぬれねずみ【濡れ鼠】ぬれねずみになる get「wet [drenched, soaked] to the skin; get [be] wet through; be dripping wet; be thoroughly drenched; be (as) wet as a drowned rat.

ね

ね【子】〔十二支の〕the Rat, the first of the twelve animals of the oriental zodiac. ▶ 子の日 the day of the Rat / 子の刻(こく) the hour of the Rat; 11 p.m.-1 a.m. / 子の方(かた)〔北〕the direction of the Rat; north / 子年 the year of the Rat.

ねぎ【葱】〔ユリ科の多年草; 中央アジア原産の野菜〕a Welsh onion; a spring onion;〔ワケギ〕a scallion;〔ニラネギ〕a leek;〔アサツキ・エゾネギ〕a chive.

ねぎとろ【葱とろ】the fatty flesh of tuna minced to a paste and mixed with chopped green leaves of Welsh onions.

ねぎま【葱間】yakitori of alternate pieces of chicken and Welsh onion (on a skewer).

ねじりはちまき【捩じり鉢巻き】a tightly twisted towel worn as a headband. ▶ ねじり鉢巻きで with a twisted cotton headband tied around *one*'s head;〔一生懸命に〕with all *one*'s might; as hard as *one* can; wholeheartedly.

ねつけ【根付け】a netsuke; an intricately carved ivory, coral, quartz or other toggle, worn suspended outside *one*'s kimono sash and attached by a cord to a purse tucked under the sash.

ネットいぞんしょう【ネット依存症】Internet Addiction Disorder (略: IAD).

ネットカフェ〔インターネットカフェ〕an Internet café.

ネットしょてん【ネット書店】an Internet ⌈bookshop [bookstore]; an online ⌈bookshop [bookstore].

ネットしんじゅう【ネット心中】an Internet suicide pact.

ねぶた[ねぷた]まつり【ねぶた[ねぷた]祭り】the ⌈Nebuta [Neputa] Festival; a Tōhoku region festival, celebrating Tanabata, with a colorful procession of giant human- and animal-shaped lanterns.

ねまわし【根回し】1〔樹木を移植する前に根を切り詰め, 細根を発生させておくこと〕trimming all but the main roots of a tree to foster root development a year or two before transplanting.　**2**〔計画がうまくいくようあらかじめ関係者に働きかけること〕prior consultation; doing the groundwork; forgoing making a decision until behind-the-scenes consensus-building is completed.　◐彼の根回しが功を奏し, その議案に対して反対論はまったく出なかった. His efforts in building a consensus bore fruit and not a single voice was raised in opposition to the bill. / 根回しをする lay the groundwork 《for obtaining *one*'s objective》; maneuver behind the scenes / 根回し工作 behind-the-scenes maneuvering; backstairs dealing.

ねんが【年賀】New Year's greetings; a New Year's「call [visit].　◐年賀に行く pay a New Year's「call [visit]《to…》/ 年賀に回る make (a round of) New Year's「calls [visits] / 年賀の客 a New Year's「caller [visitor] / 年賀の挨拶(あいさつ)を交わす wish each other a happy New Year; exchange New Year's greetings《with…》/ 喪中につき年賀をご遠慮申しあげます. Being in mourning, I respectfully refrain from sending you my greetings for the New Year.　■**年賀電報** a New Year's telegram.　**年賀はがき** ＝ねんがじょう.　**年賀回り**　◐年賀回りをする make *one*'s New Year's round of calls.　**年賀郵便** New Year's mail.

ねんがじょう【年賀状】a New Year's (greeting) card.　◐年賀状を出す send *somebody* a New Year's (greeting) card / お年賀状ありがとう. Thanks for your New Year's card.

ねんぶつ【念仏】〖仏教〗a Buddhist invocation; a prayer to Amitabha; repetition of the sacred name of Amitabha.　◐念仏を唱える pray to Amitabha; chant [say] a prayer to Amitabha; tell *one*'s beads.

の

のう【能】〔能楽〕(the) Noh (drama); a Noh「dance [play]. ■ 能衣裳[装束] (a) Noh costume.　能舞台 a Noh stage.　能役者 a Noh「actor [player].

のうかい【納会】the last meeting of the「year [term, month];〔取引所の〕the「last [closing] session of the month.

のうきょうげん【能狂言】〔狂言〕a Noh farce; *kyōgen*;〔能と狂言〕a Noh play and interlude.

のうめん【能面】a Noh mask.

のきまるがわら【軒丸瓦】a kind of tile with a round edge which is used at the edge of the eaves.

のし【熨斗】a *noshi*; originally a thin strip of dried abalone folded in a variety of special patterns in red and white paper (attached as an auspicious symbol to a gift), now usually printed on wrapping paper.

のしあわび【熨斗鮑】a long, thin strip of dried abalone (attached to a gift).

のしがみ【熨斗紙】(Japanese) gift wrapping paper; wrapping paper with an emblematic *noshi* decoration printed on it.

のしぶくろ【熨斗袋】a gift envelope; a special decorative envelope (with a *noshi* on it) for a gift of money.

のしめ【熨斗目】a ceremonial robe worn under the *kamishimo* by a samurai. [⇨ かみしも]

のしもち【伸し餅】a flattened *mochi*.

のだて【野点】a tea ceremony「performed [held] in the open air.

のちじて【後仕手】〔能楽〕the principal actor (in the second part of a Noh play).

のっぺらぼう〔平らなこと〕monotony; flatness;〔目・口・鼻のないお化け〕a goblin with a blank, featureless face.　〜な flat and smooth. ▷

[204]

のっぺらぼうな顔 a flat, expressionless face;〔その化け物の顔〕the smooth, featureless face of a type of Japanese goblin.　のっぺらぼうに monotonously.　◐のっぺらぼうに朗読する read「monotonously [in a monotonous voice].

のどあめ【喉飴】(a) throat candy; a throat lozenge; a cough drop.

のどじまん【喉自慢】〔人〕a person who is proud of「his [her] good voice; a person who likes to sing in front of other people;〔事〕pride in *one*'s「voice [singing ability].　◐素人のど自慢〘テレビ・ラジオ〙an amateur singing contest (on radio or television).　のど自慢大会 an amateur singing contest.　◐カラオケのど自慢大会 an amateur karaoke singing contest.　のど自慢日本一 the winner of the first prize in the National Amateur Singing Contest.

のり【海苔】laver; nori; an edible seaweed of the genus *Porphyra*.　◐のりの佃煮(つくだ) laver boiled down in soy sauce.　■青のり green laver; a species of edible seaweed of the genus *Enteromorpha*.　味付けのり dried and seasoned「laver [nori].　焼きのり toasted「laver [nori].

のりと【祝詞】a Shinto prayer.

のりまき【海苔巻き】vinegared rice wrapped in nori; a sushi roll.

のれん【暖簾】1〔店名などを書いて店先に下げるもの〕a short curtain hung outside a restaurant or shop to indicate that it is open for business; a shop curtain;〔室内の装飾用〕a split curtain (used to divide spaces within a house); a partitioning curtain.　◐のれんを掛けて開店する put out the curtain and「open [start business] / のれんをおろす〔閉店する〕(take down the curtain and) close up shop / 私は質屋ののれんをくぐったことがない. I've never「been into [had dealings with] a pawnbroker('s).　**2**〔店の信用〕credit; (a) reputation; a good name;〔店の株〕goodwill.　◐のれんに傷がつく damage the「reputation [good name] of a「store [shop, firm] / 古いのれんの店 a long-established「shop [store]; a shop with a long tradition; a shop of long standing / のれんを分ける start *somebody* [set *somebody* up] in the same business; help an employee to start up a branch of the same firm (and share *one*'s clientele with him or her).　暖簾に腕押し be like beating the air; be (a) waste of「time [labor]; have no effect at all; make no impression.

のれんわけ【暖簾分け】helping a long-term employee to set up a branch of the same shop and to share the clientele.　～する start *somebody* [set *somebody* up] in the same business.　◐ のれん分けしてもらう be given a branch of *one*'s own and a share of the clientele.

ノンけ【ノン気】〔同性愛嗜好がない人〕 a heterosexual; a straight 《man》;〈集合的に〉straights.

は

はいが【俳画】(a) *haiga*; (a) *haikai* painting; a watercolor or ink painting done in a witty and simple haiku-like style.

はいかい【俳諧】〔和歌の一形式〕popular [playful] linked verse; *haikai* (poetry);〔俳句〕haiku (poetry). [＝はいく]　■俳諧師 a *haikai* poet.

はいく【俳句】a haiku; a Japanese poem in seventeen syllables having a 5-7-5 syllabic form and traditionally containing a reference to a season.

はいじん【俳人】a haiku poet; a haikuist.

はいだん【俳壇】haiku circles; the world of haiku.

ばいにく【梅肉】plum pulp.　■梅肉エキス plum extract.

はいぶん【俳文】(a piece of) poetical prose written by a haiku poet; "haiku prose."

はいみ【俳味】refined taste as shown in haiku; marked「detachment; subdued [severe] taste.

はいめい【俳名】a pen name as a haiku poet; a haiku poet's pen name.

はえ【蠅】a fly.

はおり【羽織】a *haori* 《pl. 〜s》; a (Japanese)「half-coat [short overgarment].　■羽織袴(はかま)　◐羽織袴で in *haori* and *hakama*; in full dress.

はかたにんぎょう【博多人形】a Hakata earthenware doll.

はかま【袴】〔衣服の〕a *hakama*; loose-legged pleated trousers for formal wear;（女性の）a pleated skirt (worn over a kimono).

はかまいり[もうで]【墓参り[詣で]】a visit to a grave.　◐墓参をする visit [pay a visit to] *somebbody*'s grave.

ぱくり〔盗用・剽窃〕cribbing; lifting.　◐彼の新曲はアメリカで流行った歌のぱくりだと言われている. There are rumors that he pirated a song popular in America for his new tune. / ぱくり屋 a company or person defrauding businesses out of money or goods on credit.

ばけねこ【化け猫】a goblin cat.

はごいた【羽子板】a battledore; a wooden paddle with a picture on one side used to hit a shuttlecock. ■羽子板市 a battledore fair.

はこいりむすめ【箱入り娘】an innocent girl (brought up in the bosom) of a good family; a naive girl who knows nothing of the world; a hidden flower.

はし【箸】《a pair of》chopsticks. ◐箸が進む appetizing《food》/ 箸が転んでもおかしい年ごろ an age when even a dropped chopstick is hilarious / 箸をつける touch《the dish》; eat《the food》. ■はし置き a rest for chopsticks; a chopstick rest. はし立て a chopstick stand. はし箱 a chopstick case. 箸袋 a chopstick「envelope [wrapper]; a paper envelope for chopsticks.

はしやすめ【箸休め】a side dish served between the main courses.

はた【羽太】〔スズキ科ハタ亜科の魚の総称〕a grouper.

はたはた〚魚〛a sandfish.

はち【蜂】〔蜜蜂〕a bee;〔黄蜂〕a wasp;〔大黄蜂〕a hornet;〔地蜂〕a ground wasp;〔穴蜂〕a bumblebee. ◐蜂に刺される be stung by a「wasp [bee].

はちじゅうはち【八十八】eighty-eight. ◐四国八十八箇所〔大師の霊場〕the Eighty-eight Holy Places of Shikoku. ■八十八夜 the eighty-eighth day from the setting-in of spring.

はちのす【蜂の巣】a beehive; a hive; a honeycomb; a comb. ◐蜂の巣をつついたような騒ぎだ be in utter confusion;《俗》be [go] haywire.

はちまき【鉢巻き】〔頭の〕a headband; a frontlet (often worn as a symbol of concentration or dedication to achieving a goal). ◐手ぬぐいで鉢巻きをする wear [tie] a towel around *one*'s head.

はちまん【八幡】the God of War. ■八幡様 a Hachiman shrine.

パチンコ 1〔投石具〕a slingshot; a catapult. 2〔遊戯〕pachinko; a kind of vertical pinball game played in pachinko parlors, where the object is to increase the number of pinballs to exchange for prizes; Japanese pinball. ■パチンコ玉 a pachinko ball; a pinball. パチンコ屋〔店〕a pachinko parlor, offering patrons rows of pachinko machines and a counter for exchanging pinballs for prizes;〔人〕a pachinko parlor operator.

はつがつお【初鰹】the first bonito of the season.

はつがま【初釜】the first tea ceremony of the New Year.

はっけい【八景】近江(おうみ)八景 the eight scenic spots around Lake Biwa (in Ōmi Province, now Shiga Prefecture); the eight views at Ōmi.

はつぜっく【初節句】《celebrate》a baby's first Boys' [Girls'] Festival.

ばった【飛蝗・蝗】a grasshopper; 〔群飛する〕a locust.

はつびな【初雛】a girl's first doll's festival (3 March).

はつもうで【初詣】the practice of visiting a shrine or a temple at the beginning of the New Year.

はつゆめ【初夢】*one*'s first dream in the New Year 《symbolic images such as Mt. Fuji are held to be auspicious》.

ばとうかんのん【馬頭観音】an image of Kannon with a human body and a horse's head; an image of Kannon with a horsehead in the crown.

はなあわせ【花合わせ】〔花札ゲーム〕a game played with hanafuda or "floral cards"; 〔花札の札〕Japanese floral playing cards.

はなお【鼻緒】a「clog [sandal] thong; a strap 《of a geta》.

はながさ【花笠】a hat adorned with flowers.

はながつお【花鰹】dried bonito shavings.

はなしょうぶ【花菖蒲】〔アヤメ科の多年草; 栽培植物〕a Japanese iris 《*pl.* ~es, irides》.

はなだい【花代】1 〔花の代金〕the price of a flower. **2** 〔芸者の〕a charge for a geisha's services; a geisha's fee.

はなみ【花見】cherry blossom viewing; 〔行楽〕a picnic under the cherry blossoms. ◐ 花見に行く go to see the cherry blossoms 《at...》; go (out) cherry blossom viewing. ■ 花見踊り dancing under the cherry blossoms. 花見客 〔一団の〕a group of cherry blossom viewers. 花見酒 sake drunk while viewing cherry blossoms. 花見時[シーズン] the cherry blossom season.

はなび【花火】fireworks; 〔音を主とする〕a firecracker. ◐ そら, 花火が上がった. The fireworks have「started [gone off]! / 今夜隅田川で花火がある. There will be a display of fireworks on the Sumida River this evening. / 花火を上げる display [set off, let off, launch] fireworks. ■ 打ち上げ花火 a (sky)rocket; 〔大型の〕an aerial shell. 回転花火 a rotating firework; a Catherine wheel; a girandole. 仕掛け花火 set fireworks; (1個) a set piece of fireworks. 花火工場 a fireworks factory. 花火師 a fireworks「expert [manufacturer]; a pyrotechnist; a pyrotechnician.　花火大会 a fireworks display; a display [an exhibition] of fireworks.

はなふだ【花札】a deck of Japanese playing cards with 12 suits of 4 cards, each suit representing the month signified by a flower.

はなみち【花道】a "flower way"; an elevated walkway extending from the stage, through the audience to the rear of a Kabuki theater.　◖花道から出てくる appear at the end of the *hanamichi* / …をして引退の花道にする *do something* to adorn the final「days [page] of *one*'s career; pave the way for a happy end to *one*'s career / 彼女は東京マラソンに優勝して引退の花道を飾った. Winning the Tokyo marathon marked a brilliant close to her career.

はなや【花屋】a florist;〔栽培業者〕a floriculturist; a horticulturist;〔店〕a flower shop; a florist's;(屋台店) a flower stall.

はなわ【花輪・花環】a wreath; a garland (of flowers);(首にかける) a lei.　◖花輪で飾る deck with a garland; garland / 花輪で飾られた flower-garlanded 《ramp》 / 花輪を編む make [wreathe] a garland; twine a wreath [garland].

はにわ【埴輪】a *haniwa*; a hollow clay「figure [figurine]《of a man, of a horse》.

はねつき【羽子突き】battledore and shuttlecock; Japanese badminton.

ははのひ【母の日】Mother's Day.　◖母の日のプレゼントにカーネーションを贈る send (*one*'s mother) carnations for [on] Mother's Day.

はぶたえ【羽二重】*habutae*(-silk).　◖黒羽二重 black *habutae* / 羽二重餅 a rice cake made from refined rice flour.

はまぐり【蛤】a clam; *a quahaug; a quahog; a cherrystone (clam).　◖ハマグリの殻 a clamshell.　■焼きはまぐり a baked clam.

はまち【魬】〔ぶりの幼魚〕a young yellowtail. [⇨ ぶり]

はも【鱧】〔魚〕a pike conger; a sea eel.

ばら【薔薇】〔バラ属植物の総称〕a rose;(異名) the queen of the prairie.　◖ばら作りの名人 an expert grower of roses / ばらに刺(とげ)あり. No rose without a thorn.〘諺〙 | Every rose has its thorns.　■ばらの木 a rosebush; a rose tree　バラ園 a rose garden; a rosery.　バラ窓〘建〙a rose window.　バラ油(ゆ) rose oil; attar (of roses).

はらおび【腹帯】〔腹巻き〕a stomach band;〔妊婦の〕a [an obstetrical] binder;〔馬の〕a saddle girth; a bellyband; a surcingle; a cinch.

はらげい【腹芸】 1〔役者の〕the capacity to convey a character's state of mind without relying on gestures or words. ◐腹芸を見せる convey an implicit understanding of a「character [role]. 2〔度胸で物事を処理すること〕the implicit signaling of *one*'s needs; relying on the force of *one*'s personality to accomplish something. ◐あいつは政治家なのに腹芸ができない. For a politican, he certainly doesn't「have [show] much savvy. / 腹芸を見せる act on the strength of [use the force of] *one*'s personality. 3〔曲芸師の〕drawing a face or other picture on *one*'s stomach and animating it by flexing the abdominal muscles.

パラパラ〔ユーロビートに合わせて曲ごとに決められた手振りをする日本で生まれたディスコダンス〕para para; disco dancing with synchronized arm motions.

はりおうぎ【張り扇】 an extra large paper folding fan used by traditional storytellers to mark the beat of their narration.

はりくよう【針供養】 a memorial service for dull and broken needles.

はりこ【張り子】 papier-[paper-]mâché. ◐張り子の虎 a papier-mâché tiger;〔見かけ倒しの人〕a paper tiger; a blustering coward.

はんがん【判官】 1〔裁判官〕a judge. 2〔源義経〕Minamoto no Yoshitsune.

はんがんびいき【判官贔屓】⇨ ほうがんびいき

ばんこやき【万古焼】 Banko ware.

ばんしゃく【晩酌】 an evening [a dinner-time] drink. ～する have「an evening [a dinner-time] drink. ◐一人で晩酌する have a drink by *oneself* at dinner time / 晩酌をやる have a drink at supper.

はんじゅく【半熟】 ～の〔食物〕half-cooked[-done];〔果実〕half-ripe; unripe. ◐この卵はまだ半熟だ. The egg isn't hard-boiled, yet. / 半熟にする boil 《an egg》 soft [lightly]. ■**半熟卵** a soft-boiled egg.

はんしんよく【半身浴】〔坐浴〕a hip bath.

ばんづけ【番付け】〔順位表〕a「graded [ranking] list. ◐相撲の番付け a sumo ranking chart. ■**長者番付** a list of the richest people; a list of those who (have) paid the most income taxes in the past fiscal year.

ばんとう【番頭】〔店の〕a「head [chief] clerk; the general manager of a merchant business in pre-modern Japan. ■**大番頭** the head clerk of a large merchant firm.

はんにゃ【般若】 1〘Skt〙*Prajñā*; wisdom. 2〔鬼女の面〕(a Noh mask

with) the face of a female demon.　般若の面 a female demon's mask / 般若(波羅蜜多)経 the Wisdom sutras; *Prajñā-paramitā-sutra* / 般若心経 the Heart Sutra (it distills, in 260 Chinese characters, the essence, or "heart," of the Wisdom sutras).

はんぺん【半平】a cake of ground fish combined with starch and steamed.

ひ

ひあたり【日当たり】◐〔日光の当たり具合〕 わが家は南向きで日当たりがいい. Our house faces south and gets plenty of sun(shine). / 南側にビルが出来て日当たりが悪くなった. A building has gone up to the south and deprived us of sunlight. / 日当たりのよい部屋 a sunny room; a room which gets plenty of「sun [sunlight] / 日当たりの悪い家 a house with「no [little] sun; a house which doesn't get「the sun [much sunlight] / お宅の日当たりはどうですか. How much sunlight does your house get? | How sunny is your house? / 日当たり良好.〔不動産広告〕Sunny. | Plenty of sunlight.

ひえしょう【冷え性】冷え性である have poor circulation; have a tendency to feel the cold (in *one*'s hands and feet);「(tend to) get [always have] cold「fingers and toes [hands and feet]; be very sensitive to (the) cold;〘医〙〔病的に〕suffer from Raynaud's「disease [syndrome, phenomena]. ◐私は冷え性です. My「hands and feet [fingers and toes] always feel cold. | I tend to feel the cold. |《口》The cold gets to me. / 冷え性で悩んでいる be bothered by [suffer from] poor circulation [cold fingers and toes] / 冷え性の poor circulation; a tendency to feel the cold; cold「fingers and toes [hands and feet];〘医〙Raynaud's「disease [syndrome, phenomena].

ひがん【彼岸】〔春分・秋分の期間〕*Higan* week; the equinoctial week(s); the week of Buddhist memorial services centering on the「spring [autumn] equinox;〔彼岸会(ｴ)〕Buddhist services performed during the week of the equinox. ◐彼岸が明けた. The week of ceremonies centered on the「vernal [autumnal] equinox passed. / 彼岸の入り the first day of the week of the equinox / 彼岸の明け the final day of the equinoctial week / 春[秋]の彼岸の中日 the「spring [autumn] equinox / お彼岸の墓参り visiting [paying *one*'s respects at] the family grave(s) during *Higan* / 暑さ寒さも彼岸まで. *Higan* marks the end of both the worst of summer and the worst of winter.

ひきこもり【引き籠もり】〔他人との交流の拒否〕withdrawal from society; social withdrawal; going into seclusion; a pathological「shunning [avoidance] of other people shunning [avoidance] of other people. ◐ 引きこもりの若者 a young person who hides from the world at home.

ひきざん【引き算】subtraction. 〜する subtract [take away] 《6 from 7》.

ひきでもの【引き出物】a (take-away) gift for guests at a ceremony. ◐ 結婚式の引き出物 gifts (of specially prepared food or useful items) for guests at a wedding reception to take home.

ひきゃく【飛脚】**1**〔急使〕an express messenger; a courier; a messenger boy. ◐ 飛脚を立てる send an express messenger《to...》. **2**〔昔の郵便屋〕a courier. ◐ 飛脚問屋 a courier service; a delivery firm.

びく【魚籠】a fish basket; a creel.

ひじき【鹿尾菜】〚海藻〛hijiki; a species of edible brown seaweed.

ひしもち【菱餅】a three-colored lozenge-[diamond-]shaped rice cake.

びぜんやき【備前焼】Bizen ware.

ひたたれ【直垂】dress wear of a samurai; customary dress at court in the Edo period.

ひだりづかい【左遣い】〔文楽の〕of the three puppeteers who animate a puppet playing a leading role in a Bunraku drama, the one who manipulates the left arm.

ひちりき【篳篥】a flageolet-like instrument used in Shinto service.

ひつじ【未】〔十二支の〕the Ram, one of the twelve animals of the oriental zodiac. ◐ 未の日 the day of the Ram / 未の刻(ﾞ) the hour of the Ram(; 1-3 p.m.) / 未の方(ﾞ)〔南南西〕the direction of the Ram(; south-southwest). ■ 未年 the year of the Ram. ◐ 未年生まれの born in the year of the Ram.

ひつまぶし〔ウナギの料理〕a Nagoya dish of broiled eel on rice.

ひなあられ【雛霰】special dry cakes, made of sweetened rice flour, for the「Girls' [Doll] Festival.

ひなかざり【雛飾り】displaying [putting up, putting out] (a set of) dolls (on tiers)《for the「Girls' [Dolls'] Festival》;〔その人形〕dolls displayed《for the Girls' Festival in March》.

ひなにんぎょう【雛人形】 a *hina* doll; a set of dolls for the *hinamatsuri* festival (consisting traditionally of members of the Imperial court, but now often limited to the Emperor and Empress) dressed in period dress and displayed on a special stand.

ひなまつり【雛祭】 the *hinamatsuri* festival; the「Doll [Dolls', Girls', Peach] Festival held on March 3rd (at which families with girl children display the *hina* dolls, eat special sweetmeats, and drink *shirozake*).

ひのえうま【丙午】 the year of the Fiery Horse (formerly it was thought that girl born in this year would bring ruin on their husbands); forty-third in the sexagesimal system for counting years. ◐ 丙午の生まれの女性 a girl born in the year of the Fiery Horse.

ひのき【檜】 〔ヒノキ科の常緑高木；日本固有〕a *hinoki* cypress; a Japanese cypress; a *hinoki*.

ひのきぶたい【檜舞台】 1 〔檜の床の舞台〕a stage board (of *hinoki* cypress); a Noh or Kabuki stage made of *hinoki* (board). **2** 〔晴れの場所〕檜舞台で in the arena 《of political activity》. ◐ 世界の檜舞台で活躍した外交官 a diplomat「of international experience [who has worked on the world stage] / 世界の檜舞台に立つ stand on a world stage;《口》have made it (to the) big time / 檜舞台を踏む step into the limelight;《口》make it (to the) big time.

ひのまる【日の丸】〔旗〕the [a] Rising-Sun flag; the "Hinomaru" (flag). ■ 日の丸弁当 a boxed lunch consisting of boiled white rice with a single pickled red plum placed in the middle.

ひばくしゃ【被爆者】〔原水爆の放射能を受けた人〕a person who was exposed to radiation from an A-[H-]bomb;〔原水爆を受けた者〕a「survivor [victim] of「an A-[H-]bomb [an atomic air raid];〔広島・長崎の〕a *hibakusha*.

ひばち【火鉢】 a (charcoal) brazier (used for indoor heating); a hibachi 《*pl.* ~s》.

ひまわり【向日葵】〔キク科の 1 年草；北アメリカ原産の観賞・油料植物〕a (common garden) sunflower. ■ ヒマワリ畑 a field of sunflowers. ヒマワリ油 sunflower oil. ヒマワリの種《plant》a sunflower seed.

ひめくり【日捲り】 a「block [pad] calendar. ◐ 日めくりをめくる turn the「pages [leaves] of a block calendar.

ひもかわうどん【紐革饂飩】*udon* noodles made in flat strips.

ひもの【干物】dried fish;(塩をしない)stockfish. ◐干物にする dry fish.

ひや【冷や】〔冷水〕cold water;〔冷酒〕cold sake. 〜の unheated; cold; chilled. ◐お冷や1杯 a glass of (cold) water / 酒を冷やで飲む have [take, drink] sake cold.

ひゃくえん【百円】■百円玉 a (one) hundred yen coin. **百円ショップ** a shop in which all the goods are priced at ￥100. **百円ライター** a (100-yen) disposable lighter.

ひゃくにんいっしゅ【百人一首】One Hundred Poems by One Hundred Poets; a collection of one hundred *waka* poems, each by a different poet; chiefly that compiled in the mid-thirteenth century by Fujiwara no Teika;〔カルタ〕two sets of *hyakunin isshu* playing cards, one of which gives the full poems (*yomifuda*) and the other only the second half (*torifuda*). ◐百人一首競技かるた大会 a *hyakunin isshu* ﹁contest [tournament]; a contest in which the cards are scattered in front of competitors who listen to the start of each poem and then attempt to snatch up the corresponding card ahead of their opponents.

ひゃくやっつ【百八つ】a [one] hundred and eight; 108. ◐百八つの鐘 striking a temple bell 108 times on New Year's eve at midnight (to mark the passage into the New Year) / 百八つの煩悩(ぼんのう) the 108 ﹁passions [worldly desires] that people are subject to.

ひやけどめ【日焼け止め】(a) sunscreen; protection from [prevention of] sunburn; sunburn ﹁prevention [protection]. ◐日焼け止めの sun block; sunblock; anti-sunburn. ■日焼け止めオイル (a) ﹁sun block [sunblock] oil; (an) anti-sunburn oil. **日焼け止めクリーム** (a) ﹁sun block [sunblock] cream; (an) anti-sunburn cream. **日焼け止め化粧品** sunblock cosmetics.

ひやざけ【冷酒】unheated [cold] sake. ◐冷酒を飲む drink [have, take] cold sake; drink sake cold.

ひやしちゅうか【冷やし中華】ramen served cold with shredded ham, cucumber etc. on top.

ひやむぎ【冷や麦】thin *udon* noodles served cold.

ひややっこ【冷や奴】tofu served cold.

びよういん【美容院】a beauty ﹁salon [shop, parlour]; a hairdresser's.

ひょうさつ【表札・標札】a nameplate; a doorplate. ◐戸口に表札が掲げてある. The door has a nameplate on it. / 表札を出す put up *one*'s nameplate.

ひょうざん【氷山】an iceberg. 氷山の一角 the tip of「an [the] iceberg. ◐氷山の一角にすぎない be「just [merely] the tip of「an [the] iceberg / 今回摘発された収賄は全体から見ればほんの氷山の一角にすぎない. These arrests for bribery are just the tip of the iceberg.

ひょうたん【瓢箪】1〔ウリ科のつる性1年草〕a bottle gourd; a calabash (gourd). 2〔容器〕a gourd; a calabash; a cucurbit. ◐ひょうたんから駒が出る. A thing「said [done] in jest comes true.〔打ち消す語を伴って〕not likely to happen.

びょうぶ【屏風】a folding screen. ◐びょうぶで仕切る screen「*something* [*somebody*] off; screen off 《a bed》 / びょうぶのようにそびえる連山 a palisade of mountains. ■屏風絵 a painting on a folding screen.

ひょっとこ 1〔面〕a mask of a twisted male face (with puckered-up lips). 2〔道化者〕a clown; a jester; a funny guy;〔顔の醜い男〕an ugly guy.

ひら-【平-】ordinary; low-ranking; rank-and-file; common.

ひらがな【平仮名】hiragana; the hiragana syllabary; the cursive form of kana. [⇨かな]

ひらしゃいん【平社員】(just) an ordinary employee; a rank-and-file employee 《in the company》.

ひらめ【比目魚】〔カレイ目ヒラメ科の魚〕a flatfish; a flounder;〔その一種〕〔カレイ科のオヒョウ〕a halibut;〔シタビラメ〕a sole. ▶英語の flatfish, flounder はカレイ科の魚も含む.

びわ¹【枇杷】〔バラ科の常緑小高木; 果樹〕a loquat; a Japanese medlar;〔果実〕a loquat; a Japanese plum.

びわ²【琵琶】a *biwa*; a Japanese lute; a *biwa* with a bent neck and four or five strings. ■琵琶法師 a blind biwa player (who, from the Kamakura period, accompanied himself on the *biwa* as he narrated *The Tales of the Heike.*).

びん【鬢】sidelocks. ◐鬢のほつれを直す arrange the stray tresses of the sidelocks / 鬢を撫でつける comb [brush] up the sidelocks.

びんどめ【鬢留め】a hair pin.

ふ

ふ¹【歩】〘将棋〙a pawn. ◐なった[なり]歩 a promoted pawn / 歩を取る[打つ] take [move] a pawn.

ふ²【麩】wheat-gluten bread.

ぶ【分】1〔割合〕rate; a part;〔百分比〕(a) percentage; percent [%]. ◐3割5分 thirty-five percent [35%]. 2〔1寸の10分の1〕a *bu* (＝0.303 cm).

フィリピン・パブ a "Philippine pub"; a bar with Filipino hostesses.

ぷうたろう【風太郎】〔定職のない人〕an idle person with no regular job;〔住所不定の人〕a vagabond.

ふうちん【風鎮】a (decorative) pair of weights (for a hanging scroll).

ふうりん【風鈴】a「wind-chime [wind-bell]; a small glass, porcelain, or metal bell that rings when a strip of paper attached to its clapper flutters in the wind.

ふかあみがさ【深編み笠】a basket-like straw hat (worn to hide the face).

ぶがく【舞楽】*bugaku*; a masked court dance, transmitted to Japan from ancient China and Korea, that is performed to the accompaniment of musical instruments. ■舞楽台 a stage for performing *bugaku* dance. 舞楽面 a mask worn by a *bugaku* dancer.

ふかづめ【深爪】深爪をする cut [pare] a nail to the quick.

ふかひれ【鱶鰭】〔中国料理の食材〕a shark('s) fin. ◐ふかひれスープ shark-fin soup.

ふかむしちゃ【深蒸し茶】deep-steamed tea (steaming reduces bitterness).

ふき【蕗】〘植〙〔キク科の多年草; 食用植物〕a Japanese butterbur. ■蕗の薹(とう) a Japanese butterbur flower-bud.

ふきながし【吹き流し】a streamer; a pennon;〔風見用の〕a「weather [wind] vane. ◐五月(さつき)の風に翻る鯉の吹き流し a set of carp streamers spanking in the May wind.

ふきぬきやたい【吹抜屋台】a Yamato-e painting technique that depicts the interiors of buildings from an overhead perspective as if the roof or wall had been blown away open roof; the "blown-off roof" technique.

ふぐ【河豚】a fugu 《*pl.* ~s》; a puffer; a blowfish; a swellfish; a globefish. ■ ふぐ刺し fugu sashimi.   ふぐ汁 fugu soup; blowfish [swellfish] soup.   ふぐ中毒〚薬〛fugu intoxication; tetrodotoxism; blowfish poisoning.   ふぐちり〔ふぐのちり鍋〕a pot of fugu and vegetables cooked at table.

ふくさ【袱紗】a silk wrapping cloth;〔茶道の〕a small silk cloth used in the tea ceremony; a *fukusa*. ■ 袱紗捌(さば)き〔茶席で〕*one*'s handling of the *fukusa* 《during the tea ceremony》.   袱紗寿司 vinegared rice mixed with seafood and vegetables and wrapped in a thin sheet of omelet.   袱紗料理 a light meal of several dishes simplified from a full-course Japanese dinner.

ふくじんづけ【福神漬】sliced vegetables「pickled [preserved] in soy sauce.

ふくすけ【福助】a big-headed dwarf (believed to bring luck; he is depicted sitting on his heels wearing a kami-shimo).

ふくちゃ【福茶】"lucky tea"; tea made from sea tangle, black soybeans, pepper, pickled plums etc. to be drunk on festive occasions.

ふくつう【腹痛】a stomachache; a bellyache; an abdominal pain; a pain in the「stomach [guts, innards];〚医〛gastralgia;(急性の) abdominalgia; colic; *《口》(さしこみ, 特に月経時の) cramps;(間欠的な) gripe(s);(激しい) tormina.   ◐ ひどく腹痛がする. I have a bad stomachache. / 腹痛で苦しむ suffer from [have] a stomachache;(激痛) have severe abdominal pains.

ふくぶくろ【福袋】a grab bag; a mystery shopping bag.   ◐ お正月の福袋 a New Year's grab bag / 1 万円の福袋 a lucky grab bag costing ten thousand yen.

ふくらすずめ【脹ら雀・福良雀】**1**【脹ら雀】〔スズメ〕a fat young sparrow; a sparrow with its feathers fluffed up to keep out the cold.   **2**【福良雀】〔髪形・帯の結び方〕a Japanese「hair [obi] style mostly affected by young girls and women in previous eras.

ふくろおび【袋帯】a double-woven obi.

ふくろくじゅ【福禄寿】〔七福神の一〕*Fukurokuju*; the God of Wealth and Longevity (usually depicted with a long white beard).

ふくわらい【福笑い】a New Year's game in which blindfolded players pin facial features on a paper face.

ぶけ【武家】〔武士〕a samurai; a warrior;〔武門〕a samurai [military] family; samurai stock. ■武家造り〖建〗the style of samurai houses (in the Kamakura period). 武家屋敷 a samurai house.

ぶけしょはっと【武家諸法度】〖日本史〗Laws Governing Samurai Households.

ぶけほうこう【武家奉公】service with a samurai family.

ふじ【藤】〔マメ科の落葉つる性木本; 日本固有〕a Japanese wisteria; a *fuji*《*pl.* -s》. ▶藤の花 a wisteria flower. ■フジ棚 a wisteria trellis; a wisteria arbor. フジづる a wisteria vine.

ふじいろ【藤色】light purple; lilac; lavender; mauve.

ぶしどう【武士道】Bushido; the samurai code; the way of the「warrior [samurai]; Japanese chivalry. ■武士道精神 the samurai spirit.

ふじびたい【富士額】a widow's peak. ▶彼女は富士額だ. She has a widow's peak.

ふすま【襖】a fusuma; a sliding「door [screen, partition] (of Japanese paper on a wooden frame). ■襖絵 a painting on a fusuma. 襖紙 fusuma paper.

ぶた【豚】a pig; a hog; a swine《*pl.* ~》;《幼児語》a piggy;〔去勢されていない雄豚〕a boar;〔雌豚〕a sow. ▶豚がぶうぶう鳴いている. The「pigs [hogs] are grunting. / 豚に真珠 (casting [a case of]) pearls before swine.

ふたござ【双子座】〖天・占星〗the Twins; Gemini (略: Gem). ▶双子座生まれの人 a Gemini; a Geminian.

ふだしょ【札所】an office in a「temple [shrine] where *ofuda* are sold to worshippers.

ぶたどん【豚丼】a bowl of steamed rice topped with thinly sliced stewed pork; a pork bowl.

ぶたにく【豚肉】pork.

ぶち【斑】spots; specks; patches; dapples; mottles. ▶ぶちになる[する] spot; mottle / ぶちの spotted; dappled;〔白黒の〕piebald《horse》;〔斑点のある〕speckled;〔雑色の〕mottled; multicolored;〔虎斑(とら)の〕

brindled 《dog, cattle》. ■ **ぶち犬**〔白と黒の〕a black and white dog; a dog with black and white spots.   **ぶち猫** a tabby cat; a tabby.

ぶつだん【仏壇】a「household [family] Buddhist altar.

ぶつめつ【仏滅】**1**〔仏の死〕Buddha's death.   **2**〔六曜の〕the most inauspicious day in a recurring six-day calendrical cycle; a very unlucky day.

ふで【筆】**1**〔毛筆〕a writing brush; a hair pencil; a paintbrush;〔絵筆〕a brush;〔ペン〕a pen.   ◐筆に墨をつける dip a (writing) brush in ink. **2**〔書くこと〕writing;〔描くこと〕drawing; painting;〔ひと筆・筆致〕a touch; a stroke;〔文筆〕*one*'s [the] pen; writing;〔描写〕description.   ◐弘法も筆の誤り Even Homer nods.   **3**〔筆の跡〕handwriting; penmanship; *one*'s style of writing;〔作品〕a (literary) work; a production.

ふとうこう【不登校】truancy; school non-attendance.   ▶ かつて「登校拒否」と呼ばれたもの.   ◐不登校児 a school「truant [dropout].

ふとまきずし【太巻き寿司】a thick sushi roll.

ふとん【布団・蒲団】a futon;〔敷布団〕a (fold-up) mattress;〔掛け布団〕a quilt; a comforter;〔夜具〕bedding; bedclothes;〔座布団〕a cushion. ■ **組布団** a futon set; a mattress and quilt.   **こたつ布団** a *kotatsu* quilt.   **婚礼布団** a marriage futon.   **せんべい布団** an old「futon [mattress] that has become thin and hard.   **電気布団** a heating pad.   **羽根布団** a feather quilt.   **布団乾燥機** a「futon [bedding, quilt] dryer.   **布団叩き** a futon beater.   **布団店** a futon「store [shop].   **布団袋** a large bag for storing futons; a futon sack.

ふぶき【吹雪】a snowstorm; a snowdrift; driving snow.   ◐ひどい吹雪 a severe snowstorm; a blizzard / 吹雪が収まる[やむ] the snowstorm「abates [stops, dies down] / 吹雪が吹き荒れる a「snowstorm [blizzard] rages.

ふみえ【踏み絵】**1**〔江戸時代にキリシタン改めに用いられた板〕a plate with a crucifix or other Christian symbol to be trodden on in order to prove *one*self a non-Christian.   **2**〔個人の思想・信条を探るため強制する行為〕an allegiance [a loyalty] test.

ふみんしょう【不眠症】sleeplessness;〚医〛insomnia; agrypnia; vigilance; pervigilum.   ◐不眠症にかかる suffer from [be troubled with] insomnia.   ■ **不眠症患者** an insomniac.

ぶらんこ a swing; *a trapeze / ぶらんこに乗る get on a swing;〔乗って遊

ぶ] have a swing. ◐ ぶらんこに乗っている be on a swing; sit in a swing / ぶらんこをこぐ push a swing; rock back and forth in a swing. ■空中ブランコ a (flying) trapeze. 腰かけブランコ a seat swing. 箱型ブランコ a box-type swing.

ぶり【鰤】〔アジ科の海産魚〕a yellowtail.

ふりがな【振り仮名】kana syllables「printed [written] alongside Chinese characters to aid in reading.

ふりこめさぎ【振り込め詐欺】〔電話や手紙でだましたり恐喝したりして現金を銀行口座に振り込ませようとする詐欺; オレオレ詐欺など〕a fraud in which the victim is「deceived [threatened] into remitting money to a bank account; a remittance scam.

ふりそで【振り袖】long pendulous sleeves;〔着物〕a kimono with long pendulous sleeves.

ふろしき【風呂敷】〔元来、(銭湯の)風呂に入るときに衣類を包み, あがるときに足をぬぐうのに用いた〕a (cloth) wrapper; a wrapping cloth; a kerchief. ◐ 風呂敷で包む wrap (up) in a kerchief / 風呂敷を広げる spread (out) a kerchief / 風呂敷包み a bundle; a parcel in a wrapper / 風呂敷包みを広げる undo a cloth-wrapped parcel.

ふんがい【糞害】problems with [damage from]《bird》droppings.

ぶんかのひ【文化の日】〔11 月 3 日〕Culture Day.

ぶんきんたかしまだ【文金高島田】an upswept hairdo originating in the mid-eighteenth century.

ぶんちん【文鎮】a paperweight; a weight. ◐ 文鎮で書類を押える keep papers in place with a paperweight.

ふんどし【褌】a loincloth; a waistcloth; a breechcloth; a breechclout; a thong (for men).

ぶんらく【文楽】〔文楽座〕the Bunraku theater;〔芝居〕a puppet show. ◐ 文楽人形 a Bunraku puppet.

へ

へいあんじだい【平安時代】the Heian period (794–1185).

へいけ【平家】**1**〔平氏〕the「Heike [Taira] family [clan]; the Heikes. **2**〔平家琵琶〕chanting *The Tales of the Heike*.

べいごま【貝独楽】a top made from a seashell filled with lead.

べいじゅ【米寿】*one*'s 88th birthday. ●米寿の祝い celebration of *one*'s 88th birthday.

へそ【臍】the navel; the umbilicus 《*pl.* ~es, -bilici》; the omphalos 《*pl.* -li》;《口》the belly button;〘植〙〔種子の〕a hilum 《*pl.* hila》; a navel;〔櫓(ろ)の〕a thole; a tholepin. ●ひっこんだへそ a「deep [sunken] navel / へそのごま navel [belly button]「lint [fluff]; (the) fluff in *one*'s navel.

へそくり【臍繰り】secret savings; a secret stash (of money); a nest egg; money under the bed;〔小銭の貯金〕pin money. ●隠しておいたへそくりが見つかって[ばれて]しまった. The secret stash that I had hidden away was discovered. / へそくりをする save up 《a part of the household allowance》 secretly 《for *one*'s own use》; stash money away; put [keep] money under the bed / へそくりをためる build up a secret stash / へそくりを隠す hide *one*'s secret stash.

へそのお【臍の緒】a navel string [cord]; an umbilical cord (In former days the practice was to wrap a newborn's umbilicus in cotton, fold it in paper, and write the child's name on it before hiding it away; it was also the custom for a mother to secrete it in a chest of drawers sent off with her daughter upon marriage).

へそまがり【臍曲がり】a pouter;《口》a crosspatch; a crank.

へんか【返歌】a「poem [tanka] composed in reply.

べんけい【弁慶】〔怪力で武力にすぐれた鎌倉時代の僧, 武蔵坊弁慶のこと; 源義経の忠臣〕a Kamakura period Buddhist monk, skilled in the martial arts, who gave his loyalty to Minamoto no Yoshitsune. ●弁

慶の泣き所〔すね〕a shin;《kick a person in》the shins;〔弱点〕one's Achilles' heel; one's fatal flaw [weakness] / 弁慶の立ち往生 (a situation) where one can move neither forward nor backward (Benkei is said to have, thus, died on his feet shielding Yoshitsune from enemy arrows at the battle of Koromogawa in 1189).

べんざいてん【弁財天】〔七福神の一〕Benzaiten;《Skt》Sarasvatī; the Goddess of Eloquence, Music, and Art (usually depicted playing a lute).

へんろ【遍路】 a pilgrim. ◐ 遍路姿で dressed as a pilgrim / 遍路の旅 (a) pilgrimage.

ほ

ほうおう【鳳凰】 *feng huang*; a bird in Chinese myth whose appearance is said to herald good government under a wise king.

ほうがく【邦楽】1〔純邦楽〕music of the Edo period centering on the samisen. **2**〔日本のポピュラー音楽〕Japanese music.

ほうがんびいき【判官贔屓】〔源九郎判官義経が兄の頼朝に滅ぼされたのに同情したことに由来; 判官は京都を検察する役〕sympathy for Minamoto no Yoshitsune who was defeated in battle by his older brother Yoritomo; sympathy [admiration, respect] for a tragic hero; an inclination to side with the underdog. [⇨ はんがん 2].

ほうじ【法事】a Buddhist service on the anniversary of a person's death; a memorial service.

ぼうず【坊主】〔僧〕a Buddhist monk; a bonze; a monk. ◐ 坊主になる become a (Buddhist) monk; take the tonsure.

ぼうねんかい【忘年会】a year-end (dinner) party [social gathering]. ◐ 忘年会をする give a year-end party; celebrate the outgoing year / 忘年会シーズン the year-end party season.

ほおずき【酸漿】1〔ナス科の多年草, 観賞植物〕a Chinese [Japanese] lantern plant; a winter cherry;〔果実〕alkekengi; a winter cherry. **2**〔口に入れて鳴らすもの〕a Chinese lantern fruit calyx used as a whistle. ◐ ほおずきを鳴らす make a squeaky noise in *one*'s mouth with the calyx of a Chinese lantern fruit.

ほおずきいち【酸漿市】a「lantern plant [winter cherry] market held at Sensōji in Tokyo on July 9-10.

ホーム・センター〔家庭用雑貨・日曜大工用品などを扱う大規模小売店〕a home center; a「DIY [do-it-yourself] store.

ほくろ【黒子】a mole; lentigo. ◐ 黒子を取る remove a mole. ■ 愛嬌ぼくろ a cute mole on the cheek. 付けぼくろ a beauty spot. 泣きほ

くろ a mole under the eye.

ほしいたけ【乾し椎茸】a dried shiitake mushroom.

ぼせき【墓石】a gravestone; a tombstone; a headstone.

ぼだいじ【菩提寺】a family [an ancestral] temple; a (Buddhist) temple that retains *one*'s family grave.

ほたてがい【帆立貝】a scallop; a scollop. ◐ほたて貝の貝殻 a scallop (shell); a pilgrim shell.

ぼたもち【牡丹餅】a rice cake dumpling covered with bean「paste [jam].

ほたる【蛍】a firefly; a glowfly; *a lightning bug; 〔ツチボタル〕a glowworm; 〔ゲンジボタル〕*Luciola cruciata*; 〔ヘイケボタル〕*Luciola lateralis*.

ほたるいか【蛍烏賊】a firefly squid.

ほたるがり【蛍狩り】firefly hunting. ◐蛍狩りに行く go out to catch fireflies; go hunting for fireflies / 蛍狩りをする catch [hunt for] fireflies.

ぼたん【牡丹】【植】a (tree) peony; a moutan (peony). ◐立てば芍薬すわれば牡丹歩く姿は百合の花. Standing she's a peony, seated a tree peony, and her bearing as she walks a lily. ■牡丹園 a peony garden. 牡丹鍋 a wild-boar hot pot. 牡丹雪 large flakes of snow; heavy snowflakes. ◐ぼたん雪が降っている. Snow is coming down in large flakes.

ほっきがい【北寄貝】=うばがい.

ほっく【発句】1〔連歌・俳諧の初句〕the first line 《of a *renga*》. 2〔俳句〕a *hokku*《*pl.* ~》. [=はいく]

ほっけ【𩸽】〔アイナメ科の海産硬骨魚〕an Atka「mackerel [fish].

ホッチキス a stapler; a stapling machine; 『商標』a Hotchkiss (paper fastener).

ホッピー〔発泡酒の一種〕a low-malt beer flavored with hops.

ほめごろし【褒め殺し】mockery [ridicule] by overpraising; damning with lavish praise; a backhanded compliment. ~する praise somebody to the skies in mockery.

ほや【海鞘・老海鼠】『動』an ascidian; a sea squirt.

ほりごたつ【掘り火燵】a kotatsu built into the floor; a sunken kotatsu.

ぼん【盆】〔盆祭り〕the *Bon* Festival; the Lantern Festival; the Feast of Lanterns; the Festival of the Dead; the Buddhist All Souls' Day; a ceremony, celebrated from the 13th to the 15th of August, when, it is believed, ancestors return to their earthly dwellings; fires are lit to receive them and to send them off.

ぼんおどり【盆踊り】 *Bon* Festival dancing.

ぼんくれ【盆暮】 the *Bon* period and the year-end. ◐ 盆暮の付け届け *Bon* and year-end presents.

ぼんさい【盆栽】 a bonsai 《*pl.* ~》; a potted dwarf(ed) tree; a potted miniature plant.

ほんじん【本陣】 1 〔本営〕the headquarters. 2 〔昔の宿場の〕an officially appointed inn (for a daimyo).

ぼんせき【盆石】 a bonseki 《*pl.* ~s》; a miniature landscape of sand and stones (laid out on a tray).

ぼんぢょうちん【盆提灯】 a *Bon* Festival paper lantern.

ぼんどうろう【盆灯籠】 a *Bon* Festival stone lantern.

ほんのうじのへん【本能寺の変】『日本史』the Honnōji Incident; the Raid on the Honnōji Temple (in 1582, in which Oda Nobunaga was killed by Akechi Mitsuhide).

ぼんぼり【雪洞】 a lamp stand with a silk or paper shade. ◐ 手雪洞 a hand-carried paper-lantern.

ぼんぼん 〔良家の世間知らずの息子〕a boy from a well-to-do family who knows nothing of the world.

ほんまる【本丸】〔城の〕the castle keep; 〔天守閣〕the donjon; the dungeon. ◐ 敵の本丸を落とす reduce the main「castle enclosure [enemy stronghold].

ほんめい【本命】 1 〔競馬などの〕the probable winner; the favorite; the odds-on favorite; the most likely「horse [cyclist, etc.]; 〔最有力と見込まれている人〕the expected「winner [victor]; the most likely candidate. ◐ 次期市長の本命 the candidate most likely to be the next mayor of the city / (競馬などで)本命に賭ける play [bet on] the favorite / 本命のチームが予選で負けてしまった. The favored team lost in the preliminaries. 2 〔本当に望んでいるもの〕*one*'s heart's desire; what *one* really wants. ◐ (受験で)本命の大学 *one*'s first-choice university. ■ **本命チョコ**〔バレンタインデーの〕a heartfelt (rather than obligatory) gift of chocolate to a man on (Saint) Valentine's Day. **本命馬** the (odds-on) favorite.

ま

まいこ【舞子・舞妓】 a girl who is studying in Kyoto to be a geisha; a girl who dances at drinking parties.

まいばやし【舞囃子】〔能の〕a short Noh piece in which two performers dance, out of costume, to musical accompaniment.

まえじて【前仕手】〔能楽〕the principal actor (in the first part of a Noh play).

まえみつ【前褌】〖相撲〗the front of a sumo wrestler's belt.

まきえ【蒔き絵】 a technique of decorating lacquerware by sprinkling ⌈gold [silver] dust particles over wet lacquer designs; gold [silver] lacquering. ◐ 金蒔き絵の箱 a gold-lacquered ⌈box [casket].

まきずし【巻き寿司】 rolled sushi.

まきびし【撒き菱】〔忍者の用いる〕a spiked device for scattering on the ground to maim enemy ⌈infantry [horses]; a calt(h)rop; a caltrap.

まきもの【巻き物】〔軸物〕a makimono; a horizontal scroll; a roll; a rolled book;〔反物〕rolled drapery.

まくのうち【幕の内】〔弁当〕a variety box lunch; a box lunch containing from 10 to 15 different small portions of food along with white rice (literally, "between curtains").

まくらえ【枕絵】〔春画〕an erotic [a pornographic] picture; a picture depicting bedroom action.

まくらことば【枕詞】 a set epithet 《in classical Japanese poetry》.

まくらぞうし【枕草紙】 an erotic picture book 《of the Tokugawa period》.

まぐろ【鮪】〔クロマグロ・ホンマグロ〕a bluefin (tuna); a horse mackerel; a tuna; tuna (meat). ◐ マグロの(油漬け)缶詰 canned tuna 《in oil》/ まぐろ丼 a bowl of rice topped with tuna (meat).

まけおしみ【負け惜しみ】 unwillingness to ⌈admit defeat [resign *oneself*

[228]

to losing]; hating to lose; 《a case of》sour grapes. ◐ 負け惜しみが強い hate to lose / 負け惜しみでも何でもなく, 貧乏はいいもんだよ. This is not sour grapes or anything on my part, but I think being poor is good for a person. / 負け惜しみを言う refuse to「admit [acknowledge] *one*'s defeat; do not acknowledge *one*self beaten; yield with (a) bad [(an) ill] grace; be a「poor [sore] loser / 負け惜しみを言わない accept defeat「graciously [with (a) good grace]; be a good loser.

まげ【髷】〔女性の〕a pompadour;〔力士などの〕a topknot. ◐ 髷を結う〔女性が〕do *one*'s hair in a pompadour.

まげもの【髷物】a「story [film] treating events in the Edo days; a period「play [novel].

まご【孫】a grandchild;〔男〕a grandson;〔女〕a granddaughter.

まごのて【孫の手】a back scratcher; a scratchback.

ます【鱒】a trout 《*pl.* ~》; a sea trout; a salmon trout. ◐ 鱒釣りに行く go trout-fishing / 鱒のすむ流れ a trout stream. ■ **海鱒** a sea trout.

マスオさん〖漫画『サザエさん』でサザエの夫であるフグ田マスオから〗〔妻の実家に同居している男性〕a husband who lives with his wife in a house that belongs to her parents.

ますずし【鱒鮨】trout sushi, pressed and wrapped in a bamboo leaf.

ますせき【升席】〔相撲・芝居小屋の〕a box (seat).

まちや【町家】a tradesman's house; a traditional townhouse.

まつ【松】〔マツ科の常緑針葉高木; アカマツ・クロマツなどのマツ属 (Pinus) の植物の総称〕a pine (tree).

まつかさ【松笠, 松毬】a pinecone; a cone.

まつかざり【松飾り】the New Year's pine decorations.

まつたけ[1]【松竹】pine and bamboo decorations for the New Year.

まつたけ[2]【松茸】a *matsutake* (mushroom). ■ **松茸狩り** ◐ 松茸狩りに行く go mushroom-gathering[-hunting]; go mushrooming. **松茸御飯**〖料理〗rice cooked with *matsutake*, sake, and soy sauce.

まっちゃ【抹茶】powdered [ground] tea. ◐ 抹茶色 tea green.

まつのうち【松の内】the first seven days of the New Year; the New Year「Week [holidays].

まつぼっくり【松ぼっくり】⇨ まつかさ.

まつやに【松やに】(pine) resin; pine-tree gum.

まないた【真魚板・俎】a chopping board; a (chopping) block. ◐ まな

板の上の鯉のようなものだ be helpless; be (left) high and dry.

まねきねこ【招き猫】(a figure of) a beckoning cat (to attract customers).

ままごと【飯事】playing house; playing at housekeeping. ◐ままごとの恋「calf [puppy] love / あの若夫婦の生活はままごとのようなものです. That young couple live as though they're playing house. / ままごとをする play (at) house; play at「housekeeping [keeping house] / おままごとしよう. Let's play house.

まめしぼり【豆絞り】a spotted pattern; a pattern of tiny polka dots. ◐豆絞りの手拭 a (Japanese) towel with a speckled pattern.

まめまき【豆撒き】a bean「-scattering[-throwing] ceremony [exorcism] (performed on or about 3 February). [⇨ せつぶん] ◐豆まきをする scatter parched beans (to drive out evil spirits).

まやく【麻薬】a narcotic; a (narcotic) drug;《口》dope. ◐麻薬所持の疑いで on suspicion of drug possession / 麻薬が効いてくる the drug takes effect / 麻薬が切れる the drug wears off / 麻薬の使用 drug「taking [use] / 麻薬の濫用 drug abuse / 麻薬の濫用者 a drug abuser.
■ 麻薬シンジケート a drug syndicate.　麻薬捜査官 a narcotics agent.　**麻薬探知犬** a drug sniffing dog; a sniffer dog.　**麻薬注射** (an) injection of a drug.

まゆだま【繭玉】a New Year's festive bamboo twig hung with cocoon-shaped cakes and talismans against evil.

まよいばし【迷い箸】hovering over different morsels with *one*'s chopsticks before deciding which to take (a breach of good manners).

まよけ【魔除け】a talisman [an amulet, a charm] protecting *one* against evil.

まるがり【丸刈り】close clipping. ◐頭を丸刈りにする crop the hair; 〔刈らせる〕have a close crop; have *one*'s hair「cut [cropped] close / 丸刈りの close-cropped.

まるなげ【丸投げ】hundred-percent subcontracting; farming out to subcontractors all of a project *one* has contracted to perform; the wholesale delegation《of responsibility for...》.

まるほん【丸本】〔浄瑠璃の〕a complete text of a *Jōruri*. ◐丸本物[歌舞伎] a Kabuki drama of「*Jōruri* [puppet-play] origin.

まるまげ【丸髷】a married woman's coiffure (worn well into the Meiji period, it lay flat on the head and was composed of four oval lobes).

まわし【回し】〔相撲の〕a sumo wrestler's belt;〔ふんどし〕a loincloth.

まわりどうろう【回り燈籠】a lantern with a revolving inner shade that casts images on the outer shade.

まんが【漫画】a cartoon; a comic book; comics; (a) manga;〔新聞雑誌の(通例4コマの)続き漫画〕a comic strip; ‖a strip cartoon;《口》the comics; *《口》the funnies;〔風刺漫画〕a caricature. ■漫画映画 a cartoon film; a movie cartoon; an animated film. 漫画家 a caricaturist; a cartoonist; a comic artist. 漫画チック ▷漫画チックな manga-style; caricatured / この社会にはまだ漫画チックな習慣が残っている. Our society still practices customs that are farcical. 漫画本[雑誌] a comic 「book [magazine];《口》a comic. 漫画欄 a comic section《of a newspaper》; *《口》the funnies.

まんがきっさ【漫画喫茶】a coffee shop with a *manga* library.

まんげつ【満月】〔月〕a full moon;〔時〕the moon is at the full.

まんざい【漫才】〔演芸〕a comic (stage) dialogue; comic backchat. ■漫才師 a comic dialogist.

まんじゅう【饅頭】a bun with a bean-jam filling. ■饅頭屋 a sweet bean bun shop.

まんねんひつ【万年筆】a fountain pen. ▷自動(吸入)式万年筆 a self-filling (fountain) pen / 万年筆にインクを入れる fill [refill] a fountain pen / この万年筆はすべりがいい. This fountain pen writes smoothly.

まんばけん【万馬券】a winning horserace ticket that pays back at least ten thousand yen.

まんびき【万引き】〔行為〕shoplifting; *《俗》boosting;〔人〕a shoplifter;《俗》a lifter; *《俗》a booster. ～する shoplift; lift [steal] goods in a store; *《俗》boost. ▷万引きするところを見つかる be caught shoplifting *something* / 万引きの常習犯 a habitual shoplifter.

まんようがな【万葉仮名】a system of Japanese writing used in the 8th century poetry anthology *Man'yōshū* in which Chinese characters represent both phonograms and ideograms.

み

み【巳】〔十二支の〕the Snake, one of the twelve animals of the oriental zodiac. ◐ 巳の日 the day of the Snake / 巳の刻(ミ) the hour of the Snake(; 9–11 a.m.) / 巳の方(ホミ)〔南南東〕the direction of the Snake (south-southeast). ■巳年 the year of the Snake. ◐ 巳年生まれの born in the year of the Snake.

みあい【見合い】〔結婚のための〕an interview [a meeting] with a view to marriage; a marriage meeting; marital「talks [negotiations]. ◐ 見合いの席を設ける arrange a meeting of the principals (and their parents) for marital negotiation. ■見合い結婚 (an) arranged marriage; (a) marriage by arrangement; a marriage brokered by a go-between. 見合い写真 a photo of oneself to be shown to a prospective marriage partner.

みえ【見得】〔歌舞伎の〕a pose; a posture; a gesture. [⇨ おおみえ]

みかづき【三日月】a new moon; a crescent (moon); the「sickle [horned] moon. ■三日月形 ◐ 三日月形の crescent(-shaped); lunate; meniscoid. 三日月眉 arched eyebrows.

みかど【帝・御門】the Emperor 《of Japan》; the Mikado.

みかん【蜜柑】**1**〔果皮の柔らかいミカン類の総称〕a mandarin orange; a tangerine (orange). ◐ みかん1箱 a box of tangerines / みかんの皮 an orange peel; the rind of an orange / みかんの皮をむく peel an orange / みかんの実の1袋[房(ふさ)] a segment of a tangerine. **2** ＝うんしゅうみかん. ■みかん箱 an orange box. みかん畑 a tangerine「orchard [plantation].

みけねこ【三毛猫】a tortoise-shell cat; a calico cat.

みこし【御輿・神輿】a portable shrine; a shrine in which a Shinto deity is carried during festivals.

みざるきかざるいわざる【見猿聞か猿言わ猿】〔処世訓〕See no evil; hear no evil; speak no evil. ◐ 見ざる聞かざる言わざるを決め込む

play dumb.

みじんぎり【微塵切り】 みじん切りにする cut fine; cut into tiny pieces.

みずあめ【水飴】 thick malt syrup.

みずいり【水入り】〖相撲〗a rest break during a sumo bout.

みずがめざ【水瓶座】〖天・占星〗the Water「Carrier [Bearer]; Aquarius (略: Aqr). ◐水瓶座生まれの人 an Aquarius; an Aquarian.

みずぐも【水蜘蛛】1〖昆〗a water spider. **2**〔忍者が水上を歩く道具〕platter-shaped footwear worn by a ninja to cross the surface of a body of water.

みずたき【水炊き】◐鳥の水炊き chicken boiled in unseasoned water and eaten with a citrus-flavored dip.

みずもち【水餅】 rice cake soaked in water.

みずぢゃや【水茶屋】〔江戸時代の路上茶屋〕an Edo-period tea stall.

みずひき【水引き】 red-[black-] and-white paper strings《for tying presents》.

みずまくら【水枕】 a water「pillow [cushion].

みずむし【水虫】〔皮膚病〕dermatophytosis; athlete's foot. ◐足が水虫にやられている. I've got athlete's foot.

みずわり【水割り】〔ウイスキーの〕《whiskey》and water. ◐〔ウイスキーの〕水割り1杯 a whiskey-and-water / 水割りの watered; diluted with water.

みそ【味噌】1〔調味料〕miso; fermented soybean paste. ◐味噌味[仕立て]の miso-flavored. **2**〔味噌状のもの〕something that looks like miso. ◐カニの味噌 crab butter. **3**〔誇れる特徴〕そこが味噌なんだ. That's the beauty of it. このプリンターは携帯しやすいところが味噌です. The good thing about this printer is that it's easy to carry. 味噌も糞も一緒にする confuse [mix up] good and bad things; fail to discriminate good things from bad. 味噌を付ける〔失敗する〕make a「mess [hash] of it; make sad work of it; make a「bad [poor] show [showing];《口》make a fizzle《of *something*》. ■赤[白]味噌 dark [light] miso. 甘[辛]味噌 lightly [heavily] salted miso. からし味噌 hot pepper miso. 酢味噌 vinegar and miso. 味噌和(あ)え a salad dressed with miso and vinegar. 味噌こし a miso strainer. 味噌豆 a soybean; a soya (bean); a soy (pea). 味噌ラーメン miso-flavored ramen.

みそか【三十日・晦日】 the end [last day] of the month. ◑今月のみそかに at the end of this month / 勘定はみそかだ. Bring the bill at the end of the month. ■ **三十日払い[勘定]** month-end payment; EOM settlement. ▶ EOM は end of month の略.

みそぎ【禊】 a purification ceremony; the washing away of defilement; ablutions. ◑みそぎをする perform [make] *one*'s ablutions / その汚職政治家は，衆議院選挙で再選されてみそぎは済んだと語った. The corrupt politician said that his reelection to the House of Representatives meant that 「he had been absolved [the slate had been wiped clean].

みそしる【味噌汁】 miso soup. ◑アサリのみそ汁 miso soup with little-neck clams.

みそづけ【味噌漬け】 vegetables [meat, fish] preserved in miso; miso pickles. ◑みそ漬けにする preserve 《vegetables》 in miso.

みそひともじ【三十一文字】〔短歌〕thirty-one syllables; a tanka.

みそまんじゅう【味噌饅頭】 a miso-flavored bean-jam bun.

みぞれ【霙】 sleet. ◑みぞれが降る. It sleets. / みぞれが降っている. Sleet is falling. / 雨がみぞれに変わった. The rain has changed to sleet. / みぞれの降る日 a sleety day.

みつ【褌】〔相撲〕a sumo wrestler's obi; belt.

みっかぼうず【三日坊主】 a person who can stick to nothing; a person who quickly gives up. ◑今年も日記は三日坊主に終わった. This year as well my diary fizzled out at the start. / 彼は何でも三日坊主だ. He sticks to nothing. | He is not steady in his purpose. | He gives up all too easily.

みつご【三つ子】 **1**〔3歳の子〕a child three years old; a three-year-old (child). ◑三つ子の魂百まで. As a boy, so the man.〚諺〛| The child is father of the man.〚諺〛三つ子でも知っている. Even a child knows that. **2**〔三生児〕triplets;〔1 人〕a triplet.

みつどもえ【三つ巴】 (a crest of) three comma-shaped figures in a circle. ◑三つ巴の戦い a three-「cornered[-sided, -way] battle [fight]; a triangular 「fight [struggle].

みとめ(いん)【認め(印)】 an unregistered [informal] seal; a signet. ◑認めを押す affix *one*'s informal seal 《to》.

みどりのひ【みどりの日】〔4 月 29 日〕Greenery Day.

みなまたびょう【水俣病】 Minamata disease; Minamata mercury poisoning.

みのがみ【美濃紙】mino paper; high-quality (Japanese) paper from Mino (modern Gifu).

みみかき【耳搔き】an ear pick.

みみなり【耳鳴り】《have》a「singing [ringing, buzzing (noise)] in the ears;〚医〛tinnitus. ◐耳鳴りがする. My ears are ringing [tingling, humming].

みや【宮】**1**〔神社〕a (Shinto) shrine;〔神棚の〕a miniature shrine. **2**〔皇族〕an Imperial「prince [princess]; a「prince [princess] of the blood. ■ **高松の宮** Prince Takamatsu.

みやげ【土産】something to「take [carry] home;〔記念の〕a souvenir;〔訪問用〕a present; a gift. ◐お父さんへのみやげ something to take home to your father / 海外旅行のおみやげ a souvenir of *one*'s trip abroad / パーティーのおみやげ party favors / ロンドンみやげとして as a souvenir from London (for the folks back home).

みやだいく【宮大工】a「temple [shrine] carpenter (the skills of their trade require decades to master).

みやまいり【宮参り】〔神社に詣でること〕a visit to a Shinto shrine;〔生後30日ごろの〕=おみやまいり.

みょうが【茗荷】〚植〛〔ショウガ科の多年草〕a mioga ginger; a Japanese ginger.

みりん【味醂】a sweet sake (used as seasoning). ◐鰯のみりん干し a dried *mirin*-seasoned sardine.

みるがい【海松貝・水松貝】=みるくい.

みるくい【海松食・水松食】〚貝〛a trough shell; a「surf [hen, sea] clam.

みんしゅく【民宿】a private house providing lodging and meals to transient guests; a tourist home; ‖a guest-house.

みんよう【民謡】a folk「song [tune, air]; a (folk) ballad;〈集合的に〉balladry. ◐ドイツ民謡 a German folk song / 民謡の節 a folk melody. ■ **民謡歌手** a folk singer. **民謡大会** a hoot(e)nanny.

みんわ【民話】a folktale; a folk story. ■ **民話劇** a play based on a folktale.

む

むかえび【迎え火】 a ﹁sacred fire [*Bon* Festival bonfire] to welcome the returning souls of ancestors. [⇨ おくりび]

むかえぼん【迎え盆】 the first day of the *Bon* Festival [festival of the dead], when people meet the spirits of their ancestors. [⇨ おくりぼん]

むぎ【麦】〔大麦〕barley;〔小麦〕wheat;〔燕麦〕oats;〔ライ麦〕rye.
■麦焼酎 a spirit distilled from barley.　麦茶[湯] barley water; barley tea.　麦飯 rice boiled with barley.

むぎとろ【麦とろ】〘料理〙a bowl of boiled rice and barley with grated yam topping.

むしろ【蓆・筵】a (straw) mat;〔蓆類〕(straw) matting.

むねさんずん【胸三寸】*one*'s heart; *one*'s mind; *one*'s feelings.　◐胸三寸に納める suppress *one*'s feelings; contain *one*self.

むねやけ【胸焼け】heartburn; water brash; a sour stomach;〘医〙pyrosis; cardialgia;〔胃酸過多〕acid indigestion.　◐胸焼けがする have heartburn.

むらさめ【村雨】a passing ﹁shower [rain].

むらはちぶ【村八分】social [village] ostracism.　◐村八分にされる[にあう] be ostracized ﹁within the village [by the villagers].

むらまつり【村祭り】a village festival.

むりしんじゅう【無理心中】a murder-suicide.　～する force *somebody* to die with *one*.　◐一家(の)無理心中 a family murder-suicide.

むろまちじだい【室町時代】the Muromachi period (1392–1573).

め

めいじじだい【明治時代】the Meiji ┌era [period]┘ (1868–1912).

メイドきっさ【メイド喫茶】a coffee shop in which waitresses dress as house maids (first noted in the Akihabara district of Tokyo, they are now found in cities throughout Japan).

めいにち【命日】〔年1回の〕the anniversary of *somebody*'s death; a deathday;〔毎月の〕the monthly return of the date of *somebody*'s death. ◐ お父さんの命日を忘れてはなりません. You must not forget the anniversary of your father's death.

めいぼ【名簿】a name list; a ┌register [list]┘ of names; a nominal ┌list [register, roll]┘; a roll (of names); a roster. ◐ クラスの名簿 a class list / 名簿から除く cross 《*somebody*'s name》┌off [out]┘ from the list; remove [erase, cancel]《*somebody*'s name》from the list / 彼は名簿から除かれた. His name was struck off the list. / 名簿に記入する[載せる] put [enter] 《*somebody*'s name》on the roll; register《*somebody*'s name》; enroll *somebody* (on the list) / 来訪者名簿に名前を書く write *one*'s name in the visitors' book / 名簿に載っている be on the ┌list [books]┘.

めがね【眼鏡】**1**〔目にかける器具〕《a pair of》glasses [eyeglasses];《a pair of》spectacles;《口》specs. ◐ べっこう縁のめがね glass with a tortoiseshell frame / 度の強いめがね powerful spectacles; strong glasses;〔レンズが厚い〕thick [strong] (eye) glasses; glasses with thick lenses; thick-lensed spectacles / 遠視[近視]用のめがね glasses for ┌farsighted [nearsighted]┘ people / めがねのふち the ┌rim frame of a pair of spectacles / めがねのつる the temples of a pair of glasses / めがねの玉[レンズ] a spectacle lens / めがねをかける[する] put on *one*'s ┌glasses [spectacles]┘. **2**〔鑑識・鑑定〕judgment; discrimination; discernment; insight; a ┌critical [discerning]┘ eye. ◐ めがねが狂う misjudge / 上司のめがねにかなう gain [win] *one*'s ┌superiors' [supervisor's]┘ confidence; find favor with *one*'s supervisor; impress *one*'s superiors favorably. ■ 柄付きめがね〔老婦人用の〕a lorgnette. 遠近両用めがね bifocals; bifocal glasses. 片めがね an eyeglass; a monocle; a quizzing glass. 金[銀, 黒]縁めがね gold-[silver-, black-]rimmed glasses. 黒めがね dark glasses; sunglasses. 水中めがね〔水泳用の〕(swimming) goggles;〔水中を見る箱型の〕a water glass. 鼻めがね a pince-nez《*pl.* ~》. 飛行めがね aviation [flying] goggles. 縁なしめがね rimless「spectacles [glasses]. めがねケース[入れ] a「glasses [spectacle] case. めがね越し ▷ めがね越しに over [from above] *one*'s glasses; over the frame of *one*'s glasses. めがね違い misjudgment. めがね屋〔人〕an optician;〔店〕an optician('s)「store [shop]. めがね拭き a lens cloth.

めざし【目刺し】dried sardines (tied together in a bundle with a straw passed through the eye sockets).

めざましどけい【目覚まし時計】an alarm clock; an alarm. ▷ 目覚まし時計が鳴った. The alarm went off. / 目覚まし時計で目を覚ます wake (up) to the alarm《at five o'clock》/ 目覚まし時計を 7 時に鳴るようにセットする set the alarm clock「for [to ring at, to go off at] seven o'clock / 目覚まし時計を 7 時にかけておいた. I set the alarm to wake me (up) at seven. / 目覚まし時計を止める turn off the alarm.

めじろおし【目白押し】jostling《with one another》;《get caught up in》the crush; milling. ▷ 目白押しに並ぶ stand shoulder to shoulder (like white-eyes on a branch) / 目白押しの群衆 a milling「throng [crowd]《of spectators》; a jostling crowd《of cameramen》.

めだか【目高】a killifish; a medaka.

めだしぼう【目出し帽】《a man in》a「ski mask [balaclava].

めだまやき【目玉焼】a fried egg; an egg fried sunny-side up; a sunny-side-up egg.

めびな【女雛】the Empress doll (in a Girls' Festival display of dolls). [⇨ おびな]

めん【面】〘剣道〙〔面を打つこと〕a *men*; a stroke to the head.

めんくい【面食い】a person who is excessively concerned with good looks《in choosing a marriage partner》. ▷ あの男は面食いだ. Good looks in a woman mean more than anything else to him. | He's only interested in good-looking girls.

めんるい【麺類】noodles; vermicelli; pasta; noodle dishes.

も

もう【毛】〔貨幣の単位（＝1/10000 円）〕a *mo*;〔尺貫法における長さの単位（＝1/1000 寸）〕a *mo* 《*pl.* ~》;〔尺貫法における重さの単位（＝1/1000 匁(もんめ))〕a *mo* 《*pl.* ~》.

もうひつ【毛筆】an artist's animal-hair brush;〔書道用〕a calligrapher's brush;〔水彩画用〕a watercolor brush.

もえ【萌え】1 budding into leaf;〔若芽〕young「buds [leaves]. **2**〔アニメ・漫画ファンの間で, べた惚れ〕a fascination 《with...》; an infatuation 《with...》; a crush 《on *somebody*》. ◐ 萌えキャラ a「cute [charming] character ／ 萌え要素 a cute [an attractive, a charming] feature [characteristic].

もえぎいろ【萌黄色】yellowish green; grass green.

もくぎょ【木魚】《beat time on》a wood block 《as one chants a sutra》.

もくば【木馬】〔木製の馬〕a wooden horse;〔揺り木馬〕a rocking horse; a hobbyhorse;〔器械体操の〕a (vaulting) horse. ◐ トロイの木馬 the Trojan horse.

もくはんが【木版画】a woodcut; a wood engraving; a woodprint; a wood-block print.

もぐら【土竜】a mole. ◐ もぐらの掘った穴 a mole('s) tunnel ／ もぐらの毛皮〔モールスキン〕a moleskin ／ もぐらたたき〔ゲームの一種〕《play》Whack-A-Mole ／ もぐらたたきをする play the Whack-A-Mole game.

もくれん【木蓮】〖植〗a (lily) magnolia.

もち【餅】*mochi*; (a) rice cake; a「cake [block] of pounded rice—hard when it dried out—eaten baked, broiled or in soup, especially on festive occasions.

もちゅうはがき【喪中葉書】a postal card informing friends and acquaintances that *one* is in mourning and will not send a New Year's card this year; a mourning-notification card.

もったいない 〔無駄な・惜しい〕wasteful; wasting. ▶2004年ノーベル平和賞を受賞したケニアの環境保護活動家ワンガリ・マータイが2005年に来日した折に *mottainai* ということばを世界に広めたいと提唱した. ◐この靴はまだはける. もったいなくて捨てられない. These shoes are still wearable. It would be a waste to throw them away. / そんなに紙を何枚も使ってはもったいない. It is「a sheer waste [simply a waste, bad economy] to use so many sheets of paper.

もつなべ【もつ鍋】a「hot pot [stew] containing entrails.

もなか【最中】〔菓子〕bean-jam-filled wafers.

もふく【喪服】mourning dress. ◐喪服を着ている wear [be in] mourning (dress); wear black; be in (mourning) black.

もみじ【紅葉】**1**〔カエデ類の別名〕a maple; a「Japanese [full-moon] maple. ◐紅葉のような手 the cute little hands 《of a baby》. **2**〔秋に葉が赤や黄に変わること〕tinted autumnal「leaves [foliage]; red [scarlet-tinged] leaves;〔色〕autumnal tints [colors]. 〜する turn「red [crimson] / ◐紅葉した谷 an autumn-tinted valley / 山は紅葉して燃えるようだった. The hills were aflame with autumnal tints. ■紅葉和え〖料理〗cod roe spiced and colored with「red [cayenne] pepper. **紅葉おろし**〖料理〗daikon radish grated with red pepper;〈俗に〉grated white radish and grated carrots mixed together. **紅葉葉** scarlet maple leaves.

もみじがり【紅葉狩り】an excursion to view the autumn leaves. ◐箱根へ紅葉狩りに行く go to Hakone to see the scarlet maple leaves.

もも【桃】〔木〕a peach (tree);〔実〕a peach. ◐桃の花 a peach blossom / 桃の節句 the Doll's Festival (March 3) / 桃栗三年柿八年. The peach and chestnut take three years to bear fruit, the persimmon eight years.

ももいろ【桃色】rose (color);〔薄桃色〕blushing pink. ◐桃色の peach-[rose-]colored; rosy; pink / 薄桃色の pinkish; pale pink. ■**桃色遊戯**《indulge in》sexual play.

ももたろう【桃太郎】Momotaro; the "Peach Boy" (the Tom Thumb-like hero of a Japanese folk tale).

ももひき【股引】〔ズボン下〕(long) drawers [underpants, underwear]; long johns;〔職人などの〕close-fitting trousers. ◐股引をはいている be wearing drawers / 半股引 knee breeches; trunks.

もやし【萌し】〔麦〕(barley) malt or〔豆〕bean sprouts grown in the shade.

■ もやしっ子 a spineless 《town-bred》 child; an over-protected pantywaist.

もりじお【盛り塩】〔店の門口に塩を盛ること〕placing a heap of salt at the door (of a restaurant or bar) to keep out misfortune;〔その塩〕a heap of salt placed at the door (of a restaurant or bar) to keep out bad luck.

もりそば【盛り蕎麦】buckwheat「noodles [*soba*] served on a small wickerwork tray.

モルモット a (domestic) guinea pig. ▶「モルモット」の名は "marmot" から出たものであるが，これはまったく別の動物. ◐医学実験のモルモットにされるのはごめんだ. I refuse to be used as a guinea pig in a medical experiment.

もんご(う)いか【紋甲烏賊】〔コウイカ科のイカ〕（ヨーロッパコウイカ）a common cuttlefish.

もんじゃやき【もんじゃ焼き】〖料理〗a wheat flour pancake with cabbage and other ingredients, cooked on a griddle.

もんつき【紋付き】a garment bearing *one*'s family crest; a crested kimono. ◐黒羽二重の紋付き《wear》crested ceremonial clothes of black *habutae* silk cloth / 黒紋付き a black crested kimono. ■ 紋付き羽織 a crested *haori*. 紋付袴 a man's formal「clothes [dress] consisting of a crested kimono and「hakama [trousers].

もんめ【匁】〔尺貫法における重さの単位〕a *momme*《*pl.* ~》(＝約 3.75 g).

や

やおちょう【八百長】〔明治の初めのころ八百屋の長兵衛という人が元相撲取りと碁をやるときに勝負に手心を加えたことに由来〕《race》fixing;《match》rigging; a fix;《put in》the fix. ▶八百長で負ける〔勝ちをゆずる〕throw a「match [game, race] / 八百長のけんか a「put-up [staged] quarrel / 八百長をやる fix《a fight》; put in the fix / 八百長疑惑 (a) suspicion of「match-fixing [game-fixing, race-fixing, etc.] / 八百長競馬《口》a「fixed [rigged] horse race / 八百長試合 a「rigged [fixed] game; a put-up game / 八百長相撲 a「rigged [fixed] sumo match; a fixed sumo bout.

やがすり【矢絣】cloth with a splashed pattern of arrow-feathers.

やかたぶね【屋形船】a houseboat;〔遊覧船〕a pleasure boat.

やきいも【焼き芋】a baked sweet potato. ■焼き芋屋 a baked sweet-potato vender.

やぎざ【山羊座】『天・占星』the (Sea) Goat; Capricorn; Capricornus (略: Cap). ▶山羊座生まれの人 a Capricorn; a Capricornean.

やきそば【焼き蕎麦】〔中華料理〕chow mein. ■固[揚げ]焼きそば crispy [deep-fried] noodles. ソース焼きそば fried noodles with sauce. 五目焼きそば fried noodles with (at least) five basic toppings.

やきとり【焼き鳥】grilled chicken drumsticks and wings, as well as skewered morsels of chicken meat, hearts, gizzards, livers and skin. ■焼き鳥屋 an establishment offering skewered chicken as a specialty.

やきにく【焼き肉】(Korean-style) grilled meat. ▶焼き肉のたれ sauce for Korean-style grilled meat. ■焼き肉定食 a set meal with (Korean-style) grilled meat; a Korean-style barbecue set. 焼き肉店[屋] a Korean barbecue restaurant.

やきゅうけん【野球拳】〔野球の歌を歌ってじゃんけんをし、負けたほうが着ているものを一枚ずつ脱いでいく遊び〕a game in which two people sing a short song and pantomime playing baseball followed by a round of rock-paper-scissors, with the loser removing one piece of clothing; strip baseball.

やくすぎ【屋久杉】〔鹿児島県屋久島に自生するスギのうち, 特に樹齢 1000 年を越えるスギ〕a Yaku「sugi [cryptomeria]; a「sugi [cedar] growing on Yaku Island, Kagoshima Prefecture, some of which are more than 1000 years old.

やくどし【厄年】〔男の厄年は 25, 42, 61 歳で, 女の厄年は 19, 33, 37 歳〕an unlucky [a bad, an evil] year; 〔年齢〕a「climacteric [critical] age (by Western reckoning, 24, 41, 60 for men and 18, 32, 36 for women).

やくみ【薬味】〔香辛料〕spice(s); condiment(s); 〈集合的に〉spicery; 〔味付け〕a seasoning; a flavoring. ◐ 薬味にネギのみじん切りを添えます. 〔調理の手順で〕Garnish with finely sliced Welsh onions. / 薬味ののった garnished [flavored] 《with…》/ 薬味を入れる flavor 《a dish》with spice / 薬味をきかせた highly「spiced [seasoned]. ■ **薬味入れ** a cruet; 〔瓶〕a castor. **薬味立て** a cruet stand.

やけいスポット【夜景スポット】a「spot [place] with a (good) night view 《of the city》.

やごう【屋号】〔店の〕the「name [style] 《of a store》; 〔役者の〕a (hereditary)「stage title [Kabuki name].

やさい【野菜】(green) vegetables; greens; greenstuff; 〔根菜〕root vegetables; 〔菜園の〕garden vegetables. ■ **野菜炒め** fried [stir-fried] vegetables. **野菜サラダ[スープ]** vegetable「salad [soup]. **野菜ジュース** (a) vegetable juice.

やし【香具師・野師】〔縁日などで食べ物などを売る商人〕a street stall vendor 《at a festival》.

やじうま【野次馬】〔群集〕rabble; a mob; busybodies; bystanders; spectators; a curious crowd; the curious; (a crowd of) curiosity seekers; curious onlookers; 〔1 人〕a busybody; an intruder; a meddler; a sensation-seeker; 《口》a rubberneck. ◐ サイレンの音にたちまち野次馬が集まってきた. At the sound of the siren a crowd of「curiosity seekers [gawkers] instantly gathered. / 野次馬が現場を遠巻きにしている. Spectators are ringing the site at a distance.

やたい【屋台】**1** 〔山車(だし)の〕a float; a movable stage; a scaffold. **2** 〔屋台店〕a (street) stall; an open-air stall; a stand; a booth.

やたのかがみ【八咫の鏡】〔三種の神器の1つ〕the (sacred) mirror (an item of the three imperial regalia).

やっこだこ【奴凧】a kite in the shape of a samurai's serving man.

やながわ(なべ)【柳川(鍋)】a hotpot of loaches boiled in soy sauce with eggs and burdock.

やぶさめ【流鏑馬】the art of shooting arrows from astride a horse (popular in the late Heian and Kamakura period); horseback archery.

やまかけ【山掛け】a dish of「sliced fish [buckwheat noodles, bean curd, etc.] covered with grated yam. ■ 山かけそば a bowl of「soba [buckwheat noodles] topped with grated yam.

やまかん【山勘】◐ やまかんが当たった. My「hunch [guess] was right.｜I「was [guessed] right. / やまかんで〔あてずっぽうで〕by guesswork; by guessing; on a hunch;〔山を張って〕《buy》at a venture; on speculation;《口》on spec / やまかんで当てる guess right.

やまと【大和】Yamato; (old) Japan ■ 大和絵〔唐絵に対して〕a Yamato-e painting (a traditional painting of the late Heian and Kamakura periods dealing with Japanese themes, in contrast to Kara-e paintings dealing with Chinese themes);〔浮世絵〕an ukiyo-e. 大和言葉〔和語〕the distinctive language of Japan; a word of (purely) Japanese origin; a native (Japanese) word;〔和歌〕⇨ わか. 大和魂 the Japanese spirit. 大和朝廷〖日本史〗the Yamato「court [state](, Japan's first imperial government). 大和撫子(なでしこ) a woman who exhibits the fresh grace of the Japanese feminine ideal; an elegant term for a Japanese woman. 大和煮 beef cooked in soy sauce.

やまとたけるのみこと【日本武尊】Prince Yamatotakeru; a prince of the legendary Emperor Keikō.

やまぶき【山吹】〔バラ科の落葉低木〕a Japanese rose; golden kerria.

やまぶきいろ【山吹色】bright [golden] yellow.

やまぶし【山伏】a mountain ascetic; an itinerant priest; a hermit.

ゆ

ゆいのう【結納】〔式〕a ceremonial exchange of betrothal gifts 《between …》;〔品物〕a betrothal [an engagement] present [gift]. ▶結納を取り交わす exchange betrothal「presents [gifts]. ■結納金 betrothal gift money.

ゆうげん【幽玄】 quiet beauty; elegant simplicity; the subtle and profound; the occult. 〜な subtle and profound; quiet and beautiful; simple and elegant; occult. ▶幽玄な雰囲気をかもす能舞台 a Noh stage creating an atmosphere of quiet and elegant beauty / 幽玄の美 subtle and profound beauty / 茶道に見る幽玄の世界 the elegant simplicity of the tea ceremony.

ゆうぜん【友禅】■友禅染め〔方法〕the Yūzen process (of dyeing);〔物〕a Yūzen-printed kimono. 友禅模様 a Yūzen pattern.

ゆうやけ【夕焼け】 the evening [the sunset] glow; the afterglow of the sunset; a red sunset; the blazing red of the setting sun;〔高山の頂上から見たもの〕an alpenglow. ▶夕焼けで西の空が真っ赤になっている. The sky in the west was aglow with the setting sun. ■夕焼け雲 sunset clouds. 夕焼け空 the sky aglow with the setting sun.

ゆうれい【幽霊】 a ghost; an apparition; a specter; a phantom; a bog(e)y; a spirit; a spook; a supernatural visitor. ▶あの家には幽霊が出る. That house is haunted. ■幽霊屋敷 a「haunted [《口》spooky] house.

ゆかた【浴衣】 a yukata; an informal cotton kimono (for summer wear or after a bath). ■浴衣帯 a sash for a yukata. 浴衣地 cotton cloth for a yukata.

ゆきかき【雪搔き】〔排雪〕snow shoveling; shoveling [clearing, sweeping] snow away; snow removal;〔雪かき具〕a snow「shovel [scraper, pusher, push]; *a snowplow; ‖a snowplough;〔雪かきする人〕a snow shoveler. ▶道の雪かきをする remove the snow on the road; clear the road of snow.

ゆきがっせん【雪合戦】a snowball「fight [battle]; snowballing.　◐雪合戦をする have a snowball「fight [battle]; snowball.

ゆきだるま【雪達磨】a snowman; a snow figure.　◐雪だるま式に[雪だるまのように]大きくなる snowball; increase [grow, multiply, expand, accumulate] at a rapidly accelerating rate / 国債[利子]が雪だるま式に増え続けている. The government bond [The interest] is snowballing. / 雪だるまを作る make a snowman.

ゆきみしょうじ【雪見障子】a shōji whose papered bottom half slides up so one can view the snow through the glass window behind it.

ゆきみどうろう【雪見灯籠】a stone lantern with a broad headpiece placed in an ornamental garden; a「*yukimi* [snow-viewing] lantern.

ゆず【柚子】a citron; a small citrus fruit.　■柚子湯 a hot citron bath.

ゆでたまご【茹で卵】a boiled egg.　◐半熟[かたゆで]のゆで卵 a soft-[hard-]boiled egg.　■ゆで卵立て〔食卓用の〕an eggcup.

ゆどうふ【湯豆腐】boiled bean curd.

ゆのはな【湯の華・湯の花】incrustations [deposits] of hot spring water; flowers of sulphur; geyserite; sinter.

ゆば【湯葉】*yuba*; boiled-soymilk skim (it is used, either fresh or dried and reconstituted, in Japanese cooking).

ゆびずもう【指相撲】finger [thumb] wrestling.

ゆべし【柚餅子】〔ユズの香味をつけた餅菓子〕a sweet citron-flavored steamed dumpling.

ゆめまくら【夢枕】夢枕に立つ appear in *one*'s dream; appear [come] to *one* in「sleep [a dream].

ゆり【百合】a lily.　◐谷間の(姫)百合 a lily of the valley　▶スズランのこと.　■鬼百合 a tiger lily.　黒百合 a black lily.　山百合 a golden-banded lily.　百合根 a lily bulb.

ゆりかご【揺り籃】a swinging cot; a cradle;〔幌(ほろ)つきの〕a bassinet.　◐揺りかごで揺られる be rocked in a cradle / 揺りかごを揺する rock《a child》in a cradle / 福祉国家では揺りかごから墓場まで生活が保障される. In a welfare state the people are guaranteed「security from (the) cradle to (the) grave [cradle-to-grave security].

よ

よいどめ【酔い止め】〔乗り物酔いの薬〕a travel sickness pill; medicine to prevent motion sickness.

よいのみょうじょう【宵の明星】the evening star; Venus.

ようかん【羊羹】a thick sweet jelly of adzuki beans. ■水羊羹 thin adzuki-bean jelly. 蒸し羊羹 steamed adzuki-bean gelatin.

ようきょく【謡曲】《chant》a Noh song.

ようし【養子】an adopted「child [son]; *one*'s son by adoption; a son-in-law《*pl.* sons-》. ◐養子にする adopt《a child》(as *one*'s son); make an adopted child of《a boy》; receive《a nephew》into *one*'s family as a son; affiliate / 養子に行く be adopted into《a family》; become *somebody*'s adopted child; enter《a family》as an adopted「son [daughter] / 養子にやる give *one*'s child《to *somebody* as his heir》/ 養子に出す be put up for adoption. ■婿養子 *one*'s adopted son-in-law. 養子縁組み an adoption arrangement / 姪(めい)を跡取りにするために養子縁組を決めた. An adoption was arranged so that their niece would become their heir. / 養子縁組み届出 notification of the adoption of an heir. 養子先 the adoptive family; *one*'s family of adoption.

ようじ【楊枝】〔つま楊枝〕a toothpick. ◐楊枝で重箱の隅をほじくる make quibbling distinctions.

よこづな【横綱】a *yokozuna* wrestler; a sumo wrestler of the highest rank; a grand champion. ◐酒豪番付の横綱《stand at》the top of the list of truly great drinkers / 横綱になる win the rank of sumo grand champion; be promoted to the position of a grand sumo champion. ■横綱審議(委員)会 the Yokozuna Promotion Council. 横綱相撲 a match in which a *yokozuna* overpowers his opponent. 横綱総見 an inspection of top wrestlers by the Yokozuna Promotion Council.

よこれんぼ【横恋慕】◐横恋慕する love another person's「wife [husband]. / あの男はいつも他人の奥さんに横恋慕してはふられている. He is always falling in love with other people's wives and being rejected.

よざくら【夜桜】◐ 夜桜を見に行く go to see the cherry blossoms「at night [in the evening]; go to enjoy the night view of the cherry blossoms.

よしず【葦簀・葭簀】a reed「screen [blind]. ◐ 葦簀張りの《a hut》sheltered with marsh-reed screens.

よせ【寄席】a storytellers' hall; *a vaudeville「theater [house]; ⁞a variety「hall [house, theatre]; a music hall. ◐ 寄席に出る appear in a「vaudeville [variety house]. ■ **寄席演芸** *a vaudeville (performance); ⁞a variety entertainment; a variety show. **寄席芸人** a「music-hall [variety] artiste [artist, entertainer]; *a vaudevillian.

よなきそば【夜鳴きそば】*soba* [buckwheat noodles] sold from a cart at night; a nighttime *soba* vendor.

よびぐん【予備軍】〔控えの軍隊〕a reserve (corps); the reserves; a reserve army. ■ **サラリーマン予備軍** students about to graduate and become office workers. **失業予備軍** the《growing》ranks of workers who are about to lose their jobs. **中年予備軍** those who are nearing middle age. **糖尿病予備軍** incipient diabetics.

よびだし【呼び出し】**1**〔呼び出すこと〕a call; calling out; 〔召喚〕a summons; citing; 〔裁判所の〕a subpoena; 〔誘い出し〕decoying out; 〔電話口への〕calling [ringing] up. **2**〔相撲の〕a ring announcer.

よみせ【夜店】〔夜市〕a night fair; 〔個々の店〕a night「stall [booth]. ◐ この通りは毎晩夜店が出てにぎわう. This street is alive with a row of night stalls every evening. / 夜店を出す open [set up] a night stall.

よみふだ【読み札】〔百人一首で, 取り札に対し〕(in the game of hyakunin isshu) cards containing the first lines of a poem read out to players.

ら

ラーメン【拉麺】〔中華そば〕Chinese ｢noodles [vermicelli] in soup; Chinese soup noodles; ramen. ■ラーメン屋〔店〕a Chinese noodle shop;〔人〕a Chinese noodle vendor. ラーメン・ライス〔食堂の品目〕ramen served with rice; ramen and rice.

らくがん【落雁】〔干菓子〕a hard dry sweet made of soy flour and sugar.

らくご【落語】traditional Japanese comic storytelling; a comic story (told by a professional storyteller); a story ending with a punch line. ■落語家 a professional comic storyteller.

ラジオたいそう【ラジオ体操】the radio ｢gymnastic exercises [gymnastics].

らっかせい【落花生】〚植〛a peanut; a groundnut; a pignut; a monkey nut.

らっきょう【辣韮】〚植〛〔ユリ科の多年草〕*rakkyō*; a ｢Chinese [Japanese] scallion. ■ラッキョウ漬 pickled *rakkyō*.

らっぱ【喇叭】〔楽団の〕a trumpet;〔軍隊の〕a bugle; a horn.

ランドセル a backpack; a knapsack; a satchel; a school rucksack.

らんま【欄間】〚建〛a carved wooden panel used as a decorative transom above fusuma or shoji; a fanlight.

り

り【里】〔尺貫法における距離の単位〕a league; a *ri* 《*pl.* ~》 (=約 3.92 km).

りきゅうねずみ【利休鼠】greenish gray (a hue much favored by the early tea master Sen no Rikyū).

リストカット〔手首を刃物などで切る自傷行為〕 wrist-cutting. ◯ リストカットする cut [slash] *one*'s wrist(s).

りゅう【竜・龍】a dragon. ◯ 竜の頷(あぎと)の玉を取る beard the lion in his den / 竜の雲を得たるが如し be in *one*'s element.
■ 竜に翼 a double advantage.

りゅうきん【琉金】〖魚〗a ryukin goldfish.

りゅうず【竜頭】〔時計の〕a (winding) crown; (軸部まで含めて) a stem;〔釣り鐘の〕the cannon 《of a bell》. ■ 竜頭巻き時計 a stem-winding watch; a stem-winder.

りょうがえ【両替】exchange (of money); money exchanging. ~する (ex)change 《dollars into yen, American money into Japanese》; change 《a 1,000-yen note》.

りょうてい【料亭】a Japanese-style (luxury) restaurant.

りょくちゃ【緑茶】green tea.

りん【厘】〔貨幣の単位〕a *rin* (=1/1000 yen);〔尺貫法における長さの単位〕a *rin* 《*pl.* ~》 (=約 0.3mm);〔尺貫法における重さの単位〕a *rin* 《*pl.* ~》 (=約 0.0375g).

る

るすばん【留守番】〔留守を預かること〕caretaking 《during *somebody*'s absence》; housesitting;〔留守を預る人〕a caretaker; a「housesitter [house sitter]. ◐ 留守番をする stay [remain] at home; house-sit; take「charge [care] of a house 《during *somebody*'s absence》; look after a house 《while *somebody* is away》. ■ 留守番電話 an [a telephone] answering machine;《leave a message on *somebody*'s》answerphone. ◐ 彼に電話したら留守番電話だった. When I called him,「I got his answerphone [the answering machine was on]. 留守番(電話)サービス an answering [a telephone answering] service.

るすろく【留守録】1〔ビデオ・ラジオなどのタイマー録画[録音]〕automatic「video [audio] recording. 〜する set the timer to record a「TV [radio] program. **2**〔電話などに残されたメッセージ〕a message left on the answering machine. ◐ 自宅に電話して留守録が入っていないかどうか確認する call home to「see [check] if there are any messages on the answering machine.

るつぼ【坩堝】 a crucible; a melting pot. ◐ 人種のるつぼ a melting pot of races; a racial melting pot.

るりいろ【瑠璃色】 sky [bright] blue; lapis lazuli (blue); azure.

るんるん ◐ るんるん気分で in a happy mood; in (the) seventh heaven.

れ

れい【礼】〔礼儀〕etiquette; decorum; propriety; politeness; courtesy; civility.

れいきゅうしゃ【霊柩車】a hearse.

れいしゃぶ【冷しゃぶ】〖料理〗boiled sliced meat served cold with a sauce; *shabu-shabu* served cold. [⇨ しゃぶしゃぶ]

れいしゅ【冷酒】cold sake.

れいぞうこ【冷蔵庫】a refrigerator;《口》the fridge;〔冷凍用〕a freezer; an icebox. ◐ 冷蔵庫に入れる put《food》in a refrigerator / 冷蔵庫に魚肉を入れておく keep fish in the refrigerator / 冷蔵庫の扉 a refrigerator door / 電気[ガス]冷蔵庫 an electric [a gas] refrigerator.

れいふく【礼服】full [formal] dress; a dress suit;〔夜会の〕《wear》evening dress;〔軍人の〕a dress uniform.

れいめん【冷麺】cold noodles (in Korean style).

レジぶくろ【レジ袋】a supermarket bag.

れんが【連歌】〔形式〕verse linking;〔歌〕a linked verse; a *renga*.

れんく【連句】a linked verse.

れんげ【蓮華】**1**〔ハスの花〕a lotus flower.　**2**〔匙〕a ⌈china [porcelain] spoon.

れんこん【蓮根】a (sacred) lotus ⌈root [rhizome].

ろ

ろうか【廊下】 a passage(way); a corridor; a gallery; a hall; a hallway; 〔劇場などの〕a lobby. ◐ 廊下伝いに along a passage.

ろうがん【老眼】 presbyopia; aged eye; farsightedness [weak eyesight] due to old age. ◐ 老眼になった. His eyes had gotten dim with age. / 老眼の presbyopic / 老眼の人 a presbyope. ■ **老眼鏡** reading「glasses [spectacles]; farsighted (eye)glasses.

ろうにん【浪人】 **1** 〔浪士〕a *rōnin* 《*pl*. ~(s)》; a「masterless [lordless, free] samurai. ◐ 浪人になる lose *one*'s master; be dismissed by *one*'s lord. **2** 〔学生の〕a high-school graduate who failed the university entrance examination and is cramming for another try (the following year). **3** 〔失業者〕a jobless person. ■ **就職浪人** a school graduate who hasn't found a job.

ろうにんぎょう【蠟人形】 a wax「doll [figure]. ■ **蠟人形館** a wax museum; a waxworks.

ろくしゃくふんどし【六尺褌】 a traditional Japanese loincloth for men.

ろくはらたんだい【六波羅探題】〚日本史〛〔鎌倉幕府の朝廷監視機関〕Rokuhara Tandai; the Kamakura Shogunate's agents stationed in Rokuhara, Kyoto; 〔その長〕the commissioner of Rokuhara Tandai.

ろくまいびょうぶ【六枚屏風】 a (decorative)「six-leaved [six-paneled] screen.

ろくよう【六曜】 a recurring six-day cycle of lucky or unlucky days that is incorporated into the Japanese calendar. 先勝, 友引, 先負, 仏滅, 大安, 赤口の順.

ろくろくび【轆轤首】 a monster, usually female, with an extensile neck; a long-necked woman 《at a carnival》.

ろてんぶろ【露天風呂】 a hot spring bath set in the open; an open-air bath.

わ

わ【和】〔日本風〕◐ 和定食 a Japanese-style「set [table d'hôte] meal.

ワイシャツ a shirt;〔胸の固い礼装用〕a dress shirt;〔カラー・カフスのついたもの〕a utility shirt. ◐ ワイシャツのすそを出して《wear》*one*'s shirt with the tail hanging out.

わか【和歌】a 31-syllable Japanese poem; a tanka.

わかさぎ【若鷺・公魚・鰙】a pond smelt; a fresh-water smelt.

ワキ〘能〙a deuteragonist; a supporting player.

わけぎ【分葱・冬葱】〘植〙a Welsh onion; a cibol; shallot.

わごと【和事】〘歌舞伎〙a love scene《in a Kabuki play》; the production style of a love scene. ■ **和事師** the actor playing a love scene; an actor accomplished in playing love scenes.

わさび【山葵】〔アブラナ科の多年草; 日本・サハリン固有の香辛料植物〕(a) wasabi; (a) Japanese horseradish. ◐ わさびがきいている be「highly seasoned [pungent] with wasabi / 刺身をわさびで食べる eat sashimi with wasabi / わさびのきいた鮨 sushi flavored with wasabi / わさびをすりおろす grate (a) wasabi / 話にわさびをきかせる spice (up) [pepper, flavor] *one*'s speech. ■ **おろしわさび** grated wasabi. **生わさび** fresh wasabi. **わさびおろし** a wasabi grater **わさび醤油** soy seasoned with grated wasabi. **わさび漬け** wasabi cut up and mixed with sake lees.

わし【和紙】Japanese [Japan] paper; (traditional) Japanese paper; *washi*.

わじまぬり【輪島塗】wajima-nuri lacquerware.

わたりどり【渡り鳥】a「migratory [passage] bird; a bird of passage;〈集合的に〉migrants.

わび【侘び・佗び】《have a》taste for the simple and understated. ■ **わび茶** a simple, austere, frugal tea ceremony.

わふく【和服】Japanese clothes; (a) kimono 《*pl.* ~s》.

わらじ【草鞋】straw sandals. ◐ わらじをはく wear [put on] straw sandals.

わらにんぎょう【藁人形】a straw ⸢man [effigy, figure]; a man of straw; a jackstraw; a Jack of straw

-わり【-割】〔十分の一〕a tenth; one-tenth; 10 percent. ◐ 2割7分 27 percent / 9割9分 99 percent.

わりかん【割り勘】〔合計の人数割り〕an equal split;〔各自自分持ち〕each paying for his own account;《口》going Dutch. ◐ 割り勘でいこう.《口》Let's split the tab. | Let's go Dutch. / 割り勘にする split the cost; share the expenses;〔2人が〕《口》go halves《on a gift》/ 割り勘にしてください. Separate checks, please.

わりざん【割り算】division. ◐ 割り算をする divide; do a problem in division / 割り算を2題やる do [work out] two division problems.

わりばし【割り箸】disposable [throwaway] chopsticks (made of unfinished wood or bamboo). ◐ 割り箸を割る split the chopsticks《before using them》.

わんこそば【椀子蕎麦】noodles in small bowls (holding only about one mouthful each, served up continuously until the customer signals to stop).

ワンタン【雲呑】won ton; Chinese flour dumplings with pork inside served in soup. ■ ワンタン麺 Chinese noodles with won ton in soup.

KENKYUSHA'S BILINGUAL
DICTIONARY OF JAPANESE CULTURAL TERMS

和英 日本文化表現辞典

2007年3月30日　初版発行
2007年5月20日　　2刷発行

KENKYUSHA

編　者	研究社辞書編集部
発行者	関戸雅男
発行所	株式会社　研究社

〒102-8152　東京都千代田区富士見2-11-3
電話　編集 03 (3288) 7711
　　　営業 03 (3288) 7777
振替　00150-9-26710
http://www.kenkyusha.co.jp

印刷所　研究社印刷株式会社

ISBN 978-4-7674-9053-3　C0582　PRINTED IN JAPAN
装幀　清水良洋 (Malpu Design)　　装画　クボアヤコ